A JOURNAL OF CONTEMPORARY WRITING

IRISH PAGES
DUILLÍ ÉIREANN

IRISH PAGES is a biannual journal (Spring-Summer, Autumn-Winter), edited in Belfast and publishing, in equal measure, writing from Ireland and overseas. It appears at the end of each six-month period.

Its policy is to publish poetry, short fiction, essays, creative non-fiction, memoir, essay reviews, nature-writing, translated work, literary journalism, and other autobiographical, historical, religious and scientific writing of literary distinction. There are no standard reviews or narrowly academic articles. Irish-language and Scots writing are published in the original, with English translations or glosses. IRISH PAGES is a non-partisan, non-sectarian, culturally ecumenical, and wholly independent journal. It endorses no political outlook or cultural tradition, and has no editorial position on the constitutional question. Its title refers to the island of Ireland in a purely apolitical and geographic sense, in the same manner of The Church of Ireland or the Irish Sea.

The sole criteria for inclusion in the journal are the distinction of the writing and the integrity of the individual voice. Equal editorial attention will be given to established, emergent and new writers.

The views expressed in IRISH PAGES are not necessarily those of the Editors. The journal is published by Irish Pages Ltd, a non-profit organization.

Submissions are welcome but must be accompanied by return postage or an international reply coupon. No self-addressed envelope is required. Reporting time is nine months. If work is accepted, a copy on disk may be requested.

Your subscription is essential to the independence and survival of the journal. Subscription rates are £16stg/€26/$45 for one year. Visit our website at www.irishpages.org for a subscription form or to order online. Credit cards are welcome.

IRISH PAGES
129 Ormeau Road
Belfast BT7 1SH

Advisory Board
Jonathan Allison
William Crawley
John Gray
Maureen Mackin
Bernard O'Donoghue
Daniel Tobin

Legal Advice: Kathy Mathews, Johnsons Law, Belfast/Dublin/London

IRISH PAGES is designed by Alicia McAuley Publishing Services and set in 12/14.5 Monotype Perpetua. It is printed in Belfast by Nicholson & Bass.

This issue has been generously assisted by Foras na Gaeilge and the Arts Councils of Northern and Southern Ireland.

Copyright remains with IRISH PAGES and the authors. All rights reserved. No reproduction, copy of transmission, in whole or part, may be made without written permission.

ISBN 978-0-9561046-2-5

IRISH PAGES

CHRIS AGEE, *Editor*

CATHAL Ó SEARCAIGH, *Irish Language Editor*

ANDREW PHILIP (Scotland) *and* STEPHEN DORNAN (Ulster),
Scots Language Editors

SEÁN MAC AINDREASA, *Managing Editor*

ELIZABETH SWITAJ, *Assistant Managing Editor*

AONGHAS MACLEÒID, *Editorial Assistant*
KATE MIDDLETON, *Editorial Assistant*

EDITED IN BELFAST
VOLUME 8, NUMBER 1

IRISH PAGES
DUILLÍ ÉIREANN

VOLUME 8, NUMBER 1

CONTENTS

Inheritance

On Absolute Darkness	7	Leslie Van Gelder
Standing Stone	21	Manus Charleton
Epiphanies	26	John F. Deane
Slaughter (historical fiction)	32	Ruth Gilligan

PORTFOLIO

Albania's Spaç	i-xvi	Peter Geoghegan
The Road to Granada	41	Gerard McCarthy
Dear Orson Welles …	52	Mark Cousins
Visiting John Hewitt	63	Patricia Craig
Two Stories	76	Ron Rash
Figures	94	Chris Preddle
The Stupid Skirt and Other Interludes (extract)	98	Emma Marx
A Suite of Poems	119	John Glenday
Bye-child (screenplay)	122	Bernard MacLaverty
60 Degrees North: Shetland & Greenland	138	Malachy Tallack
In His Eighty-Eighth Year	148	Francis Harvey

Three Poems from the Irish (Circa 900, Anno Domini)	150	Seán Hewitt
Druma an Chongó	154	Ailbhe Ní Ghearbhuigh
Cultúrlann Rant	157	Aodán MacPóilin

from THE OTHER TONGUES

A Trilingual Meitheal	162	Chris Agee
Still Singing Strong	166	Cathal Ó Searcaigh
Lasting Links	176	Peter Mackay
The Mither Tongue	179	Andrew Philip
Sleekit Loanens	184	Stephen Dornan
Auspices	188	Iain Galbraith
Bends in the Road	193	Tom Mac Intyre

Spaç Prison Camp
by Peter Geoghegan

ON ABSOLUTE DARKNESS

Leslie Van Gelder

Seeing it all.

"Everything has its wonders, even darkness and silence, and I learn, whatever state I may be in, therein to be content."
(Helen Keller)

We are sitting in the darkness before a drawing of a black horse. It rests, as it has for the last 17,000 years, in a low alcove along the cave wall in Hornos de la Peña. We are three: Raul, our guide, Jessica, my assistant, and me.

"What do you see?" I ask.

We have turned out the lights and are sitting in the depths of absolute darkness.

We all say nothing at first, adjusting to the completeness of the darkness. I call out in a deep voice and a high voice testing the echo of the space in the cave. "Hola … Hola … Hola!"

Though the sound reverberates it doesn't hit me in the solar plexus the way it does in some caves. If I had to give it a number from one to 10 in the same way nurses in hospital ask patients to rate their pain, it would be a four, as the sound is round and warm, but it does not move me. I would not sing here, or ask Raul to offer up some Spanish bass notes to warm the space as he had done in Las Chimeneas's deer chamber a few days before.

We sit for a while longer. I am waiting quietly for the others to tell me what they see.

"Azul" Raul says after a long pause. "Lineas azules." Blue lines.

That's what I see, too. In almost every cave where we have done this exercise of sitting in the darkness and playing with our voices against the walls, I have seen the same. A faint glow of light in shades of blue. Sometimes long strands of light that seem to follow the curvature of how I imagine the ceiling to be. Oftentimes, though I know it is impossible, I believe I can see the outline of my hand as I hold it up to my face to examine. It is in shadow but I see the outlines of my fingers against a sort of quietly radiant blue.

"I see green." Jess says.

Raul laughs and in Spanish that even I can understand clearly says, "That's because you are an extra terrestrial. Si?"

We laugh. "Blue is the normal color" Raul teases. "You?" He shakes his head at Jessica, or I imagine him shaking his head as I cannot see it, "You … I don't know."

We sit for a while longer in the darkness as it is soft, comfortable, and we have worked hard in this cave for two days so the few moments of simply resting our eyes against the pillow of darkness is most welcome.

Raul asks me if I will come back to do a study on sound some day. I tell him I would like to, but I don't know how or what it would say. "You didn't know much when you started this one either," he says quietly in a way that does hit me in the middle of my chest, "And now you do."

He is right. For twelve years I've been involved in the study of finger flutings – lines drawn on the walls of Paleolithic caves with fingers. In the beginning I knew nothing, but over time some aspects, some stories, some people who've been quietly dormant in the darkness for tens of thousands of years, have come, even if only a little way, back in the light.

The experience of working in the caves is like no other. I should tell you that I am not inherently drawn to caves. In fact, the opposite. I am a creature of light who tends to wither in grey places. The crepuscular gloom of an English November or a Kiwi May leaves me clawing at my skin. I built a house of windows in New Zealand and travel often there with a friend there who is even more light conscious than I. She times departures and arrivals on our itineraries so as to catch a particular slant of light on hills or to amplify the possibility of seeing lenticular clouds over Omarama – the valley the Maori's called "the place of clear light".

Equally, I admit that I don't understand the current fashion of "man caves" or inhabiting windowless sheds. Curtains are a complete mystery to me. My one foray into a floatation tank was traumatic. I still don't quite understand how spas, thinking they are clever, have adopted a form of torture outlawed by the Geneva Convention and have turned it into "therapy".

And yet despite all of this, I am comfortable, or at least at ease in the caves. There is something alluring and powerful about the experience of absolute darkness and about being deep inside a space which is in itself, inherently deep inside space. Some of my favorite places in the caves have been the furthest sections that one can access. In there, all motion stops. If there were a fermata in the signature of the world I believe I would find it there.

The caves are unique spaces. There is no horizon in a cave. No place upon which to rest one's eyes to steady oneself. Instead, there is a narrowing down of vision to that which is caught in the web of light you have cast. In a way, you are the source of your vision and the act of choosing where to put your gaze is a continuously conscious act, not one left to randomness, laziness, or chance.

I find I become profoundly conscious of where I am in space when I am in a cave in a way that does not happen so much in the outer world. At any given time, within the cave, I know where my head is. I know where my head is in relation to stalactites hanging down from ceilings, or crevasses, or edges of alcoves beneath which I've crouched. I know where my feet are all the time. I am aware that the ground is smooth or uneven, or that if I do not place my feet just so, I will slide down the clay floor into a bear pit and then have a very hard time climbing back out. I am far more aware than I am in the outer world that each step has a consequence and one that I have to consciously measure and choose, and as such my world becomes reduced to the radius of space around my body that is roughly the same length as my arm. I have to know that arm's length in a way that is about safety, not because I am worried about my own safety, but I am desperately worried about the safety of the cave. I need to protect it from me.

The lines I study were drawn in the soft walls of caves as much as 40,000 years ago. In some caves, the walls are still soft, like talc or wet concrete, and in others a thin layer of clay rests where it arrived after one or many floods in the distant past. If I were to brush my fingers against the talc – which is called most poetically, *moonmilk* – or the clay, it would leave a mark.

As my goal is to look at the marks other people left behind, the last thing I want to do is add my own. Worse, still, many of these flutings are also near pieces of artwork we recognize and treasure. Gracile deer leaping from the wall, tender muzzles of reindeer with soft eyes, thick-shouldered mammoth who've been asleep for 20,000 years, and then me. So, no, I do not want my hands to come close to them and yet many times when I am close in to the wall to look at and measure lines, I am aware that I am as close to them as I was once to my husband, Kevin, in the moment before kissing him. It's that intimate. And perhaps, like my mammoths, and reindeer, that moment of intimacy is now for me, too, only a remnant of the distant past. But in the warm light of the torch, where that is all I can see, that time feels closer than it does when I am out beneath in the wider arc of the sky.

My father and grandfather both built darkrooms into their homes. Both ardent photographers, the darkrooms were central to their psyches as both an escape from their overly talkative wives, and also a place to bring to light the photos that occupied such a large place in their personal geographies. If my father were to be bottled as a perfume scent he would be a heady mix of Dektol and formaldehyde crossed with Old Spice and Kent cigarettes. Perhaps not the blend that would win friends and influence people, but that was rarely his agenda anyway.

The smell of Dektol has probably disappeared from the world in the instant nature of digital photography and instant visual gratification. For me, I'm sorry that we have lost something of the mystery that came out of the darkness of the darkroom.

I remember vividly the sensation of having to know by feel how to open a film canister and develop the film in darkness. Something done by feel, by touch, without the need for sight. And then, there were the next stages, done after the long strands of film had been pegged on a washing line, and the contact sheets had been made to decide what was truly worth developing. Everything came down to weighing up the relationship between darkness and light and knowing that to have one always meant sacrificing something of the other.

In a windowless room an image was projected the enlarger onto the whiteness of photo paper and then dipped in the chemicals until magically it appeared from the whiteness into the dark. There are perhaps few things in life that move in that direction from the empty space of the pure white sheet to catch instead the shadows and the darkness. We all fancied ourselves Ansel Adams, a family hero, hoping that our contrasts between our whites and our blacks could be as pure as his. They never were, but in the darkness of the darkroom we were, in our own way daily alchemists of darkness, shadow, and light.

I do not remember the sensation of absolute darkness in the darkroom as the giant square timer (by which we used to know how long to soak things) glowed in the dark, and a single red light bulb cast an eerie glow over the enlarger and the pans of chemicals. When I think back on it now, I wonder when else in life are we ever warmed by the cast of red light except beneath stained glass windows in cathedrals. Though, on the night my husband died, the hospice nurse thinking she was kind, had brought in a red lamp and had bathed the room in a red light which I can only imagine she thought should rightly accompany the sound of a heart, my heart, like a wave, breaking against the darkness.

———

In the caves, I have the unique privilege of moving in and through these places at my own pace. When I have to be a tourist at a cave I am often unnerved by being encouraged to move along too quickly to fit the time frame of a 45 minute visit. The caves have their own time. They *insist* on their own time. There is a requirement of sweeping a light along a space in front of you and having it come clear for a moment and then recede again. One moves in waves.

So one of the aspects I note in the caves is that time stops there or slows to an unknowableness. I am one of those people who instinctively knows roughly what time it is all the time. In the cave, though, an hour will go by, or two, and I will have thought it to be 10 or 15 minutes. I don't know what accounts for this slowing of time for it seems I am taking in so much but it may be that it is being taken in at depth. I am seeing all there is to see. I don't know whenever that is the case in the world of light.

———

After Kevin died I didn't fear darkness as much as I feared immobility. I was afraid that the space I was in I would inhabit forever. I was endlessly asking anyone who would listen, *Where am I on this map of grief?*, as I wanted to know how long I was going to be in the woods and how much of it was I going to have to traverse on my knees. I wanted to know where I was so I would know how much energy I needed to endure this.

But I never believed in an absolute darkness there.

My hell is not black or deeply dark but is grey. It is most often peopled with academics who give the illusion of passion but are actually strange soulless creatures who have traded the theoretical for the heart and yet insist, often in very beautiful language, that they have not.

My one week in deepest hell took place in Victoria, British Columbia the June after Kevin died. I was at an environmental literature conference on a college campus that was temporarily overrun with black and white rabbits. It was surreal to continually go into sessions in dark rooms discussing nature while outside the campus was multiplying before our eyes. It was the only conference I've ever been to where one of the keynotes believed he was the Elton John of Environmental Lit and gave a paper on why we should embrace the Apocalyptic vision of the future since it was, in his way of seeing, already here. He advocated that movies should be even more violent than they already are, so they could mirror reality, and thought this especially essential for children's viewing. I secretly hoped he would be attacked by a posse of mottled bunnies on his way back to his dorm room one night. I would have slipped baby carrots into the pockets of his shiny leather post-modern suit if I could have gotten close, enough but he was protected by his eco-entourage.

In almost every session, I fell asleep. As soon as the speaker began, I was out. I tried everything to stay awake but it wasn't possible except the day Jan Zwicky read her poetry. I realized things that were pure and light still spoke to me, if they were pared down to the essentials, as her poetry was. She, through a simple poem about the joy found in doing dishes, fought back the grey.

We went whale watching and saw no whales. A giant wave came up on the ship and doused one person, me. A kind woman who saw I was trapped in a palpable misery told me that Karen Blixen had written that there were only three things in the world that held salt – blood, tears, and the ocean. Salt was what was there when the liquid had burned away. I held onto that thought and the pared down poetry through a long painful week of grey. If one waited long enough, the slow liquid of the grey world would drain away leaving crystals of something pure. I heard that. Or I made it up.

But while I felt like I was a dinner plate for a whole host of demons that week, I never once felt that I was in the space of darkness. Greyness, yes. Torpor and immobility, sure. A place where passion had drained from the world leaving behind the clown faces of illusion, absolutely. But not the depth of darkness.

I wonder now if it is because darkness does not frighten me. In darkness one can always see the contrast of light when it comes. In the greyness that is not so.

A perpetual grey is a nothing space. There is nothing to see or not see except in gradients and that world becomes so small as to never know where moments of change happen, and perhaps all things become relative instead of being able to see what is clear, light, true.

Is it any wonder that Wittgenstein went to Connemara, the furthest point west, to look back and see something clearly in what he called Europe's *last pool of darkness*?

If I want to know what is true in life – what is light – is it any wonder that I need the absolute darkness to see the light so clearly?

———

Each time I have moved in my life it has required a deep re-orientation. Moving to England required learning to drive left-handed stick shift and to change sides of the road. At the same time I was learning this, I was also learning a mirror form in tai chi where I was literally learning the exact opposite of a form I had been doing for ten years. For many years the effect of re-siding myself was unnerving, until I moved to New Zealand where it somehow became fluid and now it doesn't matter to me which side I am on as I am equally facile. I don't know how this happened within my brain but it became smooth.

When I moved to the Southern Hemisphere it was the stars that required me to realign myself. I had come from places of tremendous light pollution so the idea of living someplace where the Milky Way was so visible was a great part of the allure. My home is called *Te Mangaroa*, which is the Maori name for the Milky Way. On winter's nights when the sky is clearest I am aware that I built myself a star house.

The first time I saw the night sky in New Zealand I had the distinct feeling of sliding off the earth, as none of the stars looked familiar. These were the stars of another planet for sure, as I knew *my* night sky, and only the seven sisters of the Pleides seemed to still be familiar friends, though there they went by the name of Matiriki there and their rising signified the Maori new year. In time, my eyes adjusted and I saw my old friend Orion standing on his head and renamed the teapot. Gone were the great bears of the sky, the crown of Casseopia, the Scorpion's tail.

Instead, for solace, I had the coal sacks. In the midst of the bands of the southern hemisphere's view of the Milky Way are places of absolute darkness where there are no stars. They are so striking that they appear like spilled ink against the white backdrop of the night sky. The Aborigines of Australia saw them as part of the great emu in the sky. The first European explorers, coming across them as early as 1499 called them the Coal Sacks. Astronomers say that they are "a dark nebulae in the constellation Southern

Cross whose dust obscures the light of the Milky Way". I say they are a taste of absolute darkness in the night sky.

There was something quiet about them to me. I befriended them as my first familiars in the sky there. They are still the first place my eyes go when I encounter the wash of the Milky Way. Perhaps they are the great void or the nothingness of space, but because they are bounded by a cascade of stars, they do not seem lonely, only a pause, a four bar rest, in the riot of the sky.

My friend Patrick tells me that he thinks absolute darkness is the visual equivalence of silence. I agree. Like silence, I am fairly certain that there is a difference in the encounter between one chosen and one enforced. It may be in those defenseless places like silence and darkness that intention is amplified, because the usual layers of buffering and distraction are removed. Solitary confinement kills people. I know I starve without human touch. And yet when I willingly choose to go into absolute darkness of the caves, I do not fear what I will find there, for I have already chosen the space as one in which I am consciously exploring instead of relegated.

I spoke to a friend who meditates regularly about my interest in absolute darkness. He told me that his only internal experience of it was "the void". *"I loved the void when I got there"*, he told me, which I once thought was a story of avoiding life, but now I think he must be right. If you know that your visit to these places is not forever, and that you are not stuck there, then it is a place of peace. Or it can be.

Helen Keller wrote in her memoir of her childhood, "Have you ever been at sea in a dense fog, when it seemed as if a tangible white darkness shut you in, and the great ship, tense and anxious, groped her way toward the shore with plummet and sounding-line, and you waited with beating heart for something to happen? I was like that ship before my education began, only I was without compass or sounding-line, and had no way of knowing how near the harbour was. "Light! give me light!" was the wordless cry of my soul, and the light of love shone on me in that very hour."

A white darkness she called it. Is that what the blind see? Does it matter what color the light is or simply that there is always light in places we imagine to be the definition of absolute darkness? I don't know.

ON ABSOLUTE DARKNESS

In the spring of 2013, I visited Newgrange, Ireland's enormous passage tomb site in County Meath, with a group of rock art specialists. Rock Art is a good discipline for cultivating humility, as every presentation at the conference ended with, "We don't really have any idea what it means ... ", which I thought a useful experience for academics who so often think they know what they mean, but probably don't. Here, in the face of stones which were quarried far further afield and transported through no doubt difficult means, there is a sense of purposefulness. In looking at the artwork pecked into them, the overriding sense of "why" continually gives way to a feeling of "we have no idea".

It rained briefly and then the sun came out brilliantly, which, according to the rock art specialists, is the most ideal way to view the rock art as for in the brief moment of sunlight the designs are illuminated against the otherwise grey canvas of stone. Spirals emerge, doubles, and singles, giant owl eyes, and chunky lozenges, chevrons with sharp tips and undulating serpentines.

Our guide cheerfully encouraged us to enter into the passage tomb warning that the ceiling is low and the walls grow close and narrow. Those who are claustrophobic or think they might be were encouraged to go last so that they may flee first. In a time-honored guide trick, she exaggerated the words around darkness, closeness, tight enclosed space, and tomb to make sure that those who were having visceral reactions to the words themselves could be identified and were kindly encouraged to perhaps stay outside in the sunshine.

A smaller group entered into the tomb. We slid past the entrance stones and indeed the walls narrowed around us until we emerged into a circular chamber. In alcoves on three sides were drawings, anchored by basin-like stones on the floor carved in even hands. In hushed tones, she told us of the winter solstice mornings when for nearly a week at dawn, the sun shines through the upper passage of the site making a perfect line of buttery light illuminating the chamber. Thirty thousand people a year compete in a lottery each year to be among the hundred who will witness this miracle each year.

To give us a sense of the experience she extinguishes the lights and leaves us for a few moments in complete darkness. As ever, I want to pay attention to what I will see.

Beige.

What?

Beige. A sort of flat light the same color as concrete. The light in my eyes doesn't move. Just a patch here and there of brownish grey.

Gone are the blues I see in the caves in France and Spain. All I can think is that I can feel that this is a built environment. It does not have the sensual curves and contours of the insides of a cave that was carved by a river, but instead has the rough hewnness of stone brought from one place to another and placed with great precision by human hands.

As the lights come back up there is a sense of illumination in the chamber, but moreso of warmth. The color of the sun against the stone walls. The beginning of things. My caves never experience this. The only light they see are our small torches, and in that it is fleeting. The black horse in the back chamber of Hornos de la Peña has never been warmed by a winter morning's sun.

I ask the guide what she sees in the darkness, since she does this tour many times a day.

"It changes. It depends on my mood, the people in the group, the weather. What I had for lunch."

I'm intrigued. I tell her of the blues I see in the caves and that it has been a consistent experience for me. I share that I saw only a beige or greyish light here, not at all as alive as what I see in the caves.

"Ah that's because you're in your place there and here I'm in mine. You don't resonate here. Sometimes, when I have migraines, I see those same chevrons that you see over there. In fact, many people think that these signs and symbols may have emerged from those kinds of experiences."

I agree, but find myself more taken with the question of how much our internal state influences what we see in complete darkness. I had imagined that to be a somewhat empirical kind of question but if what she said is true, then it is as much about resonance as it is about vision.

And while Newgrange was interesting, she was right that it wasn't a space that resonated for me the way the caves do. No one built the caves – they found them.

But it does leave me wondering if in the darkness our inner world is made outer and stripped of the distraction of sight, we see instead what we feel.

Perhaps for me, that looks like long strands of blue light.

One morning not long ago I had tea with a friend, Robin, who studies evolution and human group sizes. He has spent a lifetime trying to understand the ways in which we, as humans, come together and come apart. When I ask him of his current work, he tells me it is all about endorphins – as he is trying to work out what was the trigger for hominid brain sizes to grow at various times in the historical record.

Laughter, he tells me, is the key to it all. When we laugh together we bond, we reinforce our relationships, our sense of *belonging*. It is ancient to us. A vocal calling we did before we were this variety of humans. We were once like wolves howling together under the moon. So today, when we sing, dance synchronously, make music together, feel the pulse of a bass line right in our chests, we tie into something deep in our core. Something that has been there for hundreds of thousands of years. Something that came to us about the same time we began to gather together around the fire at night.

Perhaps that is it then. Robin tells me that we associate our feeling of endorphins with euphoria or joy. I think of it as the sensation of fullness of being – that sheer delight in existing.

And then it hits me what else he has said. That our shared laughter, our shared song, and our experience of joy within that all came together in us when we also found ourselves making fire.

Is it any wonder then that we associate so deeply the warm glow of a fire, the warding off of darkness, and belonging?

These are after all, feelings. Resonances. Something we all experience deeply inside, but almost never see.

I tell Robin of my interest in darkness in the caves (to which he laughs because it is so obvious), and I share with him my stories of the acoustics of the space and the colors of the darkness. He tells me I should look at the concept of *Blindsight*, which is the capacity to detect motion and to "see" with the unconscious part of our brain even when we have lost complete sight.

This is perhaps the ultimate form of the brain seeing in the darkness, where even without any hope of translating what the eye is absorbing, the brain can still understand if there is motion, or if everything has gone deadly still. It explains why I can see my hand moving in front of my face in the darkness of the cave.

Blindsight seems to be that part of ourselves that it is smarter than we are. The part that ignores the evidence of what we see for something else that has always been there.

It must be the part of us that keeps going even when the evidence tells us that there's nothing ahead. It is the part of us in the midst of the deepest of darks that knows that there is and always will be light again. That isn't the terrain of what the eye can or can't see. That is simply the terrain of faith. Not faith in anything external per se, but a faith which perhaps explains why I see blue light in absolute darkness.

For as far as I can tell, the darkness tells me best that there is always more here than what my eyes can see.

And I, for one, am most grateful for that.

In Gargas cave I used to ask Kevin to sing. The cave is a beautiful space of long crevassed ceilings and a white calcite floor. Handprints of red, black, yellow and white emerge from the walls, giving the distinct impression of being waved at by a crowd of people who've vanished for a moment like Alice's Cheshire cat and have left behind their hands instead of their smiles.

The cave is acoustically pure, having been formed by the harmonics of an underground river curving and eddying long ago in time. From the center of the cave you can whisper and be heard at the entrance gate.

In the furthest section of the cave are three chambers nestled into each other. The outer chamber is half the size of a room. On the walls are engravings of animals one atop another. Long lines etched into the dark clay walls where bulls and bison leap from the walls alongside long maned horses and a thin necked goose.

Climbing into a smaller space, the next chamber has a long smooth benchlike space and a place in the wall where it is as if people had dug out the clay with their fingers.

The last chamber can only be reached when it hasn't rained, for puddles form at its feet and make it hard to crawl under the wall to come into the space. But on a dry day a single person can come into the heart of the cave.

There, in a round space the size of a table, the walls pull upwards into a chimney. On the wall in front of you is a Roman Centurian's mark and a letter V. Below it is a Neolithic dagger. To the left, a Paleolithic horse with its mane blowing in the wind, and finally one single nineteenth century bit of graffiti.

I asked Kevin to go into the heart chamber of the cave to sing to me. His voice was deep and warm honed from years of church choirs. With no one but us to hear him, he sang the way you do when you're alone in the car.

I sat first in the outer chamber and then in the chamber of the engravings in absolute darkness.

He sang "Amazing Grace".

It hit me with a force right in my chest that I can still feel today.

And long before I ever knew I would lose him, I wept.

For sometimes in the darkness, you truly do see and feel it all.

―

Seven summers ago, on a late July night, the Thames flooded. I was away on the other side of the world for work while Kevin was home with my stepdaughter, M. The doctor had refused to give him chemotherapy while I was gone because she didn't think M would take good enough of him. M was a good carer, in truth, though not then, as she was just terribly afraid. And when afraid we all have the potential to default to the worst versions of ourselves. Hers scolded and shook her finger at her father and demanded that he do what he was told. She mistook a dying man for a defiant man. It happens.

I came home just as they were letting the first vehicles back into the city. M took this to mean they were letting vehicles back out of the city and she fled on the first available bus. She would have jumped a canal boat had one floated by. The only one we saw lay upended like a dead whale in the middle of the river helpless to the current. That one, unlike M, wasn't going anywhere.

It was a strikingly beautiful evening and once M was safely on her way back to London, Kevin, with tears in his eyes, told me the story of what he remembered of the weekend. Though a fifty-seven year old man, that night he was a small boy with a skinned knee telling me that he didn't understand why his daughter had become so angry at him for not eating when he couldn't eat and that she had shook her finger at him and scolded him. Once spent of his story, he finally fell asleep, his cheeks still wet, and I stepped out the back garden and onto the footpath by the Thames. The river was inches from cresting over the old limestone wall. There was something compelling about its motion, as if it were a muscle flexing itself for the first time and finding it surprised to know it was supple and strong.

I crossed Folly Bridge and began to walk down the footpath on the south side of the Thames. It did not go far and at the nadir of the Hertford Bridge I stopped because the other side of it was completely under water. As was the meadow.

Christchurch Meadow had become a boulevard of water. Burst from its bank, the Thames, or should I say Isis, absorbed the wide footpath and flowed up into the trees doubling the width of river. Though no humans could be seen, I saw two blue herons walking through the new riverbed, the park finally to themselves.

Though I know it is not possible, in my memory, I am sure I saw two herons walking hand in hand in the long shadows of a late summer's night.

Leslie Van Gelder was born in New York City in 1969 and took degrees in British and Native American literatures at, respectively, the University of Michigan and the College of New Jersey. She has published a collection of essays, Weaving a Way Home *(University of Michigan Press, 2008), as well as numerous articles on cave archaeology. She teaches at the Richard Riley College of Education, Walden University, and lives in the Rees Valley, New Zealand.*

STANDING STONE

Manus Charleton

Against the grain.

On the evening of Vivienne's twenty-first he went to buy bags of fresh ice. Cars were parked outside when he got back and the party was underway on the patio at the side of the house. He packed the ice into the plastic bins of bottled beer, white wine and champagne, responding as best he could to banter from some of her friends. Then he went into the study and poured himself a whiskey. He was far from being in the mood for a party. The older he got the more he was perturbed by the gap between what he found himself saying and what he thought and how he felt. He hated when he said or agreed with something well known for the sake of having something to say, some conventional view about an item in the news in which he didn't really believe. In the aftermath he felt he had betrayed himself. And whenever he did try to say what he meant about something which had aroused his interest, something more abstract, the words seemed beyond reach. He would end up stopping short or trailing off in incoherence. At school he'd been told he had a visual rather than a verbal mind, and maybe it was true. He liked looking at things which spoke for themselves, things which had presence. And when he had come across the stone lying in a pile in a quarry yard he immediately got it for the garden, though he knew he would be risking ridicule. But at fifty the time was long past to be hidebound by what other people thought.

Oblong, smooth and round, the stone was over two meters high, its bulk proportionate to its shape and size, and with embedded symmetrical whorls, imprints of the forces that had formed it over aeons. Before setting off for work he sat in the car at the side of the house looking at the stone through the windscreen. On returning in the evening he parked in the same spot, switched off the ignition and sat looking at the stone. The dissonances of the day began then to recede. Thoughts of things done or not done would still come and go but they were losing their hold. And whenever a difficult problem got resolved as a result of events beyond his control, it seemed in keeping with the way the ritual of looking at the stone was drawing him into a different outlook from the norm, one which took him beyond immediate things requiring his attention.

Yet he could relate to a twenty-first, all the more to his own daughter's, and he wanted to take part. A twenty-first still a rite of passage, at least in name, still a time to be excited in the face of the unknown. He sat back and drank. Above the music he could hear animated voices from different conversations and pictured the eager gestures and facial expressions. Out of the hubbub now and then a voice rose, assertive and insistent. A voice infused with an emotional investment in some understanding gained about something going on in the world; yet its very stridency betrayed the speaker's need to allay insecurity through getting other people to agree. He drank back the whiskey, poured himself another, and went out onto the patio. It was beginning to get dark, and candles lighting in the stillness added to the fervid atmosphere as inhibitions lessened and people grew more excited.

Helen came out of the kitchen carrying the candle-lit cake which she placed on a table and, withdrawing her hands in a flourish, declared "For my baby girl." People gathered round singing happy birthday, an orange glow from the flames reflecting on their faces. Someone called on Vivienne to make a wish and she closed her eyes tight and then blew out the candles to applause and cheers as champagne corks popped and flutes were filled and handed out. To calls of "speech", "speech", Vivienne thanked everyone for coming, and for their gifts; then, after banter and further comments, he looked closely at her as she spoke of her friend Evelyn, how she missed her, how she would have loved her to be here, and how she would like for everyone to remember her. "To Evelyn", someone called. "To Evelyn", and they raised their glasses and drank. Then Helen said that, though Vivienne was now officially an adult, the key she would like her to have is the key to keep open her inner child. A key to a child's way of looking at the world with curious eyes, not taking for granted people or things as they are represented. And she finished by wishing her magic and enchantment. "To Vivienne's magic and enchantment", someone quipped, and they drank.

From the marquee down the garden pulsating dance music started and some people began to move in its direction. He went over to where Vivienne stood in a group and wished her and her friends a great night; then went into the study where he poured a whiskey and took it up to the bedroom. Evelyn's death: the circumstances impossible to forget. In the middle of the day knocked down by a car that had mounted the footpath. A loss of control the driver couldn't explain other than to say it must have been momentary inattention, and the inquest concluded a failure to drive with due care. Evelyn, like Vivienne, in her element as an art student, in the fresh stimulation of being young and creative. The chance events that bring death. On the radio earlier in the day an item on the Indonesian tsunami; the scale of death and destruction was still being reported months after the chaos. The sea erupting in an onslaught on the land – he could well imagine how people would have responded before science. A reason to bow down and deify a power in nature, and to make sacrifice to appease the god's anger. A talk show had followed with a discussion about how a supposedly all powerful and benevolent Christian God could have allowed a tsunami to occur; the God who could raise his hand to part the waters of the Red Sea and allow the Israelites safe passage. No one could give a plausible explanation, and believers when pressed were hard put to say why they still held onto their faith.

Evelyn's death – its abruptness – had shocked Vivienne out of taking anything for granted. It had forced her inward, making her more uncertain, serious and careful. It showed in her intense face and voice; in the way she strained to say what she couldn't express; it lay behind all that she found inadequate. And she had pared back her art to trying to catch on canvas the brute presence of things in a visual flash. Her paintings, he thought, caught something of the sudden astonishment he had felt in early adolescence when it fully dawned on him a world was there, a world in which he was self-aware, in which other people, things and creatures appeared. An experience of strangeness as intense as it had been brief. Often since then he had hoped to have that kind of experience again. Too much had come to intervene, too much to do with conforming to the ways of the world in order to get on.

About to draw the bedroom curtains he stopped to watch a group form a ring around the stone. A few of the girls looked tipsy; others unsteady in high heel shoes which they removed, one kicking them off with abandon. Eager to join the ring, a girl left down her glass and, as it fell over and spilt he could see her exclaim "Jesus". She moved the glass away with her foot; then stumbled into the others who held her up. When they'd all linked hands someone said something and they laughed. A girl let go and stood outside the circle. A shiver ran through her body and she crossed her arms and gripped her shoulders. Then the group began to prance around the stone, lifting their legs high and laughing. He felt his annoyance flare; then shook his head and drew the curtains.

He had not intended the stone to be a symbol of any pagan religion, still less one that would be mocked. Disillusioned with religion, he had long been wary of claims that something existed for which there is no proof. The world according to science, the world based on evidence verified by the senses, the world built up with everyday devices, proves itself reliable, and when it doesn't there's an explanation, or at least an expectation of one. Yet there's more to things than can be proved, and the stone a reminder of what lies beyond comprehension.

In bed he put in earphones and fell asleep to soothing music. During the night he awoke and took out the earphones and switched off the device. Beside him Helen lay asleep. *4 a.m.* shone luminously on the digital bedside clock. In the house, in the garden, all felt quiet. He got out of bed and looked out the window. There was no sign of anyone. Then he noticed a candle had been left burning in front of the stone. More likely than not, other candles had also been left to burn. He put on his bathrobe and went down. At the kitchen door he saw he was still in his bare feet, but the night was warm and he opened the door and went out.

Candles were burning on the patio tables, casting yellow pools on the white tablecloths strewn with leftover food and empty glasses and bottles, and they were burning too in front of the dwarf cypress trees that stood like statuary on each side of the steps that led up from the patio into the garden. He looked around. Everyone seemed to have gone. The fire still glowed in the outdoor pot-bellied stove. He went over and sat by the stove and stared into the glow. He couldn't remember when he'd last sat alone by a fire outdoors in the dark. The contrast between the silence and earlier noise was stark. He would come back and sit here after he'd blown out the candles. As he lifted them from the tables and from the steps, the beady rivulets of hardened grease looming in front of his face reminded him of stalactites. And, as he crossed the garden to the candle in front of the stone, his feet tingled in the dewy grass and his shadow projected from the solar-lights in the flowerbeds. Lifting the candle from the ground, he stumbled and reached out to the stone and stopped his fall. Then, turning round, he startled as an unfamiliar shape bulked large. The marquee – he had forgotten it was there, and hadn't seen it before in the dark. He stood transfixed as his palpitations eased. Holding the lighted candle, he walked down to the marquee, parted the flap and went inside. It had been made to look like a cave. Rocks of crumpled dark-grey construction paper were fixed to the roof and sides and lay at the edges of the floor. As he moved the candle looking round, shadows loomed and the atmosphere turned strange. Then he held the candle still and felt in his bones distant ancestors shining burning torches on paintings of wild animals on the walls.

Manus Charleton lectures in Ethics and Politics at the Institute of Technology, Sligo. He is the author of the textbook Ethics for Social Care in Ireland: Philosophy and Practice *(Gill and Macmillan, 2007). He has been published previously in* Irish Pages, *in the* Dublin Review of Books *and in* Studies: An Irish Quarterly Review.

EPIPHANIES

John F. Deane

The craft of loneliness.

A small, two-roomed school, one hundred yards down the laneway towards the monastery, in off the main road. The rhododendron bushes dense, with the glisten of raindrops at times, and with an explosion of large and pink-soft blossoms. Half-way down the lane, turn in through the small green-iron gate, and there's the school, where I so often, mornings, heard my name called out, heard my own answering call, *anseo*, present, here I am, for here I was to learn what it all was about, the world, the flesh, and God. And all those friends, young and easy, too, at the small green gate of life, Paddy, *anseo*, Seamus, Thady, Seán – for this was a school run by the Franciscan brothers, boys only, the girls' school a quarter mile up the road, mother a teacher there – *anseo, anseo, anseo*.

I am walking home, the afternoon soft and easy, the schoolbag sitting easily on my back. Third or fourth class, for I had already developed a certain boldness and nonchalance as if I had mastered a great deal of what there is to know about this puzzling earth on which we live. I was excited, for in amongst the second-hand readers, the book of tables, the catechism, there was a new and a great treasure, a tiny lead cannon-gun on tiny wheels that would shoot real matches, propelled by a tiny spring, to a distance of almost two feet. I had swapped my new fountain pen for it, and was in a rush home to show it off. And there was Stokes, near neighbour, in his shirt-sleeves, laboring on the road, shoveling stones into a hole, then back out of the hole and into another hole, for that's what his labouring appeared to be. On his head he wore a white handkerchief, its corners knotted so that it fitted his skull and saved him from the worst effects of a weak sunshine. The thick grey hairs of his chest peered from his open shirt, like feathers, the muscles of his arms thrust out powerfully under the heavily-stained, rolled-up sleeves. He stopped, fitted his big hands on the handle of the shovel, leaned on it and watched me as I approached.

"Well, well, well," he said, in a mocking tone of voice, "here's the scholar, his head a-burstin' with knowledge an' I bet a shillin' to a farthin' ye cannot tell me what's the Irish word for tar."

I hesitated. "I haven't got that far in the book yet, John", I replied at last, then passed along, preserving a further dignified silence, my scholarly eyes diverted. But I heard the loud chuckling that followed me all the way home. Stokes, slow-moving, heavy-soldered, John Joe Stokes, one for the dimness of the snug and the darkness of the pints, one whose life I could not fathom, nor whose longings I could never gauge.

God, on our island, insinuated himself, like the thousand varieties of rain, everywhere. He was thudded down on our bent backs as we hummed our lessons from catechism and Bible history. He was associated with a memory of a bitter people, herded onto piers to leave the safety of these shores for impossible places: Faith of our fathers, mother sang, in spite of dungeon, fire, and sword.

> With a stump of white chalk,
> a squared-off piece of black slate,
> I inscribed, to perfection, the word
> GOD. I remember concentration, teeth
> irritating against the lips, harsh
> scraping sounds as I worked. Remember, too,
> no words of praise or acclamation but only
> small clouds of dust rising as I erased.

There was a big coloured chart on the schoolroom wall, with pictures of bellows, anvil, rasp; I had to tell the process through, in Irish; the horse coming to the forge, the darkness within, the fire, the hiss of water: *boilg*, *inneoin*, *raspa*. I had to tell of harness, cart-wheel, tongs; and there were boys to whom all this was familiar, almost everyday business. But to me it was strange and distant, pushing the language of my country into unknown territory, for we had a brand new baby Ford garaged in what had been the stable. History was a book against the English, how they pounded, and hammered, and shaped, how they stole our language and undid our souls. The Bible stories were of oppression and escape, of a vengeful God and a slaughtering Power. (God, we were told, had surrounded us for centuries with his love; why, then, did our hearts so rarely beat high with joy? The famine bodies had filed in silence to the altar-rocks, the people had been true to him till death; and we were taught to revere them, the fathers, those knuckle-breasted lovers of bitterness who had not yet ascended from the catacombs. What wonder then, that we should turn to lesser gods who have not, nor will not, love us with such gravity, such devotion.) Brother Sebastian, should we falter, curved his rod cut from the rhododendron hedge into a horse-shoe shape: begin, he'd call, *boilg*, *inneoin*, *raspa*.

I came back, eldering gentleman, several books of poems attempting to state that I had, at last, become some sort of a scholar. The monastery school was little more than a tumble of naked walls, without roof or window or door, open to the skies, weeds and grasses for floor. Now the island winds were the masters, moving through the empty spaces with authority. Thistle-dust instead of chalk-dust was blowing through the air. The only lesson left to be learned is the lesson of time, with its corollaries. In my mind, as I stood listening to the sing-song call of a thrush from the slatternly rhododendron bushes that were left, I offered roll-call: morning-time, we small boys settling, and I hear my name called out, hear my own answering call, *anseo*, present, here I am, but that call was yesterday's call and yesterday was over half a century ago. That child, that scholar, that acolyte to a stern God, that innocent, is absent now, *as láthair*, flown. I speak aloud, into the wind, to the dead in their ordered rows, their scratched-upon and ink-stained desks, Seamus, I say, Thady, Seán, I call, here I am, still willing, still learning, still studying what it is to be a human with human longings and a straining towards the Divine. And it is only the breeze that answers, only the cries of curlews echoing from the distant shore.

Two rooms, the "small" room, for the smaller boys, from lower infants up to first class; the "big" room for the big boys (and oh the pride of that, the glory) from second to sixth. In the big room we were truly scholars, we were going to get it all straight, from arithmetic to geography to the histories of God's heroes and his militias. Between the two rooms a high, wooden partition that could be concertinaed back, but which rarely was, for what had the bigger boys to do with the smaller ones? Behind the school, by the bushes, the lavatories, dale boards half-hung, skreeks from the rusting hinges. In the big classroom a coloured, mesmerizing chart of stars and moons, the plotted laneways of their elliptical voyages; there were pastel-coloured maps, too, of the known world, and a larger one of Ireland, with its counties and its sorry history offered up in cartoons of the great and wicked. In the small room, the words that Mrs Kilbane chalked up on the blackboard, words to be copied down into a headline copybook, were puzzling at first, though we could write our names in melted tar on the roadside walls. The clumpy sticks of crayons, the thin pencils, were, at first, more cumbersome than shovels in our hands but by the time we sat scared before the looming figure, in brown habit, of Brother Sebastian, we were skilled at spelling and we could use a pen with a split nib and ink from the tiny well at the top of the desk. Words our medium and our method, our praying and complaining, and words our way around the screeching games we played out on the lumpy field in the early afternoon.

The scholars, their heads a-burstin' with knowledge; I found them, when I stepped into the Burns Library at Boston College, bearing the burden of the title: "visiting scholar". Oh I was shy and scared, I, a poor scholar from the two-room school in Bunnacurry, Achill, and here I was, in a great hall of learning, to give a course to freshmen and sophomores, true scholars, in the writing of poetry. I could hear old John Joe Stokes, labouring man, his incredulous, his mocking chuckles. One may wander from the sources of one's first school lessons, but never forget the real lessons that life teaches. There, in the plush and daunting furnishings of the Irish Room in the Burns Library, I am actually calling names out in a genuine taking of the rolls, strange names, names that betoken the many immigrants from so many lands, Jessica Hincapie, Jay Lin Lang, Heather Bourke Polanczyuck, and all these bright and eager students gazing up at me as if I, scholar from the tiny monastery school of Bunnacurry, Achill Island, can dare to tell them how poetry occurs, how to catch the wonders of this creation in magical words and forms. Tonight I will give a public reading, in what appears to be an *Aula Maxima*, to an audience of professors, masters, doctors of philosophy and medal-winners, offering them poems on the crumbling of the monastery in Bunnacurry, on the harbour at Cloghmore, on the current at Bullsmouth. I shall stand before them, a-tremble, far from home, trying to hold my scholar's head on high. *Anseo*, I will whisper to myself, *anseo*, here I am, still learning, still ignorant of the Irish word for tar.

Mornings in the two-room school, mornings after rain; a shuffle-off and scuffling to hang wet coats, an abandoning of marvels, our sherbet, our lucky-bags, our marvellous show-off new acquisitions of toys or comics, and then the clattering of desk lids, the slapping of books. I learned, early, the craft of loneliness, though at playtime I ranged and rowdied with the rest and the best of them. I was stopped, often, as I have been always, by harmonies sensed among furze blossoms and the assonant humming of the bees, by the sheer exuberance and near transcendent whiteness of a herring-gull high against the light-blue sky, by the fluttering among the heathers of a swallowtail butterfly, a tortoiseshell, or the hairy crawling of a caterpillar along the steeps of a fern or a lupin stem. I did not yet see the beautiful God in these things, but I found myself stilled by unnameable longing. And then I was back indoors, accepting the rote calling out of rollicking verses, the echoes of the need to share a lunch with one who had forgotten his, or who had little enough to bring tied up in the wrapper of a loaf. It was the music of being, it was the distant whisper of that music, of harmonies certain in their ultimate structuring, a music that was grounded and pure of ego, it was a deep and satisfactory, though not understood, base prelude, the fugue yet to come. And it came, the fugue, slowly, surely, and is swelling still towards its cadenza. For I came, recently, to the Western Wall in Jerusalem and was told that here was the gateway to heaven, here was the great partition that would part, draw back, concertinaed, to reveal, at last, the glory, the fulfilment, the peace.

> I stand – a continent away
> from the crumbled walls of Bunnacurry 2-room school –
> now, at last, by the Western Wall,
> leaning my hands against its massive stones, and seeking words;
>
> "in Yerushalayim", the Spirit wrote, "shall be my name forever";
>
> to my left, black coat and pants,
> white shirt and thick grey beard, kippah, prayer shawl, a man
> sways back and forth in prayer –
> *hear, O Yisrael, The Lord our God, the Lord is one* … Torah, psalms;
>
> our little catechism asked: *does God*
>
> *know all things?* The high partition
> between the rooms squealed on its castors, folding open,
> when Father Tiernan came
> to test our souls; *God knows all things, even*
>
> *our most secret thoughts and actions.* I relished then
>
> the loveliness of the near-rhymes,
> the old-fashioned *doth*-and-*dost* of the English, leaving
> a softly-furred coating on the soul. I need to know
> the rough texture of a wall you could break your life against; and so

I have come to take possession, of the songs, the psalms, the
                                          lamentations,

Ruth and Boaz, Jonah,
Daniel in the den of lions – for these are my stories, too,
the prophet Moshe stretching out his hand
over the sea, Yermiyahu's grief before the golden throne

of Babylon, with Markos, Mattityahu, Loukas, Yohanan ...

for here is the gate of Heaven, folded open,
where we thrust our words towards the invisible, waiting for those
inaudible answers, where we thrust our prayers
into the crevices in the wall,

and speak aloud, look, here I am, oh Elohim, oh Yeshua, here I am:

John F. Deane was born in 1943 in Achill Island, Co Mayo. He is the author of two novels and ten collections of poems, most recently The Instruments of Art *(2005),* A Little Book of Hours *(2008),* Eye of the Hare *(2010), and* Snow Falling on Chestnut Hill: New and Selected Poems, *all from Carcanet Press. In 1979, he founded Poetry Ireland, the national poetry organization, and* Poetry Ireland Review. *He lives in Dublin.*

SLAUGHTER

Ruth Gilligan

In a stranger's kitchen.

(Editor's note: In the early twentieth century, kosher butchers from overseas travelled through the Irish countryside killing animals in the proper kashrut way so as to provide meat to the meagre Jewish communities dotted across the island.)

"Right so, well there're the three I'm after choosing for you, so."

Moti stared at the pen. Small enough, maybe ten by ten, with bars along three sides and then just the wall of the barn for the back, the ripples of the corrugation flaked in rust. The gate in front of them was held shut by a knot of grain-coloured string. A mess of a thing – you'd be as well just cutting through it as trying to get the twists and turns undone.

The straw inside the enclosure was filthy, matted black and wet though it had been a dry spell of late. A fresh pat sat in the corner, warm. And three large cows – two of them Irish Moiled, naturally – standing oddly still, as if knowing their fate was watching. A stranger in black overalls and a bushy beard, a *kippah* at the back of his head like a cap that had shrunk in the rain.

"Now, your one Ellie there on the left is a fine thing," Joe went on. "Guts of a hundred stone, give or take. Cautious enough with the milk, like, but I suppose that won't be a bother to you lot."

Moti shook his head. Stroked the beast with his eyes.

"And that's Maisy beyond with the missing tail. Flithered it in some barb a couple of summers back, the gobshite. She'd be a bit bigger now, only a bit older – one of the mammy's of the bunch, like. Fine bossy head on her."

The head in question was smooth and white, *maoi* being the Irish for moiled, or hornless. The body itself was a reddy brown with a stripe rubbed out along the back and the face, an empty borderline.

Maisy nudged Ellie's arse. Ellie didn't blink. Didn't so much as swat her little dressing-gown tassel tail.

"And your man here at the front is, as you can tell, our British White. Be setting you back the most, of course, but'd sort out with the largest dose of steaks. Cocky shite altogether but sure, no surprise there given his breeding, what?"

(This story continues after Portfolio.)

PORTFOLIO

Peter Geoghegan

Albania's Spaç

Main Detention Centre, Spaç Prison Camp

Spaç was the most notorious of the more than 50 forced labour camps in Enver Hoxha's Communist Albania. Opened as a "re-education centre" in the 1960s, it is in Mirdita region of northern Albania, and had been an Italian army barracks during the Second World War occupation. After a failed revolt at Spaç in 1973, the uprising's four leaders were executed, eighty-seven prisoners had their sentences extended by twenty years or more, and family visits were restricted to five minutes. When the Communist regime fell in 1991, the triumphant Democratic Party (led by Hoxha's one-time physician, Sali Berisha) promised to turn Spaç into a museum for the victims of Communism. Two decades on, the prison lies abandoned and crumbling. Peter Geoghegan writes, "When I visited in the summer of 2013, I found animals grazing in former isolation cells, order books from the 1980s left in undocumented piles, and buildings falling in on themselves."

Peter Geoghegan is a writer and freelance journalist. Originally from Co Longford, he now lives in Glasgow. He is currently writing a book about Scotland's independence referendum for Luath Press. He is the Editor of Political Insight.

Communist Slogan at Spaç

PORTFOLIO

Holding Cell, Spaç

Rows of Cells, Spaç

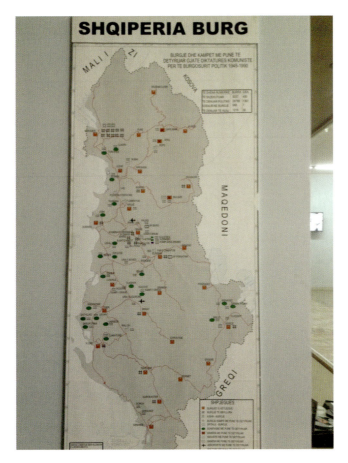

Map of Forced Labour Camps in Communist Albania,
National History Museum, Tirana

Memorial to Communist Crimes, Tirana

PORTFOLIO

Tractor on a Cooperative Farm at Hajmel, Albania

Cooperative Vineyard, Hajmel, Albania

Holding Centre, Spaç

Detention Centre, Spaç

PORTFOLIO

View from a Cell, Spaç

Holding Centres, Spaç

PORTFOLIO

Holding Centre, Spaç

National History Museum, Tirana

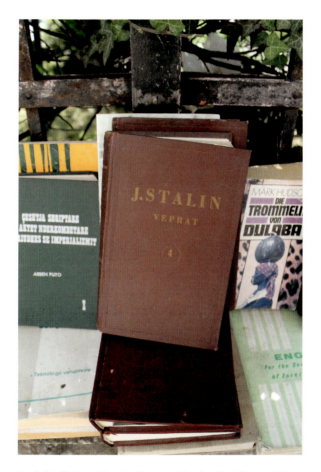

Book Stall Outside the Former Hoxha Residence, Tirana

The Former Residence of Enver and Nexhmije Hoxha, Blloku, Tirana

PORTFOLIO
is generously supported by Nicholson & Bass Ltd, Belfast.

Moti shook his head with a hint of amusement this time. Politics, yes, even in the cattle.

And Joe looked at him then, to check. "Christ, Moti – you're not giving much away today, are you? Feel I'm here trying to flog off one of me own bloody daughters!" And then, quieter: "I mean, if I had any, so to speak."

The British White had a pair of red horns and the lowest belly of the lot. If there'd been udders they would have scraped the floor, dragging the muck into patterns as he went.

"And where were ye lot now before me?"

This, at last, Moti answered: "Jim Sweeney. Down in Collooney. Very much land, you know him?"

He watched Joe cross his arms like a child's huff. "Christ, sure everyone knows Big Bollocks Sweeney, alright. Pity we mightn't. I'm only surprised he is, you know, willing to take part in your little … *scheme*, so to speak."

"Oh yes," Moti assured, unfazed. "Nine there we slaughtered today. Only, a growth on the lung had one of them so we couldn't take her after all."

"Ah the divil! Bet Jimbo was thanking his stars – a free kill."

Moti looked at the ground. "Only half price he charge us."

"A merciful fucker, aye."

Moti stayed looking down, the blood splats on his boots as if he was prone to just kicking the beasts to death.

As it happened, Jesse and Ori had said Mr Sweeney was alright. Even laid on a few sandwiches, which the wife brought down to the rest of them waiting in the carts by the gate. Thick cheese on soda, so fresh you could still taste the rennet.

They had left there about an hour ago when the light was still good. Passed a group of British Constables on the way, His Majesty's finest – they were everywhere at the moment, things getting more restless by the day. Nearly four years since the Rising but there was another one lurking, to be sure.

The Polis had glared at the butchers as they passed, but hadn't bothered to stop them, given their attire.

Are you a Protestant Jew or a Catholic Jew?

The old joke, kicked to death.

"Right well, I think the bullock I will take," Moti pronounced, eventually.

"Ah sure, a good choice, now."

"So I am hoping."

Though really it didn't matter which of them he picked. They probably had enough from the day as it was – probably a waste of time coming up here for just the one kill but Moti hadn't seen Joe in almost a year now so he had insisted. The annual chat.

Despite himself, he felt a little blush.

He had taken a shine to the farmer a while back, shortly after joining the group. He could still remember the day itself, one of the heifers growing restless until she ended up landing Moti an almighty kick, clock on the shin. A gasp off Joe, mortified entirely, before he'd insisted Moti come inside for a bandage and a wet of tea.

The warm scut of a kitchen. A chipped jug of daffodils wilting towards the table, a woman's touch.

And ever since, it had been there between them. Chatting away each year, man to man – maybe even local to local – something Moti hadn't really got from anyone else on the island. At least, not when you were dressed like this.

He looked at his friend now, the speckled patch on the head that reached a little further than last time. He reminded himself to ask about the wife.

Joe led the bullock out around the back for him into another, smaller, barn, empty but for the straw and shit.

"Be the best place now, I'd reckon."

"The usual," said Moti.

"Aye, yes. The usual."

The beast watched them both carefully. Lashes long over bulging eyes, popping from the sides of its head.

Joe held the rope in place while Moti crouched down on the ground and unrolled his leather pack, a little tinkle from the tools as they settled.

"And go on, so is it true that Sweeney's after sticking up another barn in the top field, then?" Joe asked. "Only I was down in Keogh's with the boys back Saturday and they were bending me ear that…"

But Moti wasn't listening now. Held the *sakin* up to the light to check for bumps, imperfections. The blade was in good condition, just the right size – twice the width of the British White's neck but not much more – the jowls like an old man's that flapped from side to side when telling a story.

He had noticed Joe's neck too. A bit more flap there now than before.

The knife glinted in the fading glow that had tiptoed in the door to watch. Moti took his fingernail, placed it at the base of the metal and ran it along, creating a fine white dust in the air. A magic.

He felt the four eyes watching him, two with eyelashes two without.

He lowered the blade.

"Are you right, so?" Joe said then, by way of acknowledgement. Taking a step back.

Moti stroked the beast, the whitepink hairs which swirled in ebbs and tides, a whole body of a fingerprint. He could feel the chest rise and expand, flinch at the first touch – a little quiver – but then it calmed again, giving in to the pressure of the fingers. The reassurance.

One long lazy blink and the cut was made. The windpipe and then the oesophagus. A spurt of blood onto his hand but he mustn't flinch, mustn't press down on the warm, splitting skin, only ease across to the end like drawing a line in the sand at Clifden Bay until the tide comes and seeps it all away.

And the blood, beginning like a local's confession.

"… although, I'd say we've a turn coming on," Joe continued still, rocking on his heels, chatting away as if over tea not death. "Them clouds does be awful mean-looking there beyond …"

Moti feeling the warmth of the flow. Two minutes, maybe three, until it ran dry.

The British White was already unconscious, his head slumped forward like an old man dreaming in a chair.

"… supposed to be doing some bailing myself tomorrow, like, but if the ground's getting a pissing tonight arra sure …"

Before it fell to its knees.

"… and the lads below will be gutted altogether – there was supposed to be a hop down in Keogh's hall tonight. A dance, like. Everyone in the Parish – the whole shooting match."

And suddenly Joe span around, away from the barn door towards the sunken beast, eyes all a-dazzle.

"Ye lads wouldn't think of heading down to it now, would ye?"

For the first time Moti looked up, hesitated.

But Joe was away. "Because Jaysus, just think of it now – what in Jaysus the girls would say if ye lot appeared, all dressed up to the nines in your garb, like. All … how many are ye again?"

"Ten."

"Ah yea a'course. I remember now. Need that quota yoke, don't you?"

"The *minyan*."

"Yea yea, I remember. The quota. For the praying. But come here to me now and let me tell you, there'd be a right quota of fillies going *flathúllach* over ye lads if ye were to be moseying on down – sure, they've probably never seen a pack of Jewies in their entire lives!"

The punchline burst Joe's hands out of his pockets, palms facing front, the fat in mounds between the deep lines as if they were tied with string. But as soon as they were out he was ashamed of them, probably hearing what he had said.

The beast rolled to the left just as Moti had guessed. He strained to catch, the weight massive in his arms, and then eased it to the ground.

"Ah now, I didn't mean …" Joe tried, his head low, his voice lower again. "I wasn't implying …"

The flow began to slow, the straw sodden through.

"Sure, I'm sure you all have lovely girls back home, waiting on you. Wives, like. Jew … *Jewish* wives, a'course."

Moti looked at the lashes up close. The eye which had never seen pain. Longing.

Because no, there were no wives. No homes. Just an endless loop up and around the country and then a zigzag through her middle, slaughtering as they went. They had it down to an almost perfect twelve-month cycle now – the regularity suited them. Spring in the North (though the number of koshers was dwindling up there by the day), *Pesach* in Dublin (somewhere amidst the stench of Treaty and trouble), Summer across the belly of the country, Autumn in the West and then Cork for *Chanukah*, demand for their services at its yearly peak.

But despite the movement, it all began to look the same. The seasons. The rain. The shitstraw and the tattered *geansaís* of the men themselves, a queer delight in their annual visitors even if they claimed to be embarrassed. Obliging. Secretive.

They slept in barns mostly, or down in the towns, dreaming of girls and dances though they could never admit.

Moti watched the last few drops of the British White spill out, splattering his boots. A fresh set of join-the-dots.

Of course, there were times when Ori and Jesse, the youngest of the ten, did disappear. In the pub of an evening – stand up to get in the next round of pints and not return again until morning, faintly flushed. Barely a word as to where they had been or who they had been with. Not even the time Jesse had had that tear in his shirt – a button missing, yanked away in haste – like a little mourning rip, grieving for a life which they could only taste but never really know.

The following day, over morning prayers, the jealousy of the group had hovered low. Glances. Unasked questions. But also the knowledge that, in time, these youngsters would resign to it like the rest of them – come to appreciate the littler highlights of life on the road. A decent run of dry weather. A cup of sweet tea in a stranger's daffodil-stenched kitchen.

"Right," Moti eased himself back to his hunkers, a squelch as his limbs prized free. "The organs I will now check and then I am finished."

"Right!" Joe answered, too quickly, as if he'd been waiting there in the darkness for a chance to speak again, eyebrows tight despite the attempt at a smile.

Moti took another blade from the pouch and made a new slit along the gut of the bull, ruffling the hair against the grain so it stood up around the wound like a moustache on top of a lip.

He rolled his sleeve a little further. Flexed his fingers and then, slowly, eased them in.

And it always reminded him of delivering a baby, this bit. Had even found one once by surprise – the farmer hadn't known – had to ask Sol, the eldest of them, what to do with it. The unkosher unborn.

Joe looked away again now, checking the last of the day before it went entirely. "Yes, they'll have great craic altogether down at the dance," he repeated, forcing himself, somehow, though the words came out exhausted. "Sure we all need a vent at the moment – too much killing in the air."

The left lung was fine. Very smooth.

"No one told us freedom would be such a vicious bitch, what?"

The right one too. *Glatt*.

"Ah but, that's assuming a'course the weather holds on them – sure the *cailíní* will be devastated if their hair gets all—"

At this Moti remembered, just in time. "And how is Máire, Joe? Sorry, I should have—"

"Ah don't be silly," Joe cut in. "Sure she's … grand, like. Much the same, you know yourself. Some days good, some days …"

He trailed away as the last light gave, leaving them in almost darkness.

Moti's fingers found the heart. A bit small, but otherwise perfect.

He pulled his way out with another squelch. His hand felt cold back in the air again. "Ok, Joe, well he is all fine – one to keep."

Joe took a minute. Just a second too long.

Some days ...

"Grand, so. Well for you. Now, do you need a hand down with it?"

"No, no," said Moti. "I get one of the others to come up and—"

"Arra, go way out of that!"

"No, really—"

"Sure it'd be as quick if I—"

"No!" The shout bounced off the iron, stunned it to silence. "No I am sorry it is just ... you must ..." Moti sighed then, regretting every translated word. "You cannot touch ..."

"Ah, a' course," Joe edged away, his hands back into his pockets. Fingers ashamed all over again. "A' course a' course – my mistake, Moti. Don't mind me now."

Moti stood there amidst the destruction, one arm wet to the elbow, wishing he could take it back.

Joe was right. It smelled like rain.

The cart was loaded, the front half of the cow safely stowed and the unclean hindquarters left behind. The farmers always made a joke about the beasts being *legless*, which apparently meant drunk, though they never complained about getting the bit extra to keep. Dinner no doubt.

Old Sol was in the driver's seat. The horse was restless.

"Right well, to you I give this, Joe. As agreed." Moti handed the envelope, bright white even in the darkness. "To check it, feel free."

"Ah, go way out of that – sure, there'd be no need at all for that, like."

Joe said as he shoved it into his back pocket, tucked the bottom of his fraying jumper up over it again. A sag in the wool.

They could hear the horse's breathing. Nostrils as big as eyes.

"And is the new tractor—"

"Right well, safe journey—"

They laughed, awkward laughs, thankful at least for the excuse of a smile.

"Sorry," said Moti.

"No no, go on yourself," said Joe, the encouragement almost like that you would give to a child.

But Moti was happy to take it. All the chats that had been saved for this very moment, just a few minutes more – Sol could wait. Better yet if the beast had dealt him another kick so they could head inside again, take tea and maybe a crust of something more. Watch the rain arrive at last, Biblical, so he'd have to stay the night—

But instead, he heard himself speak: "Just be sure to send my wishes to Máire." A panic that left only shame. "And no doubt I will be seeing you—"

"Well actually, Moti, I was meaning to have a little word ..."

Joe stared over Moti's shoulder now, his words aimed at someone else entirely. The shock of gorse blazed in the blackness, butteryellow.

"It's just, I ... *we* were thinking of easing up around here, you know? A couple of chickens and a bit of dairy but it's getting ... well, what with Máire needing all her looking after. And then with all this talk of overthrowing the Hun – not that an old bollocks like me would be much use to the cause at this stage, what?" He tried a smile, though it didn't quite take. "Ach, but either way I do be having my hands full enough now, you know?"

"Oh ... oh I see," Moti said, though really the darkness meant he could see very little anymore.

"And I'm awful sorry," Joe bumbled on now, his brow knotted like twine. "Don't mean to be messing you around it's just ... people are tending to talk and ... well no, no anyway, I won't be buying at the fair this year – leave all that to that fucker Sweeney, don't you know – so I won't ... there won't be much in the way to *offer* you, so to speak."

Moti listened, trying to untangle the excuses. "No no," he tried. "It is OK, Joe," lying the best he could. "I ... I understand," felt the breeze at his neck, cold now, the warmth of his *kippah* suddenly heavy on his head.

Behind him Sol drummed his knuckles on the reins, making his impatience known. Because it was late – they should have said evening prayers at least an hour ago. That was the problem with there only being ten of them – without the *minyan* they couldn't begin, so if one was delayed then the whole lot were held up. Barely enough freedom to breathe.

And suddenly Moti thought of that unborn calf. The one he had discovered, years back. Kosher, according to Sol, because of the way the mother had been killed. The barely formed limbs to be cooked up with all the rest.

"Well, the very best of luck to you, Joe." Moti offered his hand, clean except for a thin ring of red around the edge of each nail, bloodshot like eyes.

Joe looked at it, as if deciding.

"And to yourself, Moti. To the lot of ye," taking the fingers and shaking, a very different flesh somehow.

"And to Máire," Moti added. "Of course."

Before Joe nodded, just the once, and was gone.

The cart ricketed away down the lane. The steady clop of the horse's hooves and the glow of Sol's annoyance as their shoulders banged together, on now towards the dim glow of Sligo Town, a faint beacon in the distance. The first drops of a shower just beginning to spit.

And Moti pictured the girls all off to the dance – the beautiful Irish girls – skin as white as milk. Their freshly pinned hair turned frizzy in the rain, a great golden clod of straw.

Ruth Gilligan was born in 1988 in Dublin and is a graduate of three universities – Cambridge, Yale and East Anglia – and an O'Reilly Scholar from Dublin, shortly to be awarded her doctorate in English from the University of Exeter. She has published three commercial novels, one of which made her the youngest person ever to reach number one on the bestseller list. In recent years, she has turned to literary fiction, and has now completed her fourth novel, centred on the history of Irish Jews, which also provided inspiration for this story. She currently teaches Creative Writing at the University of Exeter.

THE ROAD TO GRANADA

Gerard McCarthy

How does one live one's life?

At Knock it was a crystal-clear cold early April morning. Through the window of the plane I saw a man on the platform of a low-loader fling a bucket of pale red liquid onto the wing and, with an implement one might use to clean a big window, he began to spread it vigorously; they were de-icing the plane; it was four degrees below zero. The plane rose into the clear blue sky, passing over a clutch of cattle in a boggy field. None of them looked up, intent as they were on the meagre grass beneath them. Soon the sky clouded beneath us and we could have been anywhere or nowhere, until we came down through the clouds a few hours later, into Malaga. Outside the airport I boarded a bus, which left almost immediately and brought me in through intermittent drizzle, via the bus station, onto the main street, where I got off and walked round the corner in the confidence that I would see once again the familiar sign: Hotel Sur.

After checking in, my feet took me with an inevitability down the road to the sea.

At the back of the beach I passed a woman who may have been north African, sitting looking out. I wondered was one of her kin making the short journey from their native home, across the short stretch of water in front of her. As I walked along, the sky gradually cleared and the sun came out. I sat on a spur of rocks for a long while, listening to and looking at the water rising and falling in front of me, trying to gain a measure of my own latest small journey into my unknown, my opaque ambition. On my way back along the quay I passed a Buddhist monk from India slowly walking, dwelling in his own thoughts, fingering his beads. Later, as I wandered the lively, voluble festive evening streets of Malaga, I passed an African man kneeling, his arms held out holding a large placard in front of his chest, repetitively intoning his plea like a prayer. I stood at some distance watching him before returning and throwing a few small coins into his plastic cup.

The next morning, I checked out of the hotel and walked to the bus station. I had a coffee in the cafeteria while I was waiting. There were two young north African men at another table, who seemed as if their wait was far longer than mine. A very tall, thin man came to them and spoke to them as if he had some kind of authority over them. I noticed his very long, thin hands. An old couple shuffled in slowly, and slowly settled in to their places. I think the old man was slightly deaf, and the only feature that was not old in the image of them was the woman's eyes that had the enthusiasm of a child as she leaned towards him speaking to him. I saw them outside afterwards on a bench looking out for their bus, as I loitered, gawking around me, until my time came and the old couple disappeared from my life as I joined a crowd of people at one of the bays. Two buses came in. The crowd was clustering around as the driver of the bus at my bay was barking staccatos of instructions, directing some into the bus and others around behind it. His staccato to me was accompanied by a gesture to go around, and when I showed my ticket to the driver of the other bus he nodded quickly for me to enter it. I climbed aboard without checking the destination on the front of the bus. Inside, my absurd shyness had me not seeking confirmation from another passenger, and for the beginning of the journey I had a slight unease that I might not after all be on the right bus, but as we climbed into the mountains, the signs for other destinations fell away and it became clear that it was as was meant to be, and that I was indeed on the road to Granada.

In Granada, outside the bus station I boarded a city bus in to the city centre. I got off at the cathedral and walked around it. Very quickly I was in the Plaza Bib-Rambla, and had found the Hotel Los Tilos. My room was on the fourth floor. The window overlooked a narrow enclosed space, but down the corridor was a doorway onto a balcony which opened out to the city: the square beneath, the bulk of the cathedral behind it, and the hill of the Alhambra rising above us all. I went out and first explored the square. It was crowded. Among the many traders and hawkers I watched a small human figure dressed as Mickey Mouse, selling balloons that were aloft, floating at the ends of their strings. I gave a coin to a man with one arm who was playing haunting music on a harmonium. He immediately lurched forward – I don't know was it in a gesture of thanks or to see what coin I had thrown into his box.

Soon my feet brought me up the road to the Alhambra. I made my way up to the main entrance and purchased a ticket for the Generalife Gardens. In the gardens, the atmosphere was powerfully redolent of early spring, with fresh budding and flowering. The air was crisp and cool, but the sun was warm. I loitered. I took in the prospect of the palaces below that one doesn't get filing through the crowds inside them. There were crowds in the gardens but it was possible to find more secluded places, in one of which I saw a veiled Arab woman who looked at first as if she was taking a photograph of herself with her phone, but then I realised she was taking one of her children, who had been out of my line of sight in front of her. I passed a younger man and an older man who may have been his father. The older one was determinedly choosing his steps with the younger one helping him. The younger man helped the older one sit down on a bench and left him there. The older man was a significant presence on the bench in his dark glasses, holding his stick in front of him, seeming to be taking it all in. Nearby on another bench was another young man reading a book who decades ago might have been me.

I went down to the Alhambra, and into the Hotel America, where I sat at a small table beside a sign saying "America es un continente", and had beer, and a tomato salad and bread that tasted gourmet. There were four men at a table close by. An older man was showing a younger man photographs on the back of his camera. I heard the younger man say, "I thought she was your daughter", to which the older man averred the opposite as he continued to range through the photographs, to the other man's polite dismay. I thought: far better to be sitting alone at a table than to be in company one didn't choose, watching a succession of images of people one doesn't know, interminably. I left the scene behind me and went outside to the ramparts, where I stood looking down at the city. It was a commanding prospect. Back down, when I reached the Plaza Nueva, I heard the sound of a marching band, then saw a procession, which included a big float of Christ carrying his cross, as if Easter hadn't yet happened. I headed up an alleyway that had become established as an Arab souk. My feet quickly brought me to a small square with a church at the edge of it: la Iglesia de San Gregorio Bético. I entered its shadowy light. At the bottom of the church there was a sign in a number of languages which said that God was present there, enjoining us to adore him. At the top, behind a grill from floor to ceiling, kneeling in adoration before the Host displayed in the richly ornate altar, there was the figure of a nun, all in white. All in white, she was covered completely; but for her occasional small movements it was possible to doubt that she was a real person. There was a clock on the wall beside her; its loud ticking was occasionally drowned in the noise from the streets outside when the door was opened. I wondered was she gazing rapt in adoration at the Host in front of her. For all I knew she could have been meditating on the huge blurred happening outside. I waited until another nun, also enveloped in white, appeared through a side curtain and, after joining the first one in a brief ritual, replaced her, silently.

Next day was Sunday, the first after Easter. I went into the cathedral and joined a small group of people behind a boundary cord supervised by an usher as a mass was proceeding far above us in the cavernous interior. A hymn was being sung. When it was over, a madwoman suddenly appeared down from the congregation, clapping and waving her hands into the air. The usher was affectionately firm with her as he shooed her out, parrying her attempts to embrace him. I made my exit after her and boarded a bus outside, back to the Alhambra. I headed straight for the church that was built where the mosque had stood for centuries. A mass was just about to begin. There was just a scattering of others at the top of the church. I sat at the back. The big doors were closed behind us. The priest appeared in his vestments and set about the familiar ritual. I let the unknown Spanish words wash over me. Soon he had embarked on his sermon and was in no hurry. It seemed as if he repeated a number of times the name Thomas; I guessed that doubt was his subject, and his demeanour indicated he wasn't in favour. He didn't seem disheartened by the impassive faces of his tiny congregation; he entered fully into his own flow. His voice rising, the staccato of his words carried him along against the background of the echo of his previous ones, still resounding in the almost empty church. Eventually, it seemed as if his energy was ebbing, but his voice rose for one final flourish before he gave way and carried on with the set ritual: the theatre of the consecration. When he reached the giving out of holy communion I retreated to the outside world.

I went to a bar/café across the road. The barman was friendly, and the small clientele had an easy camaraderie among them; it seemed as if they were all on brief breaks from their involvement in one way or another in the Alhambra tourist trade. It was like being backstage. One man in particular was talking jovially to a younger couple, and there was banter in Spanish between them. It seemed as if he was making fun of the foreign tour leaders that he had to deal with. As the couple were leaving he followed them to the door and as he shook their hands he repeated a few times in English with a sardonic tone, "So nice to meet you." He disappeared after them. A while later I saw him again, outside the Alhambra. He was in the midst of a group of tourists, talking to their leader with a graciousness to the point of obsequiousness. I wondered, if he were called up before a tribunal set up by his peers ... by his employers ... by God ... to which identity would he swear allegiance.

I left the Alhambra behind me and got a bus up the opposite hill of the Albaicín. When I reached the plaza of Saint Nicholas it was already crowded with hawkers and tourists and a few musicians playing flamenco. In the middle of it all sat a gypsy woman selling her castanets, clapping one of them impassively to the music. Her face lacked all enthusiasm, and had the look of someone who has seen too many things down through the years; she didn't see me. I went in search of a mosque that I had seen being built a decade before, the first to be built in Granada for centuries. A short search in the vicinity yielded it. The mosque itself was closed to visitors, but the garden was open. In the garden I asked a man who seemed to be caretaker was he aware of a Muslim cemetery in Granada. His English was poor and he didn't understand me. He went away, and came back with a leaflet in English about Muslim sites in Granada, but there was no mention of a cemetery. As I left, I heard the call from the mosque's minaret, faintly.

I came down a different way to the river right underneath the Alhambra hill. I walked along it. There were many young people out in the evening air, many with rings on their faces, some with blankets in front of them arrayed with trinkets, some playing guitars, some romancing; some drinking from bottles of beer, and occasionally a familiar waft of something heavy and sweet. I came across one young man at one of the old small bridges, with a sign saying he was giving poems away for free. There were pieces of folded paper in front of him and a receptacle for donations. When I asked for one he typed a few lines on a typewriter and he folded the paper and handed it to me. I thought how, if one were young and with a full heart, Granada is the place to be. I, with my old heart, carried on. Back in the square, most of the traders and hawkers had finished for the day. I saw the balloon-seller I had seen earlier, dressed as Mickey Mouse. This time the head of the costume was lifted up, revealing the small serious face of a south American man, talking intently to another man of the same nationality. The contrast between the expression on his face and on the mask was startling. Before going to my room, I stood outside on the balcony of the hotel. I noted the ramparts of the Alhambra. I thought how, in the heyday of the caliphate, the commanding prospect from there must have had its corollary commanding presence to the commoners living below.

That night for much of the time sleep eluded me as I wondered, perplexed: after that trio of assays on a boundary, where now can this journey and this writing go? The next morning, on the internet in the lobby of the hotel, gradually I came round to searching for the Muslim cemetery in Granada, and eventually I found a reference to it being part of the municipal cemetery, the whereabouts of which was given as a short distance past the Alhambra. I took the bus back up, and carried on along the road past it. Very quickly I had reached the municipal cemetery. A notice beside the gate mentioned different sections, called patios; off to one side, separate from the others, was mentioned "patio islamico". Another notice on the gate spoke about the cemetery providing a journey through time. I went inside.

It was an ordinary day in the life of a graveyard: lingering near the gate was a group of people in the aftermath of a funeral, some of them wearing black. One woman was crying; others were comforting her. Inside were workmen about their various roles, tending it. I walked the straight avenues with buildings either side filled with those interred, rising on each side round me, rather than in Ireland, where the graves are characteristically below. A couple of men passed by with ladders, presumably having needed them to climb to leave a tribute at the tomb of their loved one. I walked until I came to a dead end. I returned to the gate and mustered the wherewithal to ask a woman behind a counter, first apologising with the word "English", pointing to my chest, and then asking her, "patio islamico?" I didn't understand her words, but I did understand her gesture as she pointed outside and back around, past a building that was the crematorium, to a roadway behind. The road led above the crematorium, from the chimney of which a faint plume of smoke was rising. As I walked along, the road quickly became a dirt road that a sign announced to be a *camino*. Beside the road I saw an old condom in the grass. I remembered Marcus Aurelius on the transience of all mortal life: "yesterday a drop of semen, tomorrow a handful of spice and ashes." Soon I came to a walled area with a gate. The gate was closed. A sign said: "Cementario la Rawda de Granada." There was a small track around by the wall. I walked it. The graveyard looked unkempt compared to the other one. Most graves that I could see looked dishevelled and quite old, many of them unmarked. I walked around to the very back along by a high fence, wondering might there be a way in. I stopped at the back, looking out in front of me at where the hill fell in a precipitous descent. There was nothing but scrub on the side of the hill. At the bottom were some houses, then a busy main road. Lines of hills receded beyond that, until they became mountains, reaching back to the upper reaches of the Sierra Nevada. I looked around through the fence into the cemetery and, to my astonishment, it was the first thing I saw: the ultimate grave. The gravestone had the name on it, written in English: "Muhammad Asad. born 2 July 1900, died 20 February 1992." I lingered, looking open-eyed at it, amazed that I had found it.

Reader, I do not anticipate that you will know the name Muhammad Asad. I had never heard the name until a couple of years ago, when I chanced upon a documentary on Al Jazeera about his life, made by an Austrian, George Misch. There is no need for me to recount his biography; a brief perusal on the internet will yield far more than I could give. A few details are sufficient for my purposes here. He was born by the name Leopold Weiss. He was brought up in the same milieu as Franz Kafka: a western Jew in the dying world of *Mitteleuropa* at the birth of the twentieth century. Unlike Kafka, he was part of the Jewish tide into Jerusalem. Around the age of 20 he went to live there with his uncle, who had a house just inside the Jaffa Gate. It was there he had an illumination that changed the direction of his life. He suddenly realised that the Arabs he saw around him in the old city were far closer to the world of Abraham than were the Zionists who had come from Europe. Thus began for him a journey into Islam. In the middle of his life he wrote an account of that journey. The book was called *The Road to Mecca*. For a while he was at the political and religious centre of the Muslim world. Later, there was a disaffection. He lived for a couple of decades in Tangier, engaged in what he had come to see as his life's work of translating the Koran into English. At last he crossed the short stretch of water from there back to the threshold of Europe: Andalucía. He lived near Malaga until his death in his nineties. Asad was in his fifties when he wrote his autobiography. In it he repeatedly uses the metaphor of the crossing of a bridge over a chasm to characterise the journey he had made from the world of his inheritance to the world of Islam – a bridge so long that he had had to reach a point of no return before the other side became visible. The final sentence of the book imagines him riding in the midst of thousands of his new brethren. Looking behind him he sees "the bridge over which I have come: its end is just behind me while its beginning is already lost in the mists of distance." The film documentary on his life, in an echo of the title of his autobiography, is called *A Road to Mecca*. The final scene of the documentary shows an altercation in the cemetery between a Muslim cleric and a man who introduces himself as Asad's assistant. The cleric is complaining about the lack of orthodoxy of Asad's gravestone, a stone's throw from where I was standing.

Later that day I wandered around the alleyways of the city. I found myself once again in the square beside the Iglesia de San Gregorio Bético – the church of the white sisters. When I saw the door open I went into it. It was shortly after six o'clock and there were about ten of them assembled, enveloped in their white habits. Their voices were all that was revealed of them. I waited as they rhythmically said their prayers. Then they began singing, fervently. Those white sisters: why should their voices not be pure? I decided to wait until they had finished their singing and praying. It took about an hour before a couple of them, who by their set and movement looked older, made their exit through the side curtain. The others followed them, leaving one sister in still, silent, solitary prayer.

Back in the hotel, before going to my room, I stood on the balcony looking down at the square. Its day's crowds had receded. Traders were shutting up shop. In the middle of the square I saw the Mickey Mouse man, standing still and alone. A child came up close to him and stood looking at him, but it seemed he paid no heed to the child. The child was called away then, and the Mickey Mouse man was a lonely looking figure as he stood a while longer, as if he was silently considering. Eventually, he slowly made his way to one of the alleyways off the square, and disappeared.

October of that same year saw me back once again in Granada, in the lobby of the same hotel, Los Tilos, in the Plaza Bib-Rambla. Soon after checking in I was heading back up the road past the Alhambra. I walked on, across the roundabout to the main cemetery. There was a crowd gathering around the crematorium. Most of them were young people, and I imagined the deceased person was also young. I walked around along the road that soon became the dirt one that was announced as a *camino*. Looking down, I could see the crowd, and a light-coloured hearse, and the crematorium waiting. The gates of the Muslim cemetery were again closed. I walked the way I had gone before around it, and soon I was again standing looking in through the fence at the grave of Muhammad Asad, still, exactly as the last time. The sun was hot. I sought shelter beneath a tree and looked down over the valley to the mountains beyond. Meanwhile, his grave was quiet behind me. The gate was still closed when I walked back round. I carried on down past the crematorium below me. The cremation ceremony was over; the mourners were gathered outside again in a kind of alcove. I saw none of them look up to where I saw clearly the smoke rising from the chimney. If one hadn't seen the surroundings one could be forgiven for assuming that it was an ordinary social gathering. I saw some embracing long, tightly, and affectionately. Meanwhile, the smoke had all but died away, and most of the gathering had left or were leaving. I loitered around the Alhambra until evening. It was almost dark as I made my way among others into the Generalife Gardens. There was some light still left in the sky above the palaces. The gardens were lit only with small lamps along the pathways. The twilight air was resonant with crickets calling. It was only as I was leaving that the almost-full moon began to appear through the tops of the trees. Back at the hotel, from the balcony, I watched as the moon rose, floating bright, making its silent voyage through the darkness. I retired to a night divided between intervals of waking and of sleep filled with a forest of forgotten dreams.

Next morning I returned to the roundabout beyond the Alhambra, which is the boundary between the tourist world and the other world. As I approached the Muslim cemetery I saw a motorbike parked outside, and a man, who disappeared inside. The gate was open. When I asked the man could I go in he directed me to a younger man. When I mentioned Muhammad Asad, immediately the older man grinned broadly. The younger man was more reserved, with a Muslim air about him, for which I imagine I share with Asad an instinctive empathy. He asked me did I know where the grave was; I said I had seen it from the outside. I went down to it. The gravestone was supported erect by concrete spread round its base. I stood beside it, paying my respects. I placed my palm on the warm stone. I picked and pocketed the lowest cone from a cypress tree that overhung it. Again I noted the dishevelled state of most of the graves as I walked back through them. The younger man was waiting. I thanked him, and asked him did many come to visit the grave. He said people come from different countries, and then, as he made as if to begin listing them, he hesitated, into which I volunteered my own country, Ireland. He told me the cemetery was from the time of the Spanish Civil War, that about 50 Moroccans had been buried there; he mentioned Franco. As he told me the story of it I couldn't make out had they fought for Franco or against him, and I didn't ask for clarification. What I gathered was the most important: that the men buried there were killed in other men's wars, fighting for their next meal, like so many men before and after them.

The young man was locking up as I was leaving. I headed out the *camino*. A number of cars passed me. Most of the front-seat passengers seemed to be consulting their personal electronic communication devices that are the successors of mobile phones. The cars were throwing up dust in their wake. I turned off the road away from them, along a narrow track, over a broken bridge, into a quiet solitary mountainscape on which I met almost nobody. A *camino* with no particular destination. I thought of Asad's road: how all the other roads had fallen away, leaving the road that had come to this: his road that brought him back to Europe, and came to an end a short stretch of road past the Alhambra. I remembered the challenging clarity of the question in my own adolescence: how does one live one's life? A question whose answer we can never know beforehand as each of us takes our whole life to answer it. I thought, amidst the cacophony, to listen out for a tone, and to follow it, would be the height one could hope for.

That evening I returned through the crowded alleyways to the church of the white nuns. Outside, in front of its porch, there was a band playing music that was not religious, and what they were playing they were playing LOUD. Inside, the nuns, about eight or nine of them, were singing their vespers, with one of them at the back playing the harmonium. They seemed to be ignoring the noise coming in from outside. What could they do but carry on? They were repeating what I had seen and heard in April, until again, just after the clock rang seven chimes, the older ones made their exit, followed by the others, leaving the one who had been playing the harmonium kneeling in silent, solitary prayer. Outside, the band had finished, but the square was raucous. A band of young people came along in a pagan parody of a religious procession, singing and dancing in revelry. I wandered in the midst of the revelry before returning to the church again. The sister was still silent and still, with the ticking of the clock, and the sounds from the outside let in with the opening door. With what ears did she hear it, the noise of the world? Had she too, like Asad, abandoned the name she was born with, her life given direction by the charge of belief, the ritual of her days given meaning by a book? I was standing at the rails when another sister appeared and replaced her. Before she left she quickly came back to retrieve her hymn book and, in the enchantment of the moment, I imagined it was a young Arab woman coming towards me.

Back outside, the loud streets of Granada were in an unequivocally festive mood.

I made my way back through them to the Plaza Bib-Rambla. It was crowded with families: some were queuing at a tent that functioned as a planetarium; there was a mechanical roundabout for children powered by a man pedalling a bicycle; there was a couple blowing huge bubbles, to the excitement of young children, and in the middle of it all I saw the Mickey

Mouse man. This time he had company, a woman of the same nationality, even smaller than he was. It seemed that he had adopted the role of a mascot, to be photographed with children, as she was entrusted with the selling of the balloons. She was holding many of them, of many different representations, of cartoon characters and animals. She was having difficulty managing them. As she tried to fix them, a horse at the end of a string became dislodged from her bundle and disappeared up beyond the buildings into the dark yonder. Among the revellers, I saw no one look up. Then arrived in the square a troupe of flamenco dancers and musicians. The dancers soon began their dance. Their fixed smiles were a counterpoint to their flowing steps as they took their lead from the music. The people crowded round them. The Mickey Mouse man and his companion were left out on the sidelines. I saw him lift up his Mickey Mouse head and discuss with the woman what they should do. What could they but carry on? After a few tunes and dances the dancers and musicians left the square. I too soon left while the square was still in full flight, with the Mickey Mouse man and his partner still in full flight among them. In the hotel I stood out on the balcony above the noise and crowds of the plaza, and watched the full moon rising silently into the sky above the Alhambra and the city of Granada, shining silently as it did centuries ago on the old caliphate, as it will presumably continue to shine, equally and without prejudice, from orient to occident until the end of the earth.

The next day out in the square, I was standing watching the man fold up his mechanical roundabout onto a trailer when I caught sight of the woman balloon-seller again. She was walking quickly through the square with her balloons, and then she disappeared down the same alleyway where I had seen her partner disappear in April. I followed her and saw her going in through a doorway. The door was open and I followed her. She had disappeared up some stairs. I stood in the twilight of the bare, empty hallway listening to the scraping of the balloons being squeezed through the narrow space of the stairwell above me, until a door closed. That sound seemed to signal a silence. It lasted no more than a moment before I began to hear again the street-sounds coming in through the open door. The noise of the world: I went back out to it.

Recently retired, Gerard McCarthy worked as a social worker in the West of Ireland. His first published essays, "Old Istanbul", "Old Jerusalem" and "Home from Andalucia", appeared in earlier issues of Irish Pages.

DEAR ORSON WELLES …

Mark Cousins

The oar and the winnowing fan.

Dear Orson Welles,

Can we go around the world together? You're dead, of course, but that doesn't stop me imagining us as a gruesome twosome, on the road. Maybe you will accept my offer because you were a mendicant friar. When Hollywood didn't know what to do with you, you set off and out to Spain and France, Yugoslavia and Morocco, to ply your trade, to set up your baroque stall in souks and courts and on stages, between rages.

From where I'm sitting – about which more in a moment – it looks like you couldn't stop making films, Orson, from *Citizen Kane* onwards. You had a will to cinema, a longing for it – or, maybe, not quite a longing, because that implies that it was outside you, far away, something to be reached for when, in fact, it's better to say that it was inside you. You embodied movies. It's hard to write to you and not use the word "embody", Orson. Your body was like an echo-chamber, like the belly of Ahab's whale; it produced that voice of yours that rumbled, and all those kings you played.

So can we make this travelogue, Orson? We could see it, also, as an epilogue. An epilogue to your life, which was so baroque that it is begging for one. I wish this letter could be a dialogue, Orson. For me it is a kind of dialogue. Shall we make it a decalogue? Shall we visit ten places around the world, with cinema on our mind, the way Diego Rivera had Frida on his mind in that great picture he did of himself? To mention Frida and Diego is to think of Mexico, of course. Can we travel the world together without going to Mexico? Without thinking of Sergei Eisenstein's time there? Without nodding our caps now to the fact that part of the reason for travelling, the compulsion to travel, the propulsion of travel, is what Eisenstein called "exstasis" – the desire to get out of yourself, the rapture of self-loss, the hope that, if we are fleet of foot, we might be able to outwit ourselves, leave ourselves behind, reverse the polarity of self and other?

Indulge me, Orson. Let's strike out together for this travelogue, epilogue, dialogue, decalogue. Let's travel the world and, as we do, ask a simple question. What are the movies? Years ago, when I was in my twenties (and as close to handsome as I was ever going to get), I went to Naples to film a grand lady in her sixties, Flora Pinto d'Albavilla Mariata Capaldo. As her name suggests, she was from aristocratic stock. The years of Garibaldi were long gone and so was her money but, somehow, she managed to ignore this fact and live in a small apartment gussied up with chandeliers and French furniture. One evening, after filming, she told me that she'd like to take me to "*le plus beau balcon du monde*". We drove for an hour in her fancy car and arrived in Ravello, from where she took me to a balcony overlooking the bay of Naples, the Costa Amalfitana. The moon was full and twinned with its reflection in the sea. As we stood on the balcony, Flora told me that Greta Garbo took Leopold Stokowski there. It was indeed, for me, a working-class Belfast boy, the most beautiful balcony in the world. As we stood there, she said to me: "Travel the world with me. I have not long to go, but we could visit the great art galleries together. I would pay for everything. All I'd ask for in return is your company and, occasionally, for you to wear swimming trunks." Did Tennessee Williams write her lines that night? Did he write this scene, Orson? Did you? I mention it here, of course, because her invitation – "travel the world with me" – seemed to me then, and still does, one of the most risky and beautiful things that one person can say to another. And so I say it to you, Orson.

1

Can we start our journey here, where I am now? I'm in Cannes, France. I'm sitting in a cheap restaurant called La Frigate. It's lunchtime. The sky is grey – the Magritte colours are only here in the sunshine, as you well know – and, just to further dispel the glamour, I can tell you that I smell of sweat (I've been schlepping around town today) and *vin blanc provençal*. I'm away from the numbers, as someone called Paul Weller once wrote, beyond the Cannes film-festival bubble; it's where I want to be. There's a quietude in this small restaurant. Nobody's talking about the film business.

I don't need to describe Cannes to you, of course, because you were here often. In 1948, you lived in the exclusive Hôtel du Cap-Eden-Roc at the Cap d'Antibes, near here, didn't you? And in that year Rita Hayworth visited you at the Cap to try to repair your relationship. Two years later, you took a taxi from Italy to the hotel, at a cost of $500, to try to convince producer Darryl Zanuck to fund your film of Shakespeare's *Othello*. You dropped to your knees and begged him. The place went silent. Perhaps to bring the moment to an end, and out of embarrassment, he offered you $100,000 to play a part in *Prince of Foxes*. You accepted. The money helped fund your film. You charged him for the taxi. Two years later, in 1952, *Othello* won the Palme d'Or here. And, then, in 1966, you were given a prize here for your contribution to world cinema. Jean Cocteau's lover Jean Marais made the announcement. Raquel Welch, whose beauty then brought tears to our eyes, took you to the stage. Behind you stood the *président du jury*, Sophia Loren, who was from Naples and who, therefore, had probably stood on *le plus beau balcon du monde*. So I don't need to tell you about this place. Unlike me, you've seen its inner sanctum, its upper echelons, its holiest of holies, its tracking shots, its foleys.

But what does Cannes tell us about the movies, Orson? As I sit in this restaurant, ten metres from the sea, with scooters buzzing by like wasps, I notice what I've always noticed about this place. There's no smell of the sea. I've heard, several times – can this be true? – that before the Cannes film festival starts, they comb the sea to remove the seaweed. Why? To make the water look cleaner, clearer? Seaweed gives the sea its smell, so removing it makes the water more like an ideal, but also more distant, because it isn't confirmed by smell. Is it the wine that makes me see, in this, a metaphor for the movies? What we see in a film is there and not there, isn't it, Orson? Just like you're here and not here now. Movies are over-available to some senses and completely unavailable to others.

2

To think of the lack of smell here, and then the lack in film, is to start with the bad news. So let's get it out of the way, Orson. Let's fly to Krakow in Poland, then take a train to Oswiecim, a place the world knows better as Auschwitz. Let's go there in autumn, when the trees are copper. Those trees make Oswiecim a lovable place, or would do so if it wasn't so hateful. Did you go there, Orson? I know your film *The Stranger* is about a Nazi and you said that Kafka's *The Trial* is "pre-Auschwitz" – which is why you changed its ending in your film of the book. Auschwitz the mother of all elisions, isn't it? A place where people were so de-imagined that an unimaginable factory system became perfectly imaginable.

So why go here, why make this the second of our decalogue, after Cannes? To acknowledge what movies are crap it, that's why, and to cede initial ground to the cinephobes. The homicidal gas chambers of Auschwitz-Birkenau were the worst thing we made in the twentieth century, Orson.

And yet we didn't film them. There's no footage of them. We stand here in front of where they once were and look at the place where film cameras of the time did not look. Of course the Nazis didn't want their unholiest of unholies, these crematoria, to be filmed, so it's perhaps not cinema's fault that it didn't do so. But it has to accept joint responsibility, I think, because, in the mid-1940s, cameras were too big to smuggle in here to record this as evidence of the attempted extermination of the Jews and, of course, cinema was still too redolent of entertainment in those years to look into such a heart of darkness. It was morally serious sometimes, in some places, but such times and places were the exceptions, Orson, weren't they? Did you know this when you were making *Citizen Kane*, before the gas chambers here started murdering people? When did it dawn on you that movies were a bit trivial? Or did it? Or are they? Or aren't they? Claude Lanzmann released a film, *Shoah*, in the year that you died, Orson. I wonder did you manage to see it? Its nine and a half hours are Lanzmann's attempt to make something big enough and serious enough and detailed enough and evidential enough to begin to undo cinema's solecism in not filming these gas chambers whose foundations lie before us.

3

So that's the worst bit done, Orson. In our road movie to find out what movies are, or why they matter, we've started with their fatal flaw. Can we go now to our third place, Yugoslavia, where you met your beloved Oja Kodar? Let's go by train and, as we do, can I tell you that Yugoslavia is no more? It broke apart in the mid-1990s, a decade after you died. The Soviet Union collapsed and its satellites did too. The break-up of Yugoslavia was the worst European war since the time of Auschwitz. The town of Sarajevo was besieged and 11,000 people died, Orson. I mention this because I was in Sarajevo during that siege and, whilst I was there, discovered why cinema matters. I was invited by Obala Art Center to bring films to show underground, to local people, in defiance of the siege. I did so and was amazed that, during a war and at great risk to themselves, those people came out at night, during the shelling, to see films. Why? Because, I realized, cinema and art aren't the icing on the cake, they are the cake. Movies make us feel alive, connected. Cinema makes moments seem more than they were, as big as the Sphinx, as available for inspection, as gnomic, as here-and-not-here as life, as sensuous and intoxicating.

Do you agree, Orson? I think you do. You spent so much time in Hollywood, in a world where cinema was thought of as the icing, and yet you ended your film of Kafka's *The Trial* with the mushroom cloud of an atomic bomb. *The Magnificent Ambersons* and *Citizen Kane* are about hubris. You seem certain in your work that the movies aren't *loin du Vietnam*.

4

Can we pack our bags now and fly again, to the place where I live, Edinburgh in Scotland? You came here in the 1950s, Orson. You went to the Cameo cinema, where we are now, and made a state of cinema speech. Do you remember? I wish I had been there. Here are the newspaper reports about it. Look at the headline – it says that you "Limp into the Festival with a 'Moan'". You'd sprained your ankle. On the stage of the Cameo – let's climb up onto it now and stand in front of its champagne curtain – you said, "The new artist goes out to Hollywood or Rome or London … and, until they catch on to him, he does something coming out of himself, something original." Then, you argued, the industry diverts the filmmaker from such personal filmmaking to something more mainstream and formulaic because "films take too long to make, they cost too much and go out to too large an audience". You said that by having to appeal to an audience of sixty million rather than, say, three million, the art gets blunt and bland. The result of this is that cinema is "dead, dead, dead".

Guess what, Orson? Are you ready for a surprise, a good surprise, a surprise that opened up the movies? Four decades after you said these words, on this stage, in this spotlight, the medium of film started to be digitized; equipment was miniaturized, processes were speeded up, budgets dropped. A new artistic/business model emerged in which films with strong aesthetics could be seen by far smaller audiences and not be called failures. Your dream came true. Film stopped becoming an autocratic art, an art that needed a patron the way Italian fresco painters needed the Vatican. It became like oil painting on canvas – intimate, for self-starters. Here in the Cameo, you recommended "a world congress to discuss the economics of the film industry". That didn't quite happen, but technological change did and, as Le Corbusier said, the technology created the poetics.

I wish, wish, wish that we could see the films you would make with such poetics and your will to form. There's a film called *Festen*, Orson, made in Denmark by Thomas Vinterberg, and it was shot by tiny cameras planted all over the set. The imagery was rough and almost fell apart, like the paintings of Seurat, but films like it removed the inertia from the movies, their lumbering slothfulness. What your friend Gene Kelly could have done with such techniques! If you had made your film of Cervantes' *Don Quixote* with such cameras, you could have finished it in a few months.

5

Talking of *Festen* makes me want to take you to our fifth place, Orson: Copenhagen. Let's go to its outskirts, to a production company called Zentropa, housed in an old army barracks, with a tank at its entrance, an outdoor, unheated swimming pool in which to swim naked at lunchtime and garden gnomes on which to piss. The people at Zentropa – Vinterberg, a director called Lars von Trier and others – would have applauded your speech in the Cameo and, probably, also heckled you. In the mid-1990s, like latter-day surrealists, they published a manifesto called *Dogme 95*, a vow of chastity and simplicity that repudiated the complexity of filmmaking, its aesthetic gloss and Hollywood lustre. They would look for a new directness in film. Their ideas energized the movies.

So, whilst we're here in Copenhagen, shall we come up with our own manifesto, Orson, our own ten commandments for cinema today, based on your Cameo ideas, and the chutzpah of *Dogme*? Let's. To get our blood going, let's swim naked in Lars's chilly pool. No? You don't like the swimming bit? OK, I'll be back in a moment. Here goes …

The Summerhall Movie Manifesto
1. *Try to show that which, without you, might never have been seen.* – Robert Bresson
2. *Make films about what you don't know.* – Kossakovsky
3. Always remember Garbo's face.
4. Watch films like a child.
5. Never make a film whose end is foreseeable from its beginning.
6. Movie stardom should be like presidential terms – no longer than four years.
7. No clichés, reverse angles, three-point lighting or well-made scripts.
8. No advertising in cinemas – there's none in churches.
9. Death to the Oscars.
10. Shoot sex scenes with as much energy as car chases.

11. More sound design, shooting silent, pauses.
12. Put onscreen lives that have never been there before.
13. Film fights the way Ozu shot kettles.
14. Understand the full tenderness, tragedy and rapture of the movies.
15. Remember the z-axis.
16. A movie is a love letter. Poetry, not prose.

That was fun, wasn't it Orson? Let's print it up on a poster. Let's hang it on walls and paste it on multiplexes. Let's spraypaint it on the Hollywood sign. Let's write it in the sky; let's get it tattooed. I'm game if you are.

6

Our trip's starting to feel like a manifesto, a pub crawl. Shall we drink something? Brandy's your thing, I think. Let's drink some at the sixth stop on our world tour of the movies, the Hollywood sign itself. From the hill behind it, let's climb down to it at dusk. There are rattlesnakes here. The sign bangs as it cools, like there's someone trapped inside it, trying to get out. Buster Keaton, maybe? Or your ex-wife Rita Hayworth? People whom Hollywood destroyed. Those crushed by the wheels of industry. How did Hollywood destroy people, Orson? How and why did it try to destroy you? By commodifying them? By sating every material need imaginable and, at the same time, starving their existential needs? By glorifying beauty and youth – beauty and youth came out of its test tubes – and then gagging when people got old? By being repelled by the very egos that were its vast, unburyable waste product? By feeding stars and directors on the desire to be desired so that they slaver for it like Pavlov's dogs – and then standing back and watching the adulation wane, the heat go out of the day, the selfhoods begin to bang as they cooled, just like this sign?

7

As we think these things, shall we go and leave a gardenia on Marilyn's grave in Westwood Memorial Park? Our seventh of the decalogue in this travelogue? Let's. Look at it. You told Peter Bogdanovich that you met her at a party when she was a starlet. A man pulled down the front of her dress to reveal her breasts. And she just laughed. Is that right?

The marble on her grave here is pearly smooth with all those years of touching, like it is in the grotto of Lourdes. Every time I come here I'm stopped in my thoughts by the realization that she was 36 when she died. I was only getting going when I was 36, but she was already gone with the wind, a lesson unlearnt, nuclear waste. Just as Auschwitz-Birkenau was unfilmed, Marilyn Monroe was over-filmed, over-filmable, the definition of *photogénie*. The camera loved her, as it loved India, but in both cases it failed to show us that the tragedy should not be passed over. We bought our movie ticket to see Marilyn and became tourists in her beauty and sadness, visitors for a day who then upped and left, leaving her to face the mess that was mostly not of her making.

Let's leave this memorial garden, Orson. There's Josef von Sternberg's wall crypt to our left, tiny, at ground level. You and he shared Marlene Dietrich, didn't you? You each loved her; you each filmed her smoking, and saw eros in that smoking.

8

Let's jump on a plane and fly 11,500 kilometres from this place, which many think of as the centre of the movie world, to our eighth place, which in some ways *is* the centre – a centre – of the film world. Let's fly east to find out something else about the movies. Let's go to the city of Ouagadougou in Burkina Faso.

Not the first place that comes to mind when you think of the centre of the movie world, I know. But walk with me in this heat, Orson, across this red soil, to the centre of the city and look ahead. That big sculpture in the middle of the road there, that tiered thing stacked with discs, is a monument to … filmmakers. In no other city in the world is the central space, the ground zero, dedicated to film. Why is it here? Firstly, because in 1969, when Africa was trying to organize its movie industry, the Ouagadougou film festival FESPACO was established here as a pan-African, biannual colloquy and congress. But there are film festivals all around the world; what makes Ouagadougou different? Its opening night is the biggest film event I've ever been to. It takes place in the national Stade du 4-Août and feels like an Olympic event. The reason it's so big explains why film is so central to Burkinabé life. Literacy levels in this country's 15–24-year-olds are 33 per cent now and were 6.6 per cent when FESPACO was founded. Burkina Faso is, therefore, a visual and oral culture rather than a literate one like Scotland (which, because of Protestantism, had one of the highest literacy levels in the world in the 1800s). As you know, countries that value the word highly often see imagery as redolent of surface, fashion, unreason or even decadence. Hence the iconoclasm of Protestant and Islamic fundamentalism at the time of the Reformation and the destruction, in 2001, of the Buddhas of Bamiyam in Afghanistan, which had been carved in the sixth century CE.

Film, then, was a key part of how Burkinabé people were entertained and socialized. It helped this, and other francophone west-African countries like Senegal, find their place in the world, share ideas and carry out moral and aesthetic thinking. This reminds us, I think, of the fact that cinema is as close to a universal language as we can get. It clearly transcends linguistic barriers. It works interculturally as well as intraculturally. I can learn a lot about Bengali life from the movies of Satyajit Ray, and of Japanese life from the movies of Yasujiro Ozu and his onetime assistant Shohei Imamura. Cinema acts like an empathy machine.

9

We're coming to the end of our trip, Orson. I've been thinking about our manifesto and your talk in the Cameo, in which you envisaged that a new smallness of scale in filmmaking would, paradoxically, open it up and make it creatively bigger. At the time I thought of Manila in the Philippines, and wanted to bring you there, but I wasn't sure that you would be game. Now I can see your wanderlust, I think we should go there. I've never been. Shall we go together?

Here we are. It's as humid as I expected. More tragic, sordid, external. Have you ever been somewhere where you can see everything in the streets, in the fields? In golden days the glimpse of stocking was thought of as something shocking ... You never needed to be optimistic about people, did you? Or did you? The New Deal shaped you, which was progressive, which knew that people would grow if they were fertilized. That's what we are seeing here.

But in filmmaking terms, why are we here? Because the filmmakers are leading the way. They don't have a fancy film school, or film magazine, or great films on TV or large budgets but, nonetheless, directors like Khavn de la Cruz and Lav Diaz are rethinking the movies. De la Cruz makes manic montage mash-up movies, at least one a year, and sometimes one a week – like your old hero John Ford did in America in the early days. He – de la Cruz – shoots on video, mocks religion and gender, uses kitsch, pop, porn, camp, punk, melodrama, news, violence, graphics and elegy to create shanty-town cinema that feels poor, vibrant, desperate and compelling. As his movies cost little and grab our attention, they make money. This way of working is what you hoped for.

Lav Diaz's films are as slow as de la Cruz's are fast. Some shots last ten minutes. The movies run for many hours. They are numinous, modernist, symphonic, mysterious frescoes of great sadness and stillness. They could fill a cathedral.

When I say the word cathedral, I always think of the last shot of Andrei Tarkovsky's *Nostalghia*. Did you ever see it? It was made two years before you died. The shot starts on a man and a dog who are outside a small country cottage that we have seen several times in the film. Then it pulls back to reveal that the whole landscape is inside a cathedral. It's as if the whole world is sacred. And then it starts to snow in the cathedral.

10

It's been quite a trip, Orson. We've been kings of the road, the Don and Sancho Panza, maybe. Where should our last place be? There's a col in the west of Scotland called the Rest and Be Thankful – at first I thought we could stop there, but then I realized that it's good to end on a grace note, isn't it? A small thing. I have a tattoo on my arm that says "the oar and winnowing fan". You probably know the story. It comes from Homer. Ulysses has been travelling by boat (the kingdom of the oar) then walks away from the sea, carrying the oar, until he comes to an agricultural place where they no longer recognize the oar as an oar and think, instead, that it is a winnowing fan for cutting down crops.

I love this parable of misrecognition. It celebrates in-between places, nowhere places, exactly the kind of places where talent comes from and begins to apprehend the world. Such places, with their lack of expectation or hubris, have perfect sight-lines. On a clear day you can see forever from them. Shall we end our decalogue-epilogue-travelogue to try to see what cinema is today, three decades after one of cinema's greatest thinkers – you – died, in such an in-between place?

I spin the globe, as it spins at the start of movies distributed by RKO, which distributed *Citizen Kane*, and then stop it by stabbing my finger onto it. And look where the place is … it's Summerhall in Edinburgh.

Orson, you gave me the movies, and they took me in their arms.

Thank you.

A filmmaker, film critic, writer, presenter and wanderer, Mark Cousins was born in Northern Ireland in 1965 and has lived in Edinburgh since the 1980s. His filmography includes The First Film *(2009),* The Story of Film: An Odyssey *(2011),* What is This Film Called … Love? *(2012), and* Here Be Dragons *(2013). He took the Edinburgh Film Festival to Sarajevo during the siege of that city in the early 1990s, and is the author* The Story of Film *(Pavilion, 2011) and* Imagining Reality: The Faber Book of the Documentary *(Faber, 2006). His acclaimed, landmark and richly poetic cine-essay,* A Story of Children and Film *(2013), was one of* The Official Selection 2013 *of the Cannes Film Festival.*

VISITING JOHN HEWITT

Patricia Craig

Out of the Old North.

John Hewitt kept a kind of open house, though he preferred his visitors to come one at a time – or at least not to arrive in an unruly bunch. The house wasn't large enough to accommodate more than two or three visitors comfortably: I'm talking about the post-Coventry period now, the house in Stockman's Lane and the days of Hewitt's widowerhood (if that's a word). Before he left Belfast in 1957, when he and his wife Roberta lived at 18 Mount Charles, John Hewitt presided over rather more formal gatherings. Especially during the war years, there were parties at the Hewitt residence, on which converged a lot of distinguished guests, both local and non-local. You had painters such as John Luke and Colin Middleton, Markey Robinson and Rowel Friers; you had Rayner Heppenstall and Emanuel Litvinoff (both serving with the British Army and stationed for a time in Northern Ireland); you had poets W.R. Rodgers and Robert Farren. After the war, in the early 1950s, Philip Larkin emerged from his "unspeakably hideous ecclesiastical-style library" at Queen's, leaving behind colleagues he called "old Sourface" and "old Bagface", to put in an appearance at 18 Mount Charles – though what he and John Hewitt would have had to say to one another, I can't imagine. There was one – Larkin – drinking a bottle of champagne before lunch, and wishing he was rich enough to do it every day; and the other – Hewitt – setting his face against drink in deference to his Methodist upbringing. There was Larkin being lectured by his friends about taking sex too seriously, and money not seriously enough; and Hewitt – well, with Hewitt I don't think anyone would have had the temerity to broach either of these topics.

Roy McFadden, from whom I've gleaned some of the above information, had no recollection of ever encountering Louis MacNeice at the Hewitts' (though he must have been an occasional visitor). As McFadden said, MacNeice would have stayed with George and Mercy McCann in Botanic Avenue whenever he visited Belfast; and in any case, "his [i.e. MacNeice's] preferred meeting-places were licensed premises, which Hewitt did not frequent". Moreover, "no alcohol is served at the Hewitts' flat in Mount Charles, only tea", says another of their wartime visitors, Robert Greacen. Eventually, as we know, John Hewitt mellowed sufficiently to consume a half pint of beer every now and then, if the occasion called for it, but the taboos of his upbringing had struck too deep for him ever to develop a taste for strong liquor. Everyone who knew him is conscious of the irony inherent in the naming of a Belfast pub "the John Hewitt" – a tribute he would probably have relished, in fact, as much for its inappropriateness as anything else.

John Hewitt is curiously absent from Robert Greacen's autobiography *Even Without Irene*, and he doesn't loom very large for John Boyd either, though Boyd acknowledges him as "a formidable figure physically and intellectually" in mid-century Belfast; and in the same book – *The Middle of My Journey* – he recalls having met W.R. Rodgers for the first time in John Hewitt's flat in Mount Charles, so he must have been a visitor to the place himself. Hewitt, he says later in the book, "was a likeable man once you got to know him, but he took some knowing". In fact, it was only from the 1970s on, when Hewitt had turned into "a white-bearded, patriarchal figure" living in Stockman's Lane, that the two elderly men became good friends. In the early days, Hewitt's stand on "Regionalism" aggravated a number of his contemporaries, including Protestants as "liberal" as himself, but liberal in a slightly different way. His use of the word "Ulster", for example, annoyed Greacen, Boyd and McFadden, whose thinking on the matter chimed with the Catholic minority's propensity for being offended by the term. Somehow "Ulster" had acquired a decidedly Unionist ring. Speaking for myself, however, as member of that minority, I don't think I ever really took exception to "Ulster", whether it was the whole Northern province, or the crucial two-thirds of it, that was being referred to. And John Hewitt made his position absolutely clear when he wrote, "Ulster, considered as a region and not as a symbol of any particular creed, can ... command the loyalty of every one of its inhabitants". All right, the conjunction of "Ulster" and "loyalty" in the same sentence carried somewhat unfortunate connotations, but we know what Hewitt meant, and it wasn't that.

Nevertheless, by placing his emphasis on a portion of Ireland and not the whole country, he left himself open to continuing – long continuing – argument and dissent. "I fail to see," Derek Mahon wrote in an *Irish Times* review, "why his chosen 'region' should have been Ulster instead of Ireland as a whole" – and, he goes on, "it was a point on which we stuck more than once, myself sitting forward in my chair, himself puffing pugnaciously at his pipe". The setting for these more or less amicable disagreements was the small right-hand front room of the Hewitt bungalow in Stockman's Lane. I have a mental image of the two of them sitting there striking sparks off one another, Hewitt in his customary tweed-covered chair, before agreeing to disagree, the elder and the younger poet exhilaratingly opinionated, and argumentative in equal measures.

Hewitt, as everyone knows, left Belfast for Coventry a few years after his failure to secure a promotion to Director of the Ulster Museum and Art Gallery (of which he was Deputy Director). Being turned down for this post, to which many people believed he was absolutely entitled, was a considerable blow to Hewitt's self-esteem. But it wasn't, according to Roy McFadden, the great disaster it came to seem later, as far as some commentators were concerned. "To describe Hewitt's departure as some sort of expulsion is nonsense," McFadden wrote. As Hewitt saw it himself, Coventry wanted him as director of an art gallery, if Belfast didn't; and so the next fifteen years of his life fell into an unexpected conformation. And in a way, the Coventry sojourn made a productive interim between the two lengthy Northern Irish phases of Hewitt's life. If the Belfast Art Gallery disappointment continued to rankle, it was only as a mild, more or less blown-over irritation. "… Besides being a Communist," Hewitt recalled ruefully in 1970, alluding to his drawbacks for the Belfast post in the eyes of the Unionist chairman of the appointing committee – "Besides being a Communist [he wasn't a Communist], I had numerous Catholic friends, play-actors and the like …": so he was scuppered by the kind of insidious sectarianism against which he had always made a stand. He was an enemy of the Unionist administration to the point where it rose up and bit him in the face when it had the chance – which only went to underscore his principled opposition in the first place.

But – unlike Derek Mahon, whose temperament propelled him out of Belfast at the earliest possible moment, and only allows him to return briefly and gingerly – Hewitt never intended his exile from Ulster's delights and defects to be permanent. Once he reached retiring age he came home – to a city, as he put it in "The Coasters", in which "the fever is high and raging", with "the ignorant-sick" threshing about in delirium, as the inevitable result of bad policies and "old antipathies" had come to pass. It was 1972, not an auspicious year. But the Hewitts, John and Roberta, settled into the bungalow in Stockman's Lane – and into the swim of new liberal and literary

Belfast – and encouraged like-minded people to call on them. They all came, visitors to Belfast and permanent residents alike, Mahon, Montague, Heaney, Simmons, Michael and Edna Longley, Gerald Dawe, John Morrow, Frank Ormsby, Ciaran Carson, Medbh McGuckian, Paul Muldoon ... "I hardly ever visit Belfast without calling ... at John's place in Stockman's Lane," said Robert Greacen; and this was true of a good many people, including myself. I only got to know John Hewitt in the last ten years of his life, and after his wife Roberta's death in 1975, so I can't gauge the effect of the Coventry interlude on his personality. Of those acquainted with him before and after, some thought he'd got better, others worse. "The 'tight shut mouth' had become tighter," Roy McFadden said, quoting Hewitt himself, and perhaps not being quite fair. (McFadden was, by all accounts, a difficult man himself.) He also noted Hewitt's reputation, in his Ulster Museum days, for "outspokenness and brusqueness amounting almost to rudeness"; and indeed, Hewitt succeeded in permanently alienating a few of those whose noses he got up through being, as they saw it, pompous and abrasive. One of them continues to refer to Hewitt as "big fat John", regardless of his late-life slimness and amiability. I don't know what brought about the change in his appearance and demeanour – if change there was – but Hewitt, when I knew him, was anything but fat; and on his return home he quickly assumed a place in the cultural life of Belfast as an important, generally revered and extremely benign presence. The honours which had eluded him in his earlier years were now heaped on him, and they were accompanied by an astonishing burst of creativity on his part, with six new collections of poetry published between 1976 and 1986. His first *Collected Poems 1932–67* had come out in 1968 to a resounding silence in the English press. Not a single review had appeared at the time, he told me, with some natural resentment of the slight. But the attention and acclaim he eventually received made up, in a sense, for the earlier neglect. In the end, as an exemplar and friend to younger poets he had come to reign unopposed – in James Simmons's famous phrase, "the Daddy of us all, good old John Hewitt".

I have to take issue, again, with Roy McFadden (himself an admirable poet), when he has Hewitt dismissing the whole younger generation of Ulster poets as "dull". I don't believe he thought anything of the sort. He's on record as finding "that never before in my lifetime has poetry been so flourishing in the North". He was an early reviewer, and admirer, of Heaney's first collection *Death of a Naturalist*. He always spoke enthusiastically to me about the new wave of Northern Irish poetry, and worried that readers might fail to appreciate the singular strengths of Heaney and Mahon, say, or fail to take account of Michael Longley's humour and wit. Incidentally, Hewitt referred to Roy McFadden as "my most consistent critic", adding that he "even got a couple of fine satirical poems out of my shortcomings". Well, productive, as well as unproductive, friction, I suppose, has always been a feature of the Northern literary scene; and McFadden, who knew John Hewitt when he was a schoolboy (McFadden, that is, not Hewitt) and before the latter was married, has left a rather endearing image of the elder poet in his youth "aggressively reading the *Daily Herald*" on the Cavehill Road bus.

If Hewitt, at the time, was parading his socialist convictions, he was doing it to show by his own example an honourable alternative to rampant sectarian alignments disfiguring his city. We're still in the 1930s here, but Hewitt's socialism and egalitarianism never wavered throughout his life. It was partly due to his upbringing and the influence of his liberal schoolmaster father (who was only illiberal, it seems, on the subject of strong drink). Hewitt was born in Cliftonpark Avenue in 1907 – a time when the future didn't look altogether bleak. "… [T]he century / scarce offered hint we'd not by now enjoy / a tolerant and just society", he wrote in rueful mode at the start of *Kites in Spring*, his 1980 verse autobiography. Rueful, because things quickly fell apart – he lived through the street violence and disruption of the early 1920s, for example – and at the time he was writing *Kites in Spring* the North was in the throes of bloody contention and upheaval.

Frank Ormsby's exemplary edition of John Hewitt's *Collected Poems*, published by Blackstaff five years after Hewitt's death in 1987 – this wonderful collection points up, among other things, the consistency of Hewitt's concerns. Even the early proletarian poems, which are frankly propagandist and not very sophisticated, show an author who is principled and compassionate, and searching for a style to express these qualities to the full. It didn't, in fact, take Hewitt long to discard the socialist simplicity and artlessness of his early work: the grievances and tatters of the unemployed (for example) were soon subsumed under an altogether more thoughtful, complicated and lyrical engagement with social issues, political abuses, and – a particular Hewitt topic – the claims to integrity of Irishmen of Planter descent.

The last recurs over and over, and led to some of his most enticing and illuminating work.

The sullen Irish limping to the hills
bore with them the enchantments and the spells
that in the clans' free days hung gay and rich
on every twig of every thorny hedge,
and gave the rain-pocked stone a meaning past
the blurred engraving of the fibrous frost.

So I, because of all the buried men
in Ulster clay, because of rock and glen
and mist and cloud and quality of air
as native in my thought as any here.

As native in my thought as any here. I'm reminded of Edna Longley's "cliquey clerihew" which was published some years ago in the sadly defunct *Honest Ulsterman*: "John Hewitt / If he only knew it / Is that rare entity / Without problems of identity." Being native to the North of Ireland is a key assertion in Hewitt's poetry, from "The Colony" on, with its flaring beacons, uprising of the dispossessed and acknowledgement of Planter guilt ("For we began the plunder"). The narrative voice, characteristically, is thoughtful, unintense, never wishing to shirk responsibility for wrongs committed, but at the same time proclaiming a proper local attachment: "for we have rights drawn from the soil and sky". Such poems stick up for settlers – or those not activated by animosity towards the native Irish, at any rate – while advocating a due regard for whatever seems most alien in the different tradition. Tolerance: this is what it all boils down to – the quality that somehow got excised from the Northern Irish psyche, and which latitudinarians like Hewitt had been trying to reinstate ever since.

One of the ways to go about it is to engage in fruitful debate: argument for the sake of enlarging one's viewpoint. But everything said in Ireland carries considerable risks; even Hewitt's instinctive aversion to Catholicism (a matter of temperament, not bigotry) was apt to get itself misconstrued. There were those who felt this aversion was atavistic, and betokened an equally atavistic political standpoint. This is far from being true. When he comes up with lines like, "I fear their creed as we have always feared / the lifted hand against unfettered thought", Hewitt isn't pronouncing himself an Orangeman, just allowing expression to a particular cast of mind – a careful and spirited cast of mind. He goes on: "I know their savage history of wrong / and would at moments lend an eager voice / if voice avail, to set that tally straight."

I learnt a lot from John Hewitt, about long-forgotten Northern Irish writers, about his literary and other friendships, about ways of steering an enlightened and conscientious course through benighted Ulster. How did I get to know him? In the mid-1970s I was contemplating starting work on a critical study of Northern Irish writing, and I was advised to contact John Hewitt in his capacity as literature consultant for the Arts Council. So I wrote to him – I was living in London at the time – and then I arranged to see him the next time I was over in Belfast. We met, appropriately enough, on the steps of the Linen Hall Library: one of the few remaining Belfast institutions embodying the radical and dissenting spirit which spoke to Hewitt of an indigenously enlightened era. In Robert Johnstone's book *Images of Belfast* there's a charming, and characteristic, photograph of Hewitt in the library looking trig (Seamus Heaney's word) and intent, as he scrutinises the back of an eighteenth-century print. The photographer has caught him in his proper environment, his spiritual home, the place where he tracked down obscure works by the County Down and Antrim weaver-poets on whom he wrote his M.A. Dissertation back in 1950. No one had heard of Hewitt's "Rhyming Weavers" at the time or later; indeed, they remained unknown to almost everyone until he published his book under that title with a selection of their verses, in 1974. Actually, the subject of Hewitt's dissertation was Ulster poets between 1800 and 1870, not exclusively weaver-poets – though the uprightness and sturdy independence of the latter were qualities that appealed to him, and he was pleased to disinter them, along with others, from ancient stacks embedded in dust. They had names like Campbell of Ballynure, Orr of Ballycarry and Herbison of Dunclug, and, in their day, they turned out adept nature poetry and strong social criticism in an Ulster-Scots dialect: their verse, Hewitt said, "if seldom of high literary value", remains "the best, and often the only record of important aspects of our social history". One or two, such as James Orr, *did* produce work of high literary value; but I won't go into that now.

Hewitt used to tell a story about a member of the Queen's examining board, who, when he submitted his thesis, failed to find any trace of the authors under consideration in the university library, and began to wonder if Hewitt had invented the lot of them, for his own purposes. However, a visit to the Linen Hall Library put the examiner right. There, sure enough, he found what he was looking for: a lot of little books, stitched paper or in boards, with titles like *Poetical Attempts by Hugh Porter a County of Down Weaver* and *Midnight Musings, or, Thoughts from the Loom* by David Herbison.

I've now got Hewitt and myself as far as the Linen Hall steps – eventually – and from there, I think, we might have gone round the corner, at his suggestion, into Fountain Street to a near-by cafe. I can't remember, but I know I visited that cafe a number of times afterwards with John Hewitt, where a small gathering had assembled for morning coffee, including his friends James Vitty, the Linen Hall librarian, Joseph Tomelty, John Boyd and others whom I've forgotten. I suppose it was a 1970s version of long-gone Campbell's Cafe where, during the war years, people like Denis Ireland, Sam Hanna Bell, Robert Greacen and others of that ilk held sway. And John Hewitt too, I'm sure, though I don't remember him mentioning it.

That first meeting with Hewitt was the prelude to a lot of visits to 11 Stockman's Lane, over the next ten years or so, whenever I happened to be in Northern Ireland. We had a good deal to talk about, in the way of Ulster literature, even though I quickly abandoned the project that had caused me to get in touch with Hewitt in the first place. Why did I abandon it? I belatedly became aware that much of the ground I'd planned to cover had already been covered by John Wilson Foster and Terence Brown between them, and covered with infinitely more expertise than I could have mustered at that time. John Wilson Foster's pioneering *Forces and Themes in Ulster Fiction*, and Terence Brown's *Northern Voices*, published in 1974 and 75 respectively, made any further attempt to survey the territory redundant. However, partly stimulated by John Hewitt and his intriguing book collection, I continued to immerse myself in every variety of local literature from Herbison to Harbinson, and from Ethna Carberry to Ciaran Carson.

John Hewitt's books were neatly arranged on shelves in a small front room of his Stockman's Lane bungalow. It was an extensive collection, but fortunately they were mostly small books, works of nineteenth-century poets and so on, which didn't require a lot of space. I never really felt the modern nondescript bungalow was an appropriate habitation for Hewitt – I'd have preferred to envisage him in a terrace house like the one he was born in, or the Mount Charles flat next-door to the birthplace of Forrest Reid – but he had organised its interior for maximum efficiency. An inherited Methodist methodicalness informed his every action. Others besides myself were impressed by his ability to lay his hand on whatever book he needed to underscore a point he was making; and if there weren't enough walls to hang the entire Hewitt collection of paintings on, the most cherished among them were displayed to be admired. "That Luke we got when we were ten years wed," he told one journalist who came to interview him for the *Irish Times*. "… Middleton did that from sketches he made during 1941 and 42 … That's a great painting, Blackshaw's 'Conversation in a Field' …". And so on.

With great generosity and kindness, John Hewitt encouraged me to use him as a source of information. "Any enquiry you may have I'll try to answer," he assured me in one letter; and again: "Don't hesitate to shoot any questions at me." So I did. In the late 1970s, I must have been doing something in connection with Irish children's writers – not a Hewitt topic really, but even here he turned up trumps. Of Patricia Lynch, for example, he wrote: "We visited her several times. She spoke in a rather Cockney accent [surprising], looked like a boarding-house landlady and was married to R.M. Fox, a Left-wing, English-born journalist … they had two glass-fronted bookcases in their living-room, one with his few volumes, hers crowded with hers in original editions and multifarious translations. *The Turf-Cutter's Donkey* was her best-known work and is the only title I have, a handsome book with Jack B. Yeats's illustrations." He ended that particular letter by saying, unduly modestly, "I'm glad you don't dislike my verses. My new book, *Time Enough*, is a Christmas recommendation of the Poetry Book Society, which is a bit of a boost for the Blackstaff Press. I don't think I've got that much better over the years; it's just that this kind of thing tends to happen if one holds on long enough." Another letter announced: "I've just been appointed Writer-in-Residence at Queen's! The first" – a piece of news he considered deserving of his first and only exclamation mark.

John Hewitt had a keen eye for literary oddities, and I shared his amusement at the astonishing eccentricity and artlessness of a whole range of minor Ulster authors – the really amazing thing was how some of them had ever made it into print. I must have alluded, in a letter, to a few of the more egregious Ulster specimens of literary effrontery, and got their provenance wrong, for I have a reply from Hewitt correcting me. "The other gem is not Alexander's at all," he wrote. "In *Poems* by Peter Magennis, published in 1888, we have the complete poem, 'Education in Enniskillen'." It's in this remarkable composition that we find the following couplet:

Beneath my eyes and broader than my hat,
Upon the waters Inniskilling sat.

So – in Hewitt's cabinet of curiosities we have Peter Magennis sitting on a hill and looking down innocently on Enniskillen. We have a Reverend

William Boyce, author of a long poem called "The Night of the Big Wind" which branches out into an extended list of dead Ulster notables and their terrible ends: "Twas hydrophobia dragged poor Harvey down." We have Samuel Burdy whose *Life of the Reverend Philip Skelton* was a particular Hewitt favourite, with its subject's eccentricities including a habit of running up turf stacks to impress his parishioners. We have these, and many, many more, all of them pored over with a certain amount of hilarity whenever I found myself at Stockman's Lane. And of course the mother of them all, the illustrious and indomitable Amanda McKittrick Ros, came up for discussion too. At one point, both Hewitt and I were invited to contribute to a newspaper article under the heading, "I wish I'd Written That". Rather mischievously, and totally tongue-in-cheek, I chose to wish I'd written the McKittrick Ros Easter sonnet which opens with the line, "Dear Lord, the Day of Eggs is here". "I liked your piece in the *Irish Times*," John Hewitt wrote following the publication of this effort. "But your photo was a teeny bit elfin? Mine on the other hand was grim."

Hewitt always took a certain pride in the distinctiveness of the Northern Irish literary tradition, and that, as far as he was concerned, meant cherishing its idiosyncratic authors, however awful, along with others – I suppose Louis MacNeice is the most obvious example here – who became absorbed into the mainstream of English literature. Among his own contemporaries, he had an especial regard for MacNeice and W.R. Rodgers, for Peadar O'Donnell, Michael McLaverty, Sam Hanna Bell, John Boyd, Joseph Tomelty – and for the Armagh author of a single novel published in 1948: John O'Connor, whose wonderful *Come Day – Go Day* lets us in on some facets of spirited working-class life in the 1920s. Hewitt was always ready to praise any author who had made an impact in one way or another – but he was at the same time very selective when it came to the question of those towards whom he felt a temperamental affinity.

In his essay of 1945, "The Bitter Gourd", he made a point about it being essential for a writer to have ancestors, "Not just of the blood, but of the emotions, of the quality and slant of mind"; and for his own part, he allied himself with people like the weaver-poets – egalitarians to a man – with James Hope, William Drennan, Mary Anne McCracken; and, outside Ireland altogether, with those like William Blake, Tom Paine, Cobbett, John Ball, the Diggers, the Levellers, the Chartists, William Morris – socialists, reformers, people of strong views, "the asserters, the protesters", as he put it himself.

Most of the time I found myself completely in accord with John Hewitt's literary judgements; but there were exceptions. In a letter to me dated July 1977, he says: "I took a holiday last night and read Anthony West's *The Native Moment* again. There's nobody among our novelists at all like him. [At this point I might have interjected, Thank goodness.] Such sensory exuberance," he goes on. And a couple of weeks later, "Last week I had a visit from Anthony C. West, the novelist, a lovely man, beautifully honest about himself and his work. Quite by chance he arrived to see an old sister here, a day or two after the Arts Council Bursary committee had made him an award. Others went to Ian Cochrane and Francis Stuart." I'm not sure if, at this stage, I had actually read Anthony C. West, but I know, when I did, I approached him with some enthusiasm, not only because of Hewitt, but because others whose judgement I trusted had also praised his work. In 1971, John Cronin described West's *The Ferret Fancier* as "one of the most lyrically evocative novels of rural life to have appeared in recent years". Seán Ó'Faoláin had already attributed to West "a tremblingly sensitive imagination" – and he didn't mean it as disparagement. I seem to remember even Seamus Heaney had something positive to say about him. So did John Wilson Foster, who judged West's *As Towns With Fire* the nearest thing to the Great Ulster Novel he'd ever come across. (This was the only comment in his cogent and engrossing *Forces and Themes* that caused me to raise an eyebrow.) In the same West novel, John Hewitt's friend and neighbour John Kilfeather found "genius stamped on every page".

So, as I said, I was primed for enthusiasm. And what did I find when I actually got down to reading the books? On page 15 of West's collection of stories, *All the King's Horses*, "a great bosom straining the seams of a frock". On the same page, "a fine-skinned white breast", and in rapid succession, "a round plump bottom", "a flat chest without a breast-valley", "young breasts", "full breasts", "low, leathery breasts", "contours full and finished". Tremblingly sensitive, hmm. I'm having to restrain myself from going on (there's lots more in the same vein). And on top of all the wallowing in busts and bums, you find West attributing to the entire female half of the population a quality he calls "a deep Eve-greed". If you add a lot of pretentious pseudo-philosophical angst-ridden claptrap, along with the profusion of small dead animals which turn up in these books, what you get is some of the most ludicrous and disagreeable fiction written in the twentieth century.

I actually met this man on one occasion, when I was introduced to him by John Hewitt. He seemed very nice – but again, I probably hadn't read him at the time. It was at some social gathering or other, and he kindly offered to get me a glass of wine ... If I'd known what his attitudes and preoccupations were ... Sensory exuberance indeed. It is an absolute mystery to me why Hewitt and others thought so highly of him. Or perhaps the blind spot is mine. You can judge for yourselves from the above quotations. My other blind spot has to do with the poet Padraic Fiaac, but I don't have time to go into the reasons why. I don't think I ever discussed either of these writers with John Hewitt, which was probably just as well, or I might have experienced at first hand some of the famous "brusqueness amounting almost to rudeness" I mentioned earlier. John Hewitt, I believe, was still capable of mildly bad behaviour even towards the end of his life, banging his stick on the floor in a fit of pique, or declining without explanation some delicacy that was offered to him. "No one I have ever met said 'no' with such resonance," Michael Longley wrote, admiringly, after Hewitt's death. And: "Hewitt was a prickly blackthorn and no mistake," said Derek Mahon; "but he was, too, a gentleman, a gentle man, and a worthy ... descendant of the eighteenth-century radicals he admired so much." So he was, all of that.

Never mind Anthony C. West – Hewitt also introduced me to some people who became lifelong friends, including the Longleys, and it was in the company of Michael Longley that I paid my last visit to 11 Stockman's Lane. It was Easter, 1987; and two months later Michael Longley rang me in London to tell me that John Hewitt had died. He died without fuss – without illness, nurses or rumours, in the middle of the night, having attended a book launch at the Linen Hall Library on the previous day. When I came to consider what he had meant to me, I came up with the following: generous, scholarly, discerning, self-contained, humorous, reticent, not given to equivocation, full of a welcome asperity and soundness of outlook. John Hewitt stands, in his own community, for a good deal that's admirable and essential. In his life and in his work, he was neither a follower of fads nor an unthinking traditionalist.

> I wait here for this light in my own fashion [he wrote]
> not lonely on a rock against the sky,
> but as the men who bred me, in their day,
> as men in country places still, have time,
> working in some long field, to answer you.

A critic, essayist and anthologist, Patricia Craig was born in Belfast and lived for many years in London before returning to Northern Ireland in 1999. She has written biographies of Elizabeth Bowen and Brian Moore, and edited many anthologies including The Oxford Book of Ireland, English Detective Stories, Modern Women's Stories, The Belfast Anthology *and* The Ulster Anthology. *Her memoir* Asking for Trouble *(Blackstaff Press) was published in 2007. She is a regular contributor to* The Irish Times, The Independent *and the* Times Literary Supplement.

TWO STORIES

Ron Rash

THE RETURN

Emma!

Benjamin Miller awoke beneath a shroud of white petals, several of which lay like soft coins over his eyes. The ground trembled vaguely now, the cannon and mortars wheeled elsewhere. He did not hear the explosions, only felt them. All he heard was a ringing in his left ear. Benjamin rested with his eyes closed a while longer, made slight movements to assay what had struck him to the ground, how bad it was. He turned his right boot in and out and then his left, felt no pain or absence of foot or leg, arms and hands the same. He moved a hand over his groin and stomach and chest, felt no spill of intestines or stoved-in ribs. Only his head was injured, the hair on one side matted with blood. He touched the wound, gauged its width. In one place the skin unpursed and his finger slid slickly over smooth bone. Smooth, not cracked. He patted the rest of his head, then nose, jaw, and teeth and found all where they should be.

Benjamin brushed the petals from his eyes and found himself staring into a jaybird-blue sky. He knew where he was, remembered thinking how pert the peach trees looked as his regiment approached the orchard. He'd even notioned to take some seeds back with him to Watauga County. No farmer he knew had grown peaches there, probably too cold, but if anyone could, it would be Emma. Lilies and roses, cherry and apple trees, raspberry bushes – everything Emma put into the earth found life at its appointed time, as if even plants responded to her gentleness. Old Jacob Story, their one near neighbor, listened when Emma said the moon's horns were turned wrong to seed a corn field, or not to plant peas before daffodils bloomed. *I've farmed near sixty year*, Jacob said, *but I'll cover nary an acorn until Emma allows it's the time.*

Benjamin raised himself to one knee, then stood. More petals fell, puddled the ground white around him. The ringing in his ear increased and the world leaned left. On the edge of his vision a gold tinge. Benjamin blinked, hoping the world might realign, but the tilt and gold tinge remained. Because my head's been knocked off plumb, he told himself, and there ain't no tonic but to lean with it. He looked around, shifted his eyes to bead the world before moving his head. He found himself standing alone amid the fallen, friend and foe entangled like logs in a splash dam. A few yet moved but most did not. Some surely made sounds – death rattles, moans, prayer, curse, or plea. His deafness was a blessing. Two faces Benjamin knew well, recognized three others by hair and girth. All dead. His musket and cap lay side by side as if posed for a tintype. He left them where they lay. The canteen was still strapped to his shoulder and the haversack tied to his back.

He staggered from the orchard, passing trees stripped of every blossom, others branchless, some mere stumps. If an enemy soldier yet lingered, Benjamin was an easy target. But no shot came. He made his way into a small wood and came to a creek, the banks narrow and the current quick. He remembered the old belief and pondered his waking in the orchard, the pall of white petals. The throbbing in his head increased. He took a deep breath and felt it lift his lungs. No dead man need do that, he told himself, but waited a few moments before swinging his boot forward. The water let him cross over. Benjamin took off the haversack and sat with his back against an oak tree. He laid an open palm on the ground. Only the slightest vibration, like thunder murmuring after a storm.

His throat was raw from smoke and thirst so he drank what water the canteen held. Benjamin probed the wound again, tried to recall a raised musket butt, a Minie ball glancing his skull. Nothing came. What he remembered was charging into the orchard with Dobbins and Wray beside him. *Keep your lines*, a lieutenant shouted but amid the like trees and smoke all direction was lost. Men blundered into each other, shooting and stabbing all who came near. Lead filled the air like slant hail. One man climbed into a peach tree's highest branches, hunched there crying with hands over ears. Benjamin's last memory was of Wray clutching his arm for a moment, then letting Benjamin go and falling.

I give both sides their best chance to kill me, Benjamin told himself. They'll not portion another. He went to the creek and used his handkerchief and water to clean the wound as best he could. He refilled the canteen and went back to the oak. Corn dodgers and jerky were in the haversack but instead of eating he took the letter from his shirt pocket, unfolded it.

My dearest husband,

I rite you this mourning from the home that I pray soon you return to. I have sown the fields for our crops, wich you say I am good at. Now I must pray the signs hold true. May your hands and mine together reap what Ive sown. What news I have of others you may wish to here. The youngest Watson boy run off to fight with his brothers. Widow Canipe died of the flux and Jess Albrights baby died last week of putrid fever. Theys a red cross on his cabin door so even the others are sore afflicted. Joe Vickers was killed in Virginia. But that is more than plenty sad tidings. Your Father has been a heep of good to me, helping plow the fields and fixing fences. Folks say in town that this war will last not a year. I pray so if not sooner. For I feel all ways night and day the lonely in my heart and will ever so until you are with me again. I go now to town to mail this letter, dearest husband, nowing that this paper I hold you will hold to.

Your loving wife always
Emma

Benjamin refolded the letter but kept it in his hand as his eyes closed. He and Emma had grown up on adjoining farms, like brother and sister, playing leap frog and red rover together, walking to the school and church, sharing chores. He'd been a feisty boy and one day when he was twelve, he found a corn snake in the barn. Something wrong inside him wanted to scare Emma with it. She'd fallen while running away, scraping her knees and elbow. He had flung the snake into the weeds and gone to her, shut-mouth with shame. As Emma wiped tears off her face, he'd offered his hand to help her up, not expecting her to take it. But she did. He had helped her to the creek, taken his handkerchief, and gingerly wiped the dirt from the knees and elbow. They did not speak the whole time, nor mention it afterward, but that night by his bed Benjamin had prayed that God would scine all meanness forever out of him so he might be worthy of her.

He must have passed out, because when he awoke the ground no longer trembled. The ringing in his ears had lessened, as had the world's slant. The letter still lay in his hand. He placed it in the pocket closest to his heart and then shed coat and belt and all other allegiance to anyone but himself. He listened for a few moments, heard nothing but a redbird, then rose and walked through the shallow wood and into a pasture, below it a farmhouse and a wagon road. The dwelling appeared deserted, its occupants fled or hidden. When Benjamin got to the road, he looked up to gauge direction. An orange sun burned low on the tree line. Buzzards circled the battlefield. Some appeared to enter the sun, then spiral down blackly as if turned to ash. He followed the road east, not knowing where he headed, only what he left behind.

The next day he saw an old man alone in his field. *I've not come to rob or harm you*, Benjamin said as he approached. The farmer looked doubtful until Benjamin flattened the back of Emma's letter on a well guard, took a pencil from the haversack and asked the way to Knoxville. *So you had plenty enough of that tussling*, the farmer asked afterward. Benjamin answered that he had. *Even with that busted head you got more sense than them still at it*, the farmer said, and told Benjamin to wait a minute, came back from his root cellar with salt meat and potatoes. The old man would not have it otherwise, so Benjamin had stuffed the victuals in the haversack and gone on.

He traveled for two weeks, first north to Nashville and then following the Cumberland Turnpike east. Several times he'd hidden as Union and Confederate soldiers passed, once a whole regiment. Another time, at night, the clatter of cavalry. He'd been spotted only once. Two soldiers on horseback fired their rifles but did not leave the pike to pursue him.

One night a few miles from Knoxville, Benjamin felt Emma's presence. Despite the afternoon heat, he'd made good time, so near dusk bedded in a meadow. When he awoke, a wet moon had peeled away the ground dark and replaced it with a silvery sheen. No breeze rustled or night bird called. No sound of water, or distant train. A stiller moment he had never known. Benjamin stepped onto the road and whispered her name. Though Emma did not answer, he knew she was very near. Then she wasn't, and he felt a distance between them that was more than the miles yet to walk. The next morning Benjamin believed all of it, the silver light, her presence, part of a dream, until he saw his boot prints in the dust.

He followed a drover's trace into the mountains and the air quickly cooled. It was as dangerous a place as he had been. Not just soldiers traversed here but also outliers who, with no cause other than profit, took no prisoners. But the few people he met, including a pair of drovers, passed with eyes lowered. They feature me the dangerous one, Benjamin told himself. As he went higher into the mountains, dogwoods that in the lowlands had shed their white yet clutched flowers, as if time was spooling backward. The fancy pleased him.

The land leveled and somewhere unmarked he passed from Tennessee into North Carolina. Not just Carolina but Watauga County, he reminded himself. Emma was probably in the field hoeing or planting. He imagined her looking up as she wiped her brow or rubbed dirt from her hands – gazing toward the gap at this very moment, already sensing his return. Sounds eight months unheard – the chatter of boomers, a raven's caw – he heard now. Yellow ladyslippers Emma used for tonics flowered on the trace edge. A chestnut three men couldn't link arms around curved the path. Everything heard and everything seen was a piece of himself restored. He thought of the soldier in the peach tree. It had been as if the man was trying to climb out of hell itself. And now I have, Benjamin thought. A whole mountain range stood between him and the horror and meanness.

Late the next afternoon he spotted a church spire, soon after the backs of store fronts. Boone, the county seat where he'd been conscripted. He could be easily recognized here, so waited in the woods as the last farm wagons left town, shopkeepers locked or barred their doors. Night settled in and with it a breeze that smelled of coming rain. Only now, for the first time since he'd left them in the orchard, Benjamin pondered Dobbins and Wray. They too had been conscripted farm boys, Kentucky born. The three of them had been of like nature, quiet men who didn't dice or drink. At night they kept their own campfire, where they spoke of their farms in such detail that the three homesteads merged into one shared memory. There were friendly disputes over the merits of brightleaf versus burley tobacco, the best way to cure a ham. On the night before the battle, they spoke quietly of crops being tended by wife and kin. I'd nary have figured to miss staring at a mule's ass dawn to dusk, Wray said, but I surely do.

They knew from the massing of troops this was to be a battle, not a skirmish. That last morning their regiment had passed a Dunker church, beyond it a plowed field tended only by scarecrows. The braggarts and raw cobs spoke little now as the battle's racket encircled them like a noose. Officers rode back and forth on skittish horses. Those who'd gone before them littered the ground, so many Benjamin wondered if a single man yet survived. Soon they smelled gunpowder, watched its smoke drift toward them. More bodies appeared. Dobbins picked up a dirt clod, squeezed it. Habit, Benjamin thought, as Dobbins let the grains sift through his fingers. Good soil, Wray had asked. Not the best, Dobbins had answered, but I reckon it to cover our bodies well enough.

The courthouse clock chimed nine, and he stepped from the woods. As he walked a deserted side street, Benjamin thought of the peach seeds he might have placed in his haversack. He'd eaten the fruit once here in Boone, sold off a wagon up from South Carolina, the peach purpled just past ripeness, fuzzy and soft in the hand. It had been like eating pulpy honey. Better not to have brought them, he decided, for if they did grow, they might barb his memory come spring.

Once he was outside of Boone, a soft rain began to fall. Benjamin lay down in a laurel slick beside Middlefork Creek, the stream he would follow eight miles until it led him into the pasture below the cabin. Tired as he was, he could not sleep, and would have gone on had the moon and stars offered the way. The laurel leaves caught the rain, let it pool into thick drops that soaked his clothes. For the first time since leaving the battle, Benjamin wished for his field coat. A bone-deep cold entered his body. He clasped his arms over his chest, tucked his knees close. After a while his feet grew numb. Teeth clicked like struck marbles. Just the wet and cold, he told himself, but thought of last winter in camp. Putrid fever had caused the same symptoms. Eight men had died. Those not yet afflicted had filled their mouths with garlic and pinches of gunpowder. A sergeant marked red crosses on dead men's haversacks. Some had believed that, like consumption, the contagion could drowse in a body for weeks, maybe months, waiting for rain or cold to awaken it.

The rain had thinned to mist by first light. Benjamin did not eat, simply got to his feet and started walking. Fog narrowed the world as he followed Middlefork Creek up the mountain. The few farmhouses loomed briefly out of the white, sank back. A dog barked once and he heard an axe cleaving wood, but that was all. Soon the fog thinned, just wisps sliding over low ground.

Until the war, there'd not been a night he and Emma were more than a furlong apart. Trips to Boone or visits to kin might last all day, but come eventide the families returned. From age twelve until they'd married, Benjamin listened for the Watson's wagon to clatter past. Once it did, he'd watch from a porch or window as the lantern floated from barn to cabin, disappear when the Watson's front door closed. In those few moments of darkness, Benjamin teased himself into believing Emma and her family had vanished forever. He would hold his breath, feel his heart gallop until, slowly, light began to glow inside the cabin, sifting through chinks, the one glass window. As it did, he felt a happiness almost painful.

As he approached Jacob Story's farm, Benjamin saw that the corn stood dark and high. No hard frost or gullywasher had come. The signs held true, not only for the corn but also the beans and tobacco. Smoke rose from Jacob's chimney. Noon-dinner time already, he thought. Benjamin followed the trailway through a stand of silver birch, straddled a split-rail fence, placed one foot on his land and then the other. He had hoped Emma would be in the cabin. That way he could step onto the porch, open the door, and stroll in no different than he would coming from field or barn. Benjamin wanted their separation to seem that way, to never speak of the war or their months apart. He wanted it to become nothing more than a few dark moments, like a lantern carried through a cabin's low door.

Emma was not inside, though, but kneeling on the creek bank, next to the cattle guard where the water quickened. He could not see her face because she was looking down, her left arm and hand in the water. She was wearing her Sunday dress, the dress she'd worn on their wedding day. When Benjamin called her name, she did not look up. He walked faster, shouted her name. Emma's eyes remained on the water and now he saw that her right hand hovered above the creek like a dragonfly. The fingers and palm descended and touched the surface, then lifted, did the same thing again and then again.

He crossed into the corn field, not stumbling over hoe furrows because there were none. Then he was on the bank opposite Emma, the creek so narrow that he could almost jump it. *Emma*, he said, almost a whisper. She lifted her head but offered no smile or words or tears. She looked past him, as if he wasn't even there.

Benjamin tried to remember the streams he'd crossed, which ones flowed fast and which ones did not. He had stepped over the creek near the peach orchard, after that crossed smidgen branches and wide rivers, sloshing through some, walking bridges over others. But what of today, recalling last night's shivering cold. He'd not eaten or drunk, and from Boone to here not once crossed the creek. He looked past Emma, searching for a mound of dirt, a wooden cross or flat stone. He looked for his own grave.

His gaze moved across pasture and wood, corn crib and barn, seeing no sign of such until his eyes settled on the cabin. A red cross was painted on the door. For a few moments, his eyes remained there. Then he looked at Emma. Her head was down and her hand touched the water, this time entered the creek's flow a moment. When she withdrew the hand, something about her had lightened, wisped away like dandelion seeds. *Emma*, he said. She raised her hand and pointed to Benjamin's and then to the water. He lowered his hand into the current and she did the same. The water pressed against his palm. Just for a moment, Benjamin felt another hand touch his. When he looked up, Emma was gone.

Since her grave wasn't on the farm, it would be behind the church. Benjamin could walk the two miles, but that would delay his going back west into Tennessee. He turned and began the trek back to Boone. In a week he would be on the Cumberland Turnpike. He'd walk the Pike in daylight and soon enough men wearing butternut or men wearing blue would meet him. Whichever side appeared first Benjamin would join. A month or two might pass but there'd be another battle. The armies would finish their business with him. He would hold out his hand again and this time Emma would take it.

OUTLAWS

Calley and all that.

When I was sixteen, my summer job was robbing trains. I'd mask my lower face with a black bandana, then, six-shooter in hand, board the train with two older bandits and demand "loot." Fourteen times a day I'd get shot by Sheriff Masterson, stagger off the metal steps, and fall into the drainage ditch beside the tracks. Afterwards, we'd wait thirty minutes for the next train, which was the same train, to come hooting up the tracks. Years later I would publish a short story about that summer, and one of my fellow bandits would read it. But that was later.

My aunt, who worked as a cashier at Frontier Village, had gotten me the job. Despite my being sixteen, she'd cajoled Mr. Watkins, who preferred college students, into hiring me. He can play Billy the Kid, she'd told him. Anyway, with a mask on who can tell how old he is? So it was that on a Saturday morning in June I changed into my all-black outlaw duds in the Stagecoach Saloon's basement. The Levi's and cowboy shirt hung loose on my hips and shoulders, and I had to gouge another notch in my gun belt. My hat sank so low my neck looked like a pale stalk on a black mushroom. I found one a smaller size in the gift shop. The boots were my own.

My fellow outlaws, both from Charlotte, were Matt, a junior pre-med major at UNC-A, and Jason, who'd just graduated from there. His major was theatre arts, which should have been a tipoff for his performance on the last day we worked together. After stashing our clothes in the lockers, we walked over to the depot where Donald, a paunchy, silver-haired man who claimed he'd been John Wayne's stunt double in *Rio Bravo*, went over the whats and whens a last time. He sent us on our way with advice gleaned from eight summers' experience: there will always be smart alecs onboard and any acknowledgement just egged them on, and be prepared for anything: kids jabbing at your eyes with gift shop spears, teenagers kicking your shins, adults setting you on fire with cigarettes. They even do that to me, Donald said, and I'm the guy wearing the white hat.

So nine to five, five days a week with Mondays and Tuesdays off, the three of us waited for the train whistle to signal it was time for our hold-up. We had no horses, so ran out of the woods firing pistols at the sky until the locomotive and its three passenger cars halted. We entered separate compartments and Sheriff Masterson took us on one at a time. Clutching our gut-shot bellies, we'd stagger to the metal steps, roll into the ditch and lie there until the train crossed the trestle and curved back toward the depot.

Getting shot and dying was the easy part. By July, all of us had plenty of wounds besides scrapes and bruises from falling. We'd been burned, poked, tripped, and pierced by weaponry that ranged from knitting needles to sling-shot marbles. After each failed robbery, we'd retreat to a hideout with its cache of extra blanks and pistols, three lawn chairs, toilet paper, and Styrofoam cooler filled with sandwiches and soft drinks, Stretched out above it all, a green camouflage tarp kept everything, most of all us, dry when it rained. Our contributions to the hideout were some paperbacks and Jason's transistor radio, which was always tuned to the college station.

One morning in mid-July Jason nodded toward the radio.

"You don't even know what they're saying, do you kid?" Jason asked as he rolled a joint.

"Everybody look what's going down," I said, after a few moments.

"But what's it *about*?" Jason asked.

"I don't know," I answered.

"It's about not wanting to get your ass shot off in Vietnam," Jason said.

Matt looked up from a copy of *Stranger in a Strange Land*.

"I didn't hear anything about Vietnam."

"When you graduate and your deferment's up you'll hear it," Jason said, "especially when they send you one of these."

He took a letter from his pocket and gave it to Matt.

"You gonna to try to get out of going?" Matt asked as he handed it back.

"I have gotten out, for four years, but yeah, I plan on keeping an ocean between me and that war," Jason grimaced. "I never got picked for anything good in my life, varsity baseball, homecoming king, class president. Hell, I didn't even get picked for glee club, but I fucking get picked for this."

"So what will you do?" Matt asked.

"I'll convince them I'm nuts. Acting's what I'm trained for, man. I'll speak in tongues while I do handstands if I have to. Maybe shit my britches right before I go in. I've heard that works. They'll 4F me in a heartbeat."

"Don't bet on it," Matt said. "The army's on to that dirty diaper scam. A buddy of mine tried it. He walked in with shit gluing his pants to his bare ass. The army doc told him not to worry, that he'd probably shit himself even worse when the VC started shooting at him."

"I'll come up with something else then," Jason said. "Like I said, I'm an actor."

"Oh yeah," Matt said. "Sure you will."

"So you don't think I can pull it off?"

"Well, it's not like you've been giving Academy Award performances this summer," Matt said. "The kid here does a better death scene than you do."

"Maybe I'm saving up for a more challenging audience than those dipshits on the train," Jason said.

"You better be saving up for a bus ticket to Toronto."

Jason lit the joint and inhaled deeply, offered it to me as he always did before passing it to Matt.

"Bob Dylan's right, kid," Jason said. "Don't trust anybody over thirty about anything, but especially Vietnam. There's nothing good about being over there."

"I heard they got great dope," Matt said as he passed back the joint.

"Yeah, it's called morphine," Jason answered. "Medics give it to you while they're trying to stitch you back together."

"Some cool animals, too," Matt deadpanned. "Cobras and pythons. Leeches, tigers, and bears, oh my."

"Fuck you," Jason said.

"Just trying a little levity," Matt said.

"We'll see how funny you think it is when you get your letter."

"If I get in med school they can't touch my ass."

"If," Jason said. "From what you said about your GPA that's a big if."

"I've got a year to pull it up," Matt said.

Jason turned to me.

"Growing up around here, you probably believe all that shit about the evil commies, right?"

"I don't know," I said.

"What about your parents?"

"My cousin's over there and Daddy says he ought not be, him or any other American."

"Might be some hope for you hicks after all," Jason said, and held out what was left of the joint to me. "Don't you want to try it just once?"

I shook my head and he threw the remnants down, ground them into the dirt with his boot toe. The train whistle blew.

"Time to get shot," Matt grinned. "In honor of that letter, the kid and I will let you lead us into battle."

"Keep joking about it, asshole," Jason said. "They may get you yet. But me, I'll figure a way out. You'll see."

Frontier Village didn't shut down until after Labor Day, but Matt and I went back to school the last Monday in August. After that Jason would work solo. All through August, Jason talked about ways of getting a deferment, but it wasn't until our last weekend together that he'd figured out what to do.

That Saturday I'd never seen him so animated. He paced manically in front of us, grinning.

"It's radical, boys," he said, "but one-hundred percent foolproof."

"Enlighten us," Matt said.

"One of my buddies in Charlotte called last night. He ran into a guy we went to high school with, a real dumbass who sawed off his fingers in shop class. Not all of each finger, just the top joints. The thing is, it wasn't that big a deal. You hardly noticed after a while. I mean, it wasn't like girls wanted to throw up when they looked at his hand. Hell, I think it made him *more* popular with girls. They felt sorry for him so voted the fucker homecoming king. He even played on the baseball team. Here's the kicker, though. He's so dumb he *volunteers* to go, but they don't let him because he won't be able to handle a rifle well enough. All I've got to do is slice off some finger joints and I'm 4F the rest of my life."

"Don't even talk this bullshit," Matt said, and nodded at me. "Look at the kid here, he's already about to faint."

"If you want something to faint about, kid," Jason said, "let me tell you about my cousin who got killed in Nam last winter, though killed is putting it nicely. He took a direct mortar hit. All the king's horses and all the king's men couldn't put him back together again, so they kept the casket closed at the viewing. Anyway, the next morning before the funeral, my uncle gets it into his head he has to see the body and my father goes to the funeral home to stop him. He takes me with him, maybe figures he'll need me to help wrestle my uncle out of there. When we get there the undertaker comes jabbering that he couldn't stop him, that my uncle has jimmied the coffin open. So we go in the back room where the coffin is and my uncle is holding something up, or I guess I should say part of something …"

"Don't tell anymore," Matt said. "The kid's got his own cousin over there."

"You don't want to hear it," Jason asked me.

I shook my head.

"Still think I'm bullshitting about doing it?" Jason asked, "or having cause to?"

"No, man," Matt said. "I've joked with you some. You know, it's a way of dealing with bad shit like this. You're right, they may come after my ass in a year, but fucking maiming yourself, that's not acting crazy, it is crazy. Even if you could actually do it, what if they found out it was on purpose? Hell, they might take you anyway, or put you in Leavenworth."

"You think I'm going to chop them off in front of those assholes?" Jason said. "It will look like an accident, but I may need you to help me, Mr. Pre-Med."

"Sure thing," Matt said. "I can see it on my application. Medical Experience: Chopped off fingers for draft dodger. Yeah, that'll get me into Bowman Gray."

"I'm just talking about afterward, so I won't bleed to death," Jason said. "The whole point of not serving is so I *won't* die."

"Stop talking this bullshit," Matt said.

"I'm going to do it tomorrow," Jason said. "You boys just wait and see."

I didn't sleep well that night, waking before dawn. In the dark, even the worst things seemed possible. I thought of what I'd seen on TV, soldiers and civilians on stretchers, some missing limbs, some blind, some dead, worst of all the monks who sat perfectly still as they transformed into pyramids of fire. I could report Jason to Mr. Watkins, or even ask my parents what to do, but this seemed something they had no part in. Or just stay home. Yet that seemed wrong as well. But then the morning sun revealed the same window that had always been there, the same bureau and mirror. Revealed my world and what was possible in it. He won't do it, I told myself, it's just talk. When my aunt came by at 8:15, I was ready.

I went down the Stagecoach Saloon steps, Jason and Matt already undressing. As we changed into our outfits, I noticed a blue backpack beside Jason's locker.

"What's in there?" I asked.

"What would you do if I said a hatchet?" Jason asked.

When I didn't respond he grinned.

"Courage is what's in there," he answered. "At least half a bottle of it still is."

We walked down the tracks to our hideout, the backpack dangling from Jason's shoulder. Things I'd paid no mind to other mornings, the smell of creosote on the wooden cross-ties, how sun and dew created bright shivers on the steel rails, I noticed now. I was lagging behind. Matt waited for me while Jason walked on.

"Don't worry, kid," Matt said softly. "Even if he was serious, he'll chicken out."

"You sure?" I asked.

"He's just trying to mess with our heads."

Once we were in the woods, Jason opened the backpack and took out the half-filled bottle, *Beefeater* on the label.

"We'll have one successful robbery this summer," Jason said, "rob Uncle Sam of a soldier to zip up in a body bag."

He unscrewed the cap and lifted two white pills from his front pocket. He shoved them in his mouth and drank until bubbles rose inside the glass. Jason shuddered and lowered the bottle. For a few minutes he just stood there. Then he set the bottle down, took out a pocketknife, and cut the rawhide strips tethering the holsters to his legs.

"Keep them in your pocket for tourniquets," he said, offering the strips to Matt. "Once the wheel rim takes the fingers off, I'll need them on my wrists."

"No way," Matt said.

"What about you, kid?" Jason asked, his voice slurring. "You too chickenshit to help me?"

I nodded and looked at Matt's watch. Five minutes until the train would be here. Jason lifted the bottle and didn't stop drinking until it was empty. He held his stomach a few moments like he might throw up but didn't. He raked his right index finger across the left palm.

"That quick and it's done," Jason said, and pulled his pistols from their holsters, flung them to the ground. "Won't be using my trigger fingers anymore, here or anywhere else."

"You're drunk and crazy," Matt said.

"Yea, I guess I am drunk and that acid, man, it just detonated. S'cuse me while I kiss the sky."

Jason looked upward, then twirled around and lost his balance. He tumbled onto the ground, rose to his knees and saluted us, before keeling back over.

"What are we going to do?" I asked.

"I'll stay with him," Matt said. "I don't think he'll be moving for a while, but just in case you'd better stop the train before it gets near here."

I left the woods and stepped onto the track. As the train came into view, wood and steel vibrated under my feet. The whistle blew. I jogged up the track waving for the train to stop, but I was just an outlaw taking his cue too soon. Mack, the engineer, blew the whistle again. I was close enough to see his face leaning out the cab window. He looked pissed-off and he wasn't slowing down. I jumped into the ditch and the engine rumbled past.

I looked ahead and saw Jason running out of the woods, Matt trailing. Jason lay down by the tracks and stretched his arms, clamping both hands on the rail. Mack grabbed the handbrake but it was too late.

Jason's hands clung to the rail when the left front wheel rolled over them.

That's how I wrote the scene's conclusion years later, then added a couple of paragraphs about an older narrator recalling the event. A standard initiation story, nothing especially new but done well enough for *Esquire* to publish.

What actually occurred was that I didn't see Jason's hands, just that his arms stretched toward the track. Then he was rolling into the ditch, forearms tucked inside the curl of his body. Matt and I scrambled into the ditch beside him. Jason screamed for a few moments, fetus-like until he slowly uncoiled and began laughing hysterically.

"You dumb fuckers thought I'd really do it," he gasped.

"Asshole," Matt said, and walked back into the woods.

Jason turned toward the train and raised his hands and open palms.

"Don't shoot I'm unarmed," he shouted, and started laughing again.

Mack shouted back that Jason was good as fired. Passengers gawked out windows as the train wheels began turning again. Donald stood sad-faced on a top step, white hat held against his leg as though mourning our perfidy.

Back at the hideout, Matt lifted the empty bottle.

"Water?"

"Yep," Jason answered.

"And the acid?"

"Two aspirin," Jason said. "Water and two aspirin, boys. That's all the props I needed. Now what do you say about my acting ability?"

"The stuff about your cousin and uncle," Matt said. "That part of the performance too."

"Of course," Jason nodded. "You have to create a believable scenario."

"The draft notice?" I asked.

"No, kid, that's all too real, but I figure if I can convince you two that I'm crazy I can convince them. This was my rehearsal."

"You're an asshole," Matt said again. "One of us could have gotten hurt because of your prank. We could lose a day's pay too."

"Don't worry," Jason said. "I'm going to turn myself in right now, tell them all of it was my doing. They won't do anything to you when they know that."

Jason stuffed the pistols back in his holsters and picked up his backpack.

"Hey, I was just having a little fun," he said.

"I hope I never see that son-of-a-bitch again," Matt said when Jason had left. "How about you?"

"That would suit me fine."

But four decades later in Denver I did see Jason again, the cowboy hat replaced with a VFW ball cap.

"Remember me?" he asked. "We used to be outlaws together."

I didn't at first, but as he continued to talk a younger, recognizable face emerged from the folds and creases.

"It's a good story," Jason said, nodding at the *Esquire* he clutched. "You got the details right."

"Thanks," I said. "You exaggerate, of course, make characters better or worse than in real life."

"Don't worry," he said. "I know I was an asshole."

I pointed at the hat.

"You end up over there?"

"Yeah, you guys were easier to fool than the army," Jason said. "Of course, the induction center didn't provide me a train to freak them out with."

"Well, at least you came back."

"I did that," Jason said.

"My cousin, he didn't."

"I'm sorry to hear that, I truly am," Jason said, and after a few moments. "What about Matt? You ever see him after that summer?"

"No."

"I always wondered if he got sent over there. I looked for him on the wall. His name wasn't on there so maybe he got into med school. I guess I could find out on the internet. When you were writing that story, did you ever do a search on us?"

"I couldn't remember your last names," I answered. "But I don't think I would have anyway. Like I said, it's fiction."

Jason had rolled up the magazine. It resembled a runner's baton as he tapped it against his leg. The bookstore was almost empty now, just the owner and two teenagers browsing the sci-fi section.

"When I dream it isn't fiction," Jason said, "for me or for them."

"Them?"

"Yeah, them," Jason said, stashing the magazine in his back pocket. "You remember who Lieutenant Calley was?"

"I remember."

"Come with me," he said. "There's something I want to show you."

From a shelf marked MILITARY, Jason took down a book and opened it to a page of black-and-white photographs. The top two photos were of Calley, but below was one of eight nameless soldiers, helmets off, arms draped around each other.

Jason pointed at the second soldier to the left.

"Recognize me?"

Except for shorter hair, he looked the same as at Frontier Village. Jason stared at the photograph a few more moments.

"Three of these guys were dead within a month," he said. "The Vietnamese say the ghosts of American soldiers who got killed are still over there. They hear them at night entering their villages, even villages that were Viet Cong during the war. They leave food and water out for them." Jason looked up from the page. "Their doing that, I think it matters."

Jason leafed farther into the book, stopped on a page with no photographs. His index finger slid down a few lines and stopped. I read the paragraph.

"You know my last name now," Jason said, reshelving the book.

The teenagers walked toward checkout, a graphic novel in hand as the owner placed a closed sign on the door.

"After I came back to the states, I told myself that if the people around me had been through what I'd been through – three of your buddies killed and scared shitless you're next, then being in a village where any woman or child could have a grenade and all the while your superior ordering you to do it – they would have acted no differently. To see it that way allows you to move on. You got unlucky in a lottery and put in some shit most people are spared. You just followed the script you'd been given."

"Here's the thing," Jason said after a pause. "It's always been okay when I am awake. I've held down a good job at a radio station for forty years, and though my wife and I got divorced a while back, we raised two great kids. Both college grads, employed, responsible, I'm blessed that way, even have a grandchild coming. So I handle the daylight fine. But night, it used to be different, because in my dreams I'd be back there. Everything was the same, the same villagers in the same places they'd been before. In the dreams I'd already know what was going to happen, not just that day, but what would happen afterwards – the accounts and testimonies, the hearings, Calley's court martial, the newspaper articles and TV reports. But even knowing all that, when the order was given, *I would do it again*. I didn't have one dream where I didn't.

Until one day I was in the vet affairs office and I read your story. That night, I dreamed I was there again, but I had no hands, which meant I couldn't hold a rifle. I walked among them, even into their huts, and they weren't afraid, and I wasn't afraid either because I knew I had no hands to hurt them. And then, as the months passed, I'd dream that though I had no hands, I balanced a bowl of rice between my wrists. I'd go into the huts and crouch, set the bowl carefully on the floor and after they'd each taken a handful of rice, I'd lift it back up and go to the next hut."

Jason paused and took the rolled-up magazine from his pocket, held it out between us.

"I went to the newsstand and bought this copy. I read the story every night for a while, then just a few pages, and then only a few paragraphs. It wasn't long until I had those paragraphs memorized. I'd lie there in the dark and speak them out loud. Now, two, three nights a week I'm back there, but always without my hands."

Jason nodded at the magazine

"You can have this if you want."

"No," I said. "You keep it."

"Afraid I might forget?"

His smile did not conceal the challenge in his eyes.

"No," I answered.

"Okay. I'll keep it then," Jason said. "Thank you for writing the story the way you did. That's why I came, to thank you, to tell you it's helped. I want to believe it's helped more than just me. I mean, if ghosts enter villages, maybe they enter dreams too."

He held out his hand and we shook.

"If Matt ever shows up at one your signings, wish him well for me."

After Jason left, I talked to the bookstore owner a few minutes, then walked back to my hotel. It was only five blocks but I wasn't used to Denver's altitude, so I was out of breath when I got there. I had a couple of drinks at the bar, then took the elevator up to my room. The curtains were pulled back and Denver sparkled below. Jason's home was down there and I wondered if he was already asleep. In the darkness beyond the city, jagged mountains rose. On the flight back to Carolina the next morning, I saw them from the passenger window. They were different from the mountains back home. Young, treeless, no hollowed out coves. Snow lay on summits yet to be softened by time.

An Appalachian poet, short-story writer and novelist, Ron Rash was born, raised and educated in the American South. He is the acclaimed author of three collections of poems, four books of short stories and four novels. On this side of the Atlantic, his third collection of stories, Burning Bright *(2010), was published by Canongate in Scotland. He is John Parris Distinguished Professor of Appalachian Studies at Western Carolina University, North Carolina.*

FIGURES

Chris Preddle

Under the cosmic pine.

1

Let the first figure be a figurine.
Ice Age woman of Moravia hipped
with hoops of flesh, O rhombus-in-the-round
of flesh, fleshhood of the human process,
a maker, inland on a meadow-holme
of a river settlement, had made you
blank as a helm of face. O Stone Age fair,
bicone of flesh, you were no sign unless
a person, some particular Venus
loved by a maker in Moravia.

2

Gilgamesh King of Uruk made these walls
as if to keep out Death. Look at the brickwork
kiln-fired, walk along the parapet.
He felled the Cedar Forest, killed like disease
cedar cadavers, killed the cedar-hoarder
Humbaba fatter than a banker by
the fat Euphrates. He killed Ishtar's Bull.
He killed my crew of Stone Ones. He made me sail
the Ocean to its edge, to find distant
Utnapishtim, the everliving human.

Utnapishtim thus, courtoyse and humayne,
on's couch. The gods have to themselves detain'd
life; death conferr'd mankinde, and seal
the time of it. Gilgamesh, retourne to Babel
(and take this whoreson ferryman Urshanabi

should never have brought you). Any mayfly had
such time as you i'th' sunne. I am ill at ease
in Dilmun, untimely human here. Depart,
since you can. Content you in your temporal work.
Gilgamesh King of Uruk made those walls.

3

Nereids came ashore like Scarborough gulls
promenading. Thetis on the harrowed sand
foresaw, to seaward of the blithe sea-girls,
Achilles and the anvil ships at hand.

4

Aphrodite Nevertodie,
Aphrodite Withedeceit
loves you, Sappho. You shall see
her face immortal, hers of Cyprus in the sea.
As in the upper world you've sung
lovers, liars, lemans, liers-by,
Aphrodite of Artifice,
Aphrodite Forceofheart –
so in the underworld for your deserving,
deceitwithed song and tortoise lyre
you shall be honoured, no less
than Aphrodite, by the flown and honourless.

5

Let the next figure be in low relief
sculpted. Eudemos the seatrader's tomb
in Lycian Olympos, in our grief
his fellow citizens erected. Whom
the seas unself and separate from us,
whom the Euxine afflicted, is beyond
the wind's assistance and the daylight's. Form us,
seanymph, to the term we spend in bond.

6

Let the next figure, Leóndios Makhairás,
mourn for Cyprus. Panayía, let our Maker hear us
among the Greekless Moslems. We
were His East-West dominium in the sea,
sweet land
of Cyprus, between the woodlouse Thomists and
the sandflea monks of Syria. What a Christ-crusader king
we had once, havocking
the infidels of Asia! We have ruled
Jerusalem. Now I the servant of the king grow old,
and even the City,
goldleaf Byzantium may fall. Saviour, Christós Sotír,
it is not in me to complete
my mythistoria of Cyprus. Contemplate
the course of things: no honest value lasts,
though all I've seen and heard should not with my time be lost.
I see both ways in time: our own King Janus
captive in Egypt, as the coining Genoese
exact us. Panayía of the Pines, I shall be wood, would lose
the expectation of Goodness here. We pines need less.

7

Kate, dramaturge of the Demiurge,
uncasual casuist, divine
of case-divinity at the marge
with morals, make us a play, a sign

to avail one failing. On a hoop of grass
I cannot do what Katy did,
sick and saintly. No-hoper of grace,
grasper at culms, tettigoniid,

I'd imitate your own good muse's
cause and conscience. Articulate
our pity and fear. Mime eases us.
Make us a form cathartic, Kate.

8

Graham by math and footrule rakes
his courtyard garden of Japan.
He measures the world, Pythagoras
in ten square feet. Ah, Graham-san,

the golden ratio has determined
form. Elliptic stones are held
in gravel loops. A shapen pine
leafs and unleafs, its shape compelled

like clouds. A granite snow-lantern shines
no light. Snow light. Russell would say,
from form or an abstract proposition
something's taken away.

9

I am not for England. I have no idea
what England or being English might be for.
Let Issues Road come down from Ida.
Young Katy, risen like a noble fir,
trots with her sheep in Holme, uno pastourèlo
grieving, or Goethe's Schäferin Scapine
sheep's-eyed. The 'ego' is in pastoral.
Herd me, Katy, under the cosmic pine.

Chris Preddle has retired from libraries to a windy shoulder of the Pennines in West Yorkshire. His second collection is Cattle Console Him *(Waywiser, 2010); his first was* Bonobos *(Biscuit, 2001). He is translating all of Sappho's poems and fragments.*

THE STUPID SKIRT AND OTHER INTERLUDES
(extract)

Emma Marx

A safe space.

(Author's Note: The following stories drawn from "talking therapy" sessions are non-fiction, but all names and many details have been changed.)

Jonny at Sea

Jonny's mother will always be grateful to me; after seeing me a few times, he finally agreed to have a shower every morning. The daily shower, as he saw it, was the least of his problems, in fact: like most of the issues in his life, it was his mother's problem, not his.

It was not one of his mother's problems, however, that brought him to therapy. He explained that he was a sound engineer, on a large cruise ship, and had had a breakdown on the ship. This meant that he was to be sent home at the ship's next port of call. As the port was a few days away, he spent time in the medical bay thinking about what might be wrong with him. He had no idea, he said, what might have caused the breakdown, but was very worried he wouldn't be able to go back to work. His mother had taken him to the GP, who had recommended therapy and had referred him to me.

As Jonny and I explored what might have led to the episode on the cruise ship, I learned many new things from him. Internet trolling was something I knew very little about, but in this field, Jonny was an expert. He taught me that not all trolling was nasty or bullying, that there was a community of "professional trolls" who were always trying to outdo each other with more and more creative and devious trolling activities, and this was a highly skilled area.

A lot of this went above my head, but I began to get a sense of Jonny in this world where he felt very comfortable and confident, unlike the real world where he was often isolated and insecure. He said he preferred to "chat" online, rather than face to face, as it was less risky for him. He explained that he often had trouble reading people's facial expressions and would therefore frequently respond in an inappropriate way. He was also aware that he had a tendency to "butt in" to conversations with what he called "random" comments. Online friendships were much easier for him, and he felt at ease.

Jonny did go out and socialise; he often went clubbing in the city centre. To my surprise, he also mentioned several sexual relationships with girls but said he would like a "proper" girlfriend and the encounters he had had to date were just "friends with benefits." He admitted that he was always drunk during these nights out and could barely remember the sequence of events. He also told me that he frequently paid for drinks, not just for his friends or the girl he was pursuing, but often for large numbers of strangers. This made him quite popular, but skint, naturally. He also suspected he was being taken advantage of. The other habit he had was to pay for people to get a taxi home, and then walk home himself, as he had no money left for his own taxi.

When he was working on the cruise ship, alcohol was forbidden and there were no opportunities for the staff to go into clubs, so he felt at a loss as to how to socialise with his colleagues. This caused him some distress, as did the pressure from his boss, who he felt always picked on him and blamed him for everything that went wrong. Finally, his cabinmate made a complaint about him because he didn't shower and this seems to have been the last straw for Jonny.

I asked him why he thought the daily shower was so important to people. He replied that he had no idea, he thought it was just one of his mother's silly obsessions, like making his bed and plumping the cushions on the sofa. I explained that if he didn't shower, he would smell and this put people off, for example, potential friends, girlfriends and, most recently, his cabinmate. It was a lightbulb moment for Jonny and he promised that from now on, he would shower every morning.

As the shower problem had already been solved, Jonny and I focused on coping strategies for him to implement when he returned to work. I suggested he practice these when he went home, where there were also issues between him and the rest of the family (mother, step-father and sister). Jonny liked lists, so we made daily task lists for him, which included, to his mother's delight, not only the daily shower but making his bed, putting his dirty washing in the basket, and walking the dog.

When he returned to see me a couple of weeks later, he confirmed that not only were things better at home, he had met a wonderful *cool* girl at the club and, he grinned, they were together, *you know what I mean, dude?* I had never been called *dude* before but considered it a compliment.

Jonny did eventually go back to work on the cruise ship and we kept in touch for a while by email. He called me once, several months later, to say that he had been offered a job as the chief sound engineer for a play that was touring the UK and that the actors and crew were all *cool* – so he was happy.

A Sister's Tale

The first time I met Angela was at a training workshop; we were a relatively small group, about 20 people, and, in accordance with the culture of these courses, everyone introduced themselves at the beginning and there were lots of opportunities during the day to contribute and participate in the training. This all gave me some sense of Angela, a small, slim woman with a very loud voice and an elegant bob of thick grey hair.

Several years passed and then I happened to meet Angela again, in a different professional context. She came to my consulting room and was, by her own admission, ill at ease. I remarked that we had met before, but she could not remember meeting me at the workshop. She commented that there were so many people there and that she had felt quite overwhelmed. I was surprised at this, as she seemed a very confident person and they were all her colleagues to some extent. As we chatted, I was again very aware of how loudly she spoke and wondered if she was hard of hearing, but Angela did not mention it and I did not feel it was appropriate to ask.

Angela gave me an account of her life and how she became a counsellor. She had originally been a Maths teacher and had been inspired to train as a counsellor after reading *On Becoming a Person*, by Carl Rogers. However, before this, she explained, she had already entered a religious order and had taken her vows. *I am a religious sister*, she said, *I don't call myself a nun and I don't wear a wimple or robes, that is all old-fashioned nonsense and not necessary*.

Over the years, Angela worked in secondary schools teaching maths and in various missionary type jobs, which she thoroughly enjoyed, especially in Africa, where, she said, she was awed and inspired by people's attitude to death and dying. On her return to the UK, she was impressed by the support a close friend received from the hospice where her father was dying and decided to volunteer there.

Angela had been working as a counsellor at this hospice ever since and was now part of the core staff. She felt that working with bereavement and loss was her true vocation, after many years of struggling to come to terms with a personal loss of her own. *Understanding loss*, she said, *has helped me to understand myself and how I view myself.*

Angela said it was very difficult for her to speak about her own loss, even though it had happened so long ago, when she was a small child, because it was so traumatic. However, she said, she felt it was an important part of her story and therefore she had made the decision to tell me.

I was born – the distilled parable goes – *during the War and, like everyone at that time, grew up in a small house without what we take for granted today, like central heating, hot water and an inside toilet. There was a wood burning stove in the kitchen, which my mother used to heat water and cook, and it was always on. I remember my mother was careful to never let the fire go out.*

One day, I must have been about seven years old, I came home from school – everyone walked themselves to school in those days – and went to the kitchen, as I always did. My mother was cooking something and did not notice I was standing behind her as she moved the cooking pot. As she bumped into me the contents of the pot spilled onto my head and I was burned.

I do not remember anything about this incident and can only tell you what was told to me. Apparently, my mother somehow got me to a doctor and the burn was treated successfully. Unfortunately, the hair on the burned part of my scalp never grew back. I was very self-conscious about my hair as I was growing up and did everything I could to cover up the bald patch. I grew my hair long and, with my mother's careful styling and plaiting arrangements, managed to hide my shame. As I got older, it became more and more difficult to hide and I noticed that I was constantly worried about it. Visits to the hairdresser, a source of pleasure for most women, became increasingly stressful. I was in despair about this but did not tell anyone.

Much later, when I was in my forties, I found a specialist, based 300 miles away, who I visit every other month, at huge expense, and who has changed my life by giving me the hair you see today. It is a complex combination of hair extensions and a semi-permanent hairpiece and, I think you will agree, looks very natural.

People think that for a religious sister, appearance doesn't matter, but they are wrong. I am a sister, but I am a woman first, and a woman's hair is the essence of her womanhood. Think about the punishments for women through the ages, cutting their hair, shaving their head, tarring and feathering … think about all of the issues around covering a woman's hair in many cultures around the world.

I was very moved by Angela's story and reflected on all of the assumptions we (myself included) make about women like her. I thought about my own hair and how important it is to me. I remembered my own mini-trauma as a child when my mother cut my hair so short that everyone thought I was a boy, which is probably why I always keep my hair long to this day.

One of my parables, in fact.

The Hoff

One day I had a phone call from a man who sounded Irish, who asked me if I was Jewish, as he was looking for a *Jewish* therapist. I was rather surprised at this requirement, which I had not come across before, but assured him I *was* Jewish and would be happy to see him. He also had some questions about confidentiality, which I was also able to reassure him about, and we duly arranged an appointment.

Conor was in his late 30s and worked in construction. He was Irish, but had lived in Scotland for many years and had a Scottish wife. He told me he had undergone something called the Hoffman Process, which had changed his life. Apparently, this was an intensive form of therapy which one undertook in a residential setting over eight days. It was developed by Bob Hoffman in the 60s and, as Conor explained, Bob Hoffman was Jewish and therefore he needed a Jewish therapist.

I was intrigued by Conor's unusual attitude to finding a therapist and told him so. I commented that Jewish therapists were very thin on the ground in the region, giving him little choice. He laughed at this and assured me that he had checked out my credentials and assured me "the Jewish thing" was not the only criteria.

Conor was the oldest of nine but, he insisted, his family was not poor like in *Angela's Ashes* and other Irish tales of misery. They had been brought up in a big house, and his father (now retired) had a good job. However, there were some problems in the family and this was what had brought him to *the Hoff*, as he called the Hoffman Process, several years ago. *I was amused by the moniker, as it made me think of the other, more famous, Hoff, who had little in common with Bob and his Process.*

Recently, some of these issues had been bothering him again, which was why he got in touch with me. Also, his wife had told him he needed to go and talk to someone as she felt he was totally stressed out at work and this was affecting their relationship.

Conor had many issues he wanted to work on in therapy, including stress at work and his relationship with his wife, but said that before he tackled them, he wanted to address something that had been haunting him since childhood. He again checked with me that the sessions were entirely confidential, and I again assured him that I would only break confidentiality under very specific circumstances, which I had already outlined in the first session. His real identity could or would never be revealed.

The story Conor told me was that of a family that, on the outside, appeared perfectly functional. His father was a successful businessman who worked away during the week and came home every weekend when, after they had all been to Mass in their Sunday best, he took Conor's mother up to their bedroom, where, Conor said, *they made another baby*.

However, during the week, apparently unbeknown to his father, Conor's mother drank, to the point that she was unable to look after the children and was often passed out on the sofa when they came home from school. It became Conor's job to ensure his younger siblings were fed, bathed and put to bed and, as there were so many of them, his duties became more and more onerous. Not only that, his mother's drinking seemed to escalate over the years, and, as she didn't want people to know about her problem, she would insist that Conor go out and buy the alcohol for her. Conor said he tried to restrict her alcohol intake as much as he could, but it was a hopeless battle.

He mentioned that during the Hoff, when all the participants had to explain their role in the family by giving themselves a name, his was *Number One Son*.

One night, he thinks he was about twelve or thirteen, he suddenly woke up in the middle of the night and felt the bed was very damp. As he changed his position to move away from the wet patch, he realised, to his horror, that he was in his eight-year-old sister's bed, and that she was lying next to him. She also awoke and, as far as he can remember, asked him sleepily why the bed was wet. He said something to comfort her and she seemed to fall asleep again. He rushed back into his own room and his own bed, shocked to the core at what he had done.

Over the years, he had revisited and analysed this incident many times. *Do you think I am a paedophile?* he asked. I responded by saying that first of all, he was a child himself when this happened and secondly, children often touch each other without it having any sexual significance. Also, could he have been sleepwalking (a common occurrence in children who are stressed and anxious) and had simply had a wet dream in his sister's bed? *Remember, you were Number One Son.*

Conor told me to that to hear this from me was truly liberating; he had never allowed himself to tell anyone of his torment, in case they believed he had abused his sister. Not only that, he had always had a difficult relationship with this particular sister and had worried that it was due to this incident, even though she had never mentioned it and, as far as he knew, had no recollection of it.

After this session I did not see Conor for some time; he had been too busy at work. When I next saw him, several months later, he looked exhausted and there was an angry red rash on his face. He explained that there had been threats of mass redundancies at work and therefore he was pulling out all the stops in order to try to secure his job. He complained of poor sleep and admitted he had been drinking "a lot". He also said things at home were "horrendous" as he and his wife were arguing all the time.

From what Conor was describing, it sounded as though both he and his wife were extremely stressed at this time: he was worried about work and she was worried about her father, who had been diagnosed with cancer. However, there was more: it turned out that his father in law was an alcoholic, who had treated Conor's wife appallingly, and it frustrated Conor to see her "running around" after her father and neglecting Conor.

Conor admitted he also felt sexually neglected and frustrated; it seemed as though his wife's libido, never very high at the best of times, had now taken a complete nose-dive and she was refusing to have sex with him. This, coupled with the fact that they were supposed to be trying for a baby, resulted in Conor becoming enraged with his wife and, perhaps to punish her, was going to a prostitute every time they had a big argument. *I feel so dirty and ashamed*, he said, *but every time we fight, I feel I just have to go see that hooker, it's like a compulsion.*

I asked what it was like to be with the hooker. Did he feel less frustrated afterwards? He said there was some relief, but it didn't last. What he really wanted, he stated, was to have sex with his wife, whom he loved, just from time to time, and for them to have children.

I reflected that I could see he was feeling disempowered at both work and at home. We explored how he might empower himself; he agreed that the current, hooker-dependent strategy was not working. I suggested that his wife might benefit from seeing a therapist; it might result in her having more time and energy for him if she had somewhere to take her own problems.

Soon afterwards, Conor cancelled his appointment. His own father had had a stroke and Conor was going to Ireland to be with him. I did not hear from him again but was aware that his wife continued to have therapy with my colleague, a sex and relationship therapist, for several years.

Three Times a Week

Unlike all the other couples I had worked with, Angus and Irene did not seem at all angry with each other. When they sat down, I noticed they sat very close together and looked like a loving couple. When I reflected this to them later in the session, they agreed that, in spite of everything, they did still love each other and got on well.

Nevertheless, when they told me what the problem was, my first instinct was that no amount of therapy could help them. Basically, after about twelve years of apparently happy marriage and three children, Angus had had an "affair", with a *man*. He had moved out of the family home into a rented flat nearby some months ago. The affair had ended, but he was still unsure of his sexuality and of what he wanted.

I asked for more details about the affair and the man in question. How had Angus met him? How long did the affair last? What need in him did it satisfy? Angus told me that he had met the man, Craig, in a gay bar and that there was an immediate sexual attraction. They saw each other a few times over the course of a month but Angus ended it when he realised that Craig was emotionally involved and that for him, it wasn't just the sex, as it was for Angus.

Irene had found out about Craig because Angus had left his phone lying around with numerous text messages from Craig on it. I remarked that it seemed almost like Angus wanted Irene to find out and he agreed that he made little or no attempt to hide the affair. He said he felt so guilty about it that it was a relief when Irene confronted him. This also helped him to end the affair, as he had the perfect excuse to give Craig.

Irene chipped in that Craig seemed like "a really nice guy". It turned out, to my amazement, that the three of them had met for dinner, at Irene's instigation. I asked Irene why she had wanted to meet Craig and she explained that it was in order to see if the affair was serious. When she saw them together, she said, she knew that it was "just a fling" and could see that it was Craig who was infatuated, not Angus.

However, Irene was torn: she was angry with Angus for the affair and felt betrayed, but was understanding of the fact that he had "issues with his sexuality". To her, the affair seemed to be a sort of test to see if he was gay, as she put it, rather than a "real" betrayal. They both said they loved each other very much and wanted to reconcile. I checked out if there was any risk of STD and they assured me they had both been tested and had been given the all clear.

Over the next few sessions, more details about their life together emerged. Angus worked from home, so was in the house every day and helped out with the children and the household tasks. His rented flat was only a few minutes by car away and therefore he could be called on very quickly to look after the children if Irene needed to go out in the evening.

Then, the bombshell: three nights a week Irene allowed Angus to "stay over". I checked that this meant what I thought it meant and they both confirmed that yes, they had sex three times a week. Not only that, the sex was great, better than ever. I was puzzled. This arrangement did not seem any different from being married, apart from the fact that Angus slept in his flat four nights a week.

Angus agreed and added: "I am the luckiest man in the world; I have my own space, see my children every day, and three times a week I am allowed to have sex with my wife." I asked Irene how she felt, hearing this comment. She explained that until she decided how to handle the aftermath of the affair, this arrangement suited her as well. She said that Angus had never been so helpful around the house or with the children when they lived together full-time, and she was enjoying the freedom of being able to go out at night with her friends whenever she wanted. In the past, Angus had been extremely reluctant to look after the children or pick them up from school but now, he was always willing and available.

I reflected that it sounded like they were both working towards a full reconciliation. Angus and Irene agreed. In that case, I suggested, it was important to identify the issues that were still unresolved, so that they did not arise again in the future and cause another breakup. I asked them each to make a list and bring it to the next session.

The lists did not contain any surprises. Irene wanted to build up trust in Angus and wanted him to "sort himself out sexually". She also wanted to ensure that his willingness to help with the children and the house continued and that he did not lapse back into the way he used to be, i.e., *lazy*.

All Angus wanted was to move back in. He also admitted that one of the reasons he had been lazy about household tasks and childcare was that he worked from home and found it difficult to switch off from work. I suggested that in order to have a clear boundary between home and work, he use his rented flat as his office. That way, when he was at the flat, he was officially at work, and when he was at home, he could be with his family. Angus agreed this could be a solution and only required some minor logistical arrangements to be made such as transferring his desk, his files and computer equipment.

In terms of his sexuality, I suggested that he work on this issue with a gay, male therapist. Angus asked why he could not simply see me for this work. I explained that as I had seen them as a couple, I could not see him individually. Therapeutically speaking, this would not work. Also, I felt that it would be much more helpful for him to see a gay man and that he might also feel more comfortable talking about sex with him (I had noticed some hesitation during our sessions).

Angus agreed to consider this strategy and I recommended an experienced colleague for him to contact. Angus and Irene said goodbye, thanked me and left the room holding hands. They looked very happy and in love. I reflected on how satisfying it was to be proved wrong sometimes.

Hooked Too

For many years I worked in a doctor's surgery in an area of the city, south of the river, which has a very mixed population. The referrals I received from the GPs in the practice spanned all social classes; ranging from people on benefits to middle class professionals, and everything in-between. I enjoyed the variety of clients very much, although I sometimes felt uncomfortable in the very clinical setting where I saw them, surrounded by blood pressure monitors, syringes and other medical paraphernalia.

Mark was a young man in his late twenties who had been referred with "anxiety due to family issues". He arrived for his appointment punctually and was neatly dressed in dark jeans and a casual shirt. He looked a lot younger than his date of birth indicated, more like a someone in their late teens. I had noticed on his referral form that he had a very distinctive, Polish-sounding surname and asked him about it. He confirmed that it was indeed a Polish name and that his biological father was of Polish descent.

Mark was very nervous; he said that it was partly because he had never had therapy before, but also because something terrible had happened in his family and he had never talked about it to anyone. I assured Mark about confidentiality and encouraged him to disclose what had happened in his family, but Mark said he wasn't ready. He said he needed time to build up trust in me and in the relationship.

I tried very hard to be patient, but as the sessions came and went without any disclosure, I began to wonder what on earth was going on. Mark had told me snippets about his family and about himself, but so far, there was absolutely nothing that was out of the ordinary.

He told me that his mother had had him when she was very young and unmarried, and that he had never known his father. Her family was "strict Catholic" and apparently, his mother's parents had shunned her until she married his stepfather when he was at primary school. He regarded his stepfather as his real father and had a younger half-brother, who he was very fond of. He worked as a sports journalist for a newspaper, a job that he enjoyed though not especially passionate about sport, but his dream was to be a writer. He was single and I had the impression that he had never had a girlfriend. He had mentioned a girl at work that he liked, but felt unable to approach her; he was too shy.

He also told me about a trip to Poland he had undertaken recently, to trace his family roots. Unclearly, he had been very close to his apparently biological Polish *grandfather*, and after he died last year Mark decided to travel to the village in Poland his grandfather had come from and learn as much as he could about the family. The trip had been a great success and Mark had been very moved by what he described as a life-changing experience.

Soon after my third session with Mark, I had my fortnightly meeting with my supervisor. I told her about Mark and my increasing frustration with him. I also disclosed, somewhat shamefully, that I had Googled his name, to see if I could find out anything about the family. Unfortunately, the search had not yielded anything, apart from a couple of articles Mark had written about football matches, and a review he had posted on a film enthusiasts website.

My supervisor's response to my account was that Mark had clearly "hooked" me with the promise of an exciting story about his family. Her theory was that he felt so insecure about himself that he was convinced that I would lose interest in him if he didn't provide me with a "hook".

I reflected on what she had said and decided I would challenge Mark in the next session. In any case, we were running out of time. There was a limit of six sessions for my clients at the surgery, unless there were special circumstances. When Mark arrived for his session, I explained that we were now half-way through the sessions, and if he wished to work through his family issue in any depth, he would need to talk about it now.

Mark looked very uncomfortable as I was speaking. After a few moments, he said, somewhat ruefully I thought, that he would now tell me. His story, which came out in dribs and drabs, initially made no sense to me whatsoever and I had to ask Mark a number of questions in order to understand what his experience had been.

This is what I *think* he was telling me: after the death of Mark's Polish grandfather and his trip to Poland, he somehow found out that he was not of Polish descent at all, but had been adopted by his stepfather, whose surname he bore. *He* was the Polish one, not his biological father and he was therefore not related biologically to his beloved grandfather. He said he came across his birth and adoption certificates and suddenly realised his identity, which he believed to be Polish, was false.

When I asked him why he had not realised this before, or why his mother had not mentioned it to him in the past, Mark became very angry with me. He said that he *did* know the truth about his origins, but somehow it did not seem real to him until he saw the documents. His mother had apparently counselled him all along against going to Poland, but he would not listen to her and made the journey anyway.

When I tried to gently explore why Mark had chosen not to believe his mother and what his feelings were around this issue, Mark started shouting at me. At this point, the session completely deteriorated, and Mark stormed out of the room. As he slammed the door, he seemed to be muttering that the counselling had been a mistake and that he should never have trusted me.

I told my supervisor what had happened and that I felt very upset about the way the relationship with Mark had ended. Had I perhaps been *too* challenging? On the other hand, Mark had not given me or the therapy a chance. Could I have handled it differently, better?

Like all good supervisors, she just listened.

The Thumb Ring

Sonya seemed to me a very *russian* Russian, not that I had met many Russians in Scotland. She had the high, Slavic cheekbones and the passion and drama in her voice was, to me, reminiscent of the great Russian writers. Like one of Tolstoy's tragic heroines, she seemed to have an aura of suffering about her. Not only that, she was a violinist, and I wondered, playfully, if she was also a tortured artist, for that would complete the stereotype perfectly.

She was in her late thirties but looked much younger. Her clothes, however, were at odds with her youthful face. She was dressed conservatively in a skirt and long sleeved blouse, with skin-coloured tights and flat shoes. She wore large, old-fashioned glasses with a thick brown frame, and no make-up.

The problem, she stated, was her husband, who had betrayed her with another woman. This was causing her terrible distress and pain, and she believed that she needed to decide whether she should leave him or not. She was hoping that therapy would help her make the right decision. She still loved him, she declared, but she didn't know what to do. Would couples counselling be helpful, she asked, or should she see me on her own?

In order to answer her questions, I asked her to tell me about the relationship with her husband and the background to the alleged affair. She and her husband, a Scot called Callum, had met in a pub frequented by musicians about seventeen years ago. She had won a scholarship to the prestigious musical academy in the city and had moved here from Russia. At that time, she didn't know anyone and spoke very little English.

Callum, who was some twenty years older than her, was a "fiddler" who specialised in traditional Scottish music and was a regular in the classical music scene in the city. Apparently, he was very charming and chatted her up in the pub. They ended up falling in love and getting married soon afterwards. They had a son, who was now sixteen, and also a talented musician. She taught violin and they lived in Callum's flat on the outskirts of the city.

A few years after they married, Sonya noticed that Callum seemed to be drinking "a lot" and became concerned that he might have an alcohol problem. She herself barely drank and explained that she could not understand the "drinking culture" in Scotland, which to her seemed even worse than in her native Russia. Callum always denied that he was dependent on alcohol, but about eight years ago, he ended up in a coma, as a result of severe seizures caused by his drinking.

She described the period following his seizure as very traumatic. It seemed for a long time, perhaps four months, that he would not wake from his coma. She was preparing for herself for widowhood and her son for a life without his father. Against all the odds, he did wake up and somehow managed to learn to speak and walk again, after almost a year in the rehabilitation part of the hospital. He even managed to re-learn how to play the fiddle and, apart from a severe limp, made a complete recovery. He never drank again.

Unfortunately, the new sober Callum was not, as she had hoped, a happy man, quite the opposite. He was unable to find work, not because of any physical impairment, but because he had fallen out with everyone in the traditional Scottish music world. He was bitter about this and, she felt, took it out on her and their son.

They also had issues around money. He expected her to pay for everything from her income, pleading poverty, but always seemed to have plenty of money for his gambling habit. She had no idea where this money came from and, as they had completely separate finances, bank accounts and there was no mortgage on the flat, simply accepted that she had to support the family. Fortunately, she earned a good salary and was very careful with her spending. Also, Callum's elderly parents paid for their son's private school fees, for which she was very grateful. She suspected they gave Callum money too, but had never confronted him about it.

I remarked that it sounded like he had replaced his alcohol habit with a gambling habit. Like his drinking, he claimed to be in complete control of his gambling and accused Sonya of "fussing over nothing." The other pastime he had was going to his cottage (inherited from his family), which was located in a fishing village in the northeast of Scotland. He would spend several nights a week there, even in the winter. "What does he do there?" I asked. Sonya said until recently she thought he just liked the peace and quiet. However, it was here that the affair had taken place, with a woman who had a holiday caravan by the marina.

"How did you find out about this woman?" Sonya explained that Callum was an avid user of Facebook and that she had simply gone into his Facebook account (easily accessible, as she had guessed his password). There she had found numerous messages to and from the woman, as well as photos that they had sent each other. Some of the messages, she said, were very flirtatious and full of sexual innuendo. One of the photographs she thought looked like it was of Callum's genitals, but she wasn't sure. When she confronted him about her findings, his explanation was that the messages were just "between friends" and that the photo she thought was odd was of "something in the garden". He denied any affair and stated that Sonya was crazy and jealous.

Sonya showed me the photo in question and asked what I thought. To me, it *did* look like a close-up of a man's genitals, and I was (privately) amazed at his audacity in claiming the image was botanical. I noticed that the penis in the photograph was curved and asked Sonya if Callum's was shaped like this. Sonya confirmed that he had contracted Peyronie's disease a few years earlier, and that since then, his penis was curved. I commented to Sonya that if Callum *had* had an affair with this woman, he would not have been able to have intercourse.

Sonya's response was that it was the principle of betrayal that bothered her, far more than the prospect of sex. She disclosed that they had not had penetrative sex for years, but that she didn't mind too much. "Sex is for having children and we don't want any more children." However, she added with a shy smile, he would, very occasionally, "pleasure her with his hands."

Sonya also showed me photos of Callum's "friend", who looked like a typical middle-aged woman, slightly overweight and reasonably but not exceptionally attractive. She was dressed in cropped trousers, a sleeveless top and sandals. Sonya pointed out that she was wearing a thumb ring and told me she had never seen that type of jewellery before. She also commented on how much make-up the woman was wearing (Sonya never wore make-up) and that maybe Callum preferred a woman who looked "like that".

At the end of our first session, Sonya said that she found it very helpful and would like to come and see me regularly, on her own. She was concerned that if she came with Callum as a couple, he would make me believe *his* version of events. *He is very charming and persuasive,* she added, *especially with women.*

When Sonya arrived for her next session a couple of weeks later, I almost didn't recognise her. She was dressed in cropped trousers, a sleeveless top, sandals and was sporting a thumb ring. Not only that, she was wearing make-up and had done something different with her hair. Her explanation was that she had decided to dress like this because she liked this style and also, she hoped Callum would find her attractive like this.

I asked if the strategy had been successful and she said that things had improved between them. She had decided to give him another chance, on the condition that he would cut off contact with this woman. However, there had been another drama at the weekend, when she found text messages on his phone, in which he told the woman that "his wife was crazy and that they would need to be discreet". After a blazing row, he went to the cottage. Later on that evening, she felt guilty and booked at taxi to take her to the cottage, where she arrived at 4am. It cost her £80, she said, but felt it was worth it, as they did manage some sort of reconciliation.

Over the coming weeks, there were many more dramas. Sonya and Callum attempted a trial separation, but they stayed together. Eventually, Sonya said she was ready to end her therapy sessions and thanked me for my help. I told her that I didn't feel that I had been of much help, but was happy that she felt more confident and empowered.

Six months later, just before Christmas, the receptionist at my office told me that someone had dropped off a parcel for me. It turned out to be a huge box of chocolates and a Russian calendar. The accompanying card expressed effusive thanks for my help and wished me and my family a *Merry Christmas, from Sonya.*

Safed

From time to time, when I worked in the Health Service, I was referred clients who did not speak English. These types of clients were usually refugees or asylum seekers from war-torn countries and the work was very challenging, least of all because of the language barrier. In these instances, I was permitted to book an interpreter, which I did through a translation agency.

However, on one occasion, I was referred a foreign client who did not fit the normal profile. She was Spanish and her English was good but, she felt, not good enough for sessions with a therapist. She was not a migrant of any kind but was coming for relationship issues. I checked with the powers that be and they agreed she could have an interpreter.

I therefore contacted the agency and booked a Spanish interpreter for the next session. As was my habit, I requested that the interpreter come a few minutes early. This was not just to explain about client confidentiality and therapeutic matters, but also to go through some common linguistic issues. For example, the term *counselling* as I understand it does not exist in many languages.

The person who arrived to do the interpreting was, to my astonishment, not Spanish or South American, but *Russian*. She had a degree in Spanish from a university in Siberia and was completely fluent in the language. Ana, for that was her name, attended and interpreted the remaining few sessions with my Spanish client, and so I got to know her a little over that time.

I learned that Ana had grown up in Siberia, in a Jewish family. When it became possible for Russians to leave the country, she and her family emigrated to Israel. She lived there for several years and spoke fluent Hebrew. When I asked how she had come to Scotland, she explained that she met her Scottish husband in Israel and that he had brought her here. Being of Israeli origin myself, I was delighted to meet someone like Ana and enjoyed chatting to her in Hebrew.

A few months later, I was again astonished. Ana, who lived in the area, had asked her GP to refer her to me and so she became my client some weeks later. When she arrived for her first appointment, she explained that she had been so impressed by the way I worked with the Spanish client that she realised that she herself could benefit from some sessions. She also had relationship problems and was at her wit's end and couldn't cope any longer.

This time, when she told me her story, it was quite different. The childhood in Siberia had been difficult. Her parents worked hard but because they were Jewish, they were unable to progress in their respective careers. The family was not religious or observant in any way, but, Ana explained, in the former Soviet Union ethnic origin was everything. The whole family believed that the move to Israel would solve all of their problems but they were bitterly disappointed.

First of all, the practical adjustments they had to make were very difficult. Everything was different; the weather, the food and the people. Also, they didn't speak the language and ended up working in menial jobs for low pay. They lived in a small flat, much like in Siberia. Ana, who was younger and learned Hebrew with ease, was happy but her parents were not.

A few years later, Ana was studying at the Hebrew University in Jerusalem. There she met Joshua, who was also a student and, according to Ana, it was love at first sight. They had a whirlwind romance and began to plan their wedding. Ana explained that Joshua was a mystic who was really into Kabbalah. She also became interested in this type of mysticism and they decided to have their wedding in Safed (*Tsfat*, in Hebrew). I was aware that Safed has always been considered a holy city and that it is the centre of Kabbalah.

Their wedding was apparently a magical day. Ana said everyone could feel the mystic atmosphere as the rabbi conducted the ceremony and afterwards, she felt what she described as being completely in harmony with Joshua and the world. She said it was the most amazing feeling she had ever had.

Unfortunately, the feeling didn't last. Ana became pregnant very quickly and their daughter Sarah was born within the year. During this time, Israel was experiencing large numbers of suicide bombers, especially in Jerusalem where they lived, and Ana and Joshua no longer felt safe. They decided to return to his home town in Scotland, where they would have safety, the support of his family and, hopefully, job opportunities.

It seemed as though once Joshua was away from Israel, he became a different person. Ana noticed that he was very impatient and would fly off the handle over the smallest thing. He even got angry with little Sarah, who was a toddler, and Ana was worried about leaving him alone with her. Also, it became clear that Joshua did not have a good relationship with his parents as they argued constantly, especially when they first arrived in Scotland and were living with Joshua's parents.

Once they moved into their own flat, Ana was busy looking for work but Joshua seemed in no hurry. His behaviour became more and more peculiar and he began to neglect his appearance and personal hygiene. "He looks like Jesus Chris now with his long beard and long hair." I asked if he was perhaps taking drugs and Ana replied that yes, to her horror, she discovered used syringes on the floor under the bed. She confronted him about the drugs but he became enraged and shouted at her and told her to leave him alone.

At this point, I asked if he had hit her or Sarah. She said no, but she was terrified that it was just a matter of time. I asked about support for her and her daughter; perhaps Joshua's parents could help? She said she would speak to them but she was not sure they could do anything as they were frightened of Joshua.

She had only just found out that Joshua was schizophrenic and was under the care of a psychiatrist. For some reason, while he was in Israel his symptoms were under control, but since returning to Scotland he had stopped his medication and his condition had deteriorated. He was convinced that the GP, the psychiatrist, his parents and Ana were all conspiring against him and that the medication would "take away his soul."

I continued to see Ana for a few more sessions and eventually, she reached crisis point. Joshua's behaviour became more and more threatening and she finally fled, with Sarah and a few bags, to a women's refuge. She then began to rebuild her life, with a little help from social services, and managed to find another flat. During all of this time, she somehow managed to continue to work as an interpreter. She even enrolled in a training course for interpreters, which, when she obtained her certificate of proficiency, qualified her to interpret in court and for legal matters.

About a year after Ana finished her sessions with me, I bumped into her in front of the doctor's surgery. She was there to interpret for a patient and looked well. When I asked how she was doing, she told me that things were fine; she was very busy with work, Sarah was at school and Joshua had stabilised to the point that he was allowed to look after Sarah a couple of times a week. Also, she said, she was just about to start another degree course at the university, this time in Psychology.

Once again, I was astonished.

Airport Hotel

Soon after I started my private practice, I obtained a contract with one of the large train companies. This meant that I was on their list of therapists authorised to work with their employees. These were often train drivers or other train staff affected by a suicide on the track and, as these events seemed to be an eerily regular occurrence in the region, I had a steady stream of traumatised clients.

Willy was a train driver, but he was off work for a completely different reason. He was recovering from prostate cancer and his GP had recommended counselling in order to help facilitate his return to work. He was a sprightly man of 61, with a great sense of humour and lots of funny stories to tell me. He had worked for the railways since leaving school at the age of 15 and had worked his way up the ranks to driver. He was married with grown-up children and, as he put it, *had never had a day's illness in his life until he got cancer*.

It was difficult to discern exactly what was troubling Willy, as he was so cheery and positive. He told me that he was very grateful to be alive, and, apart from some pain in his groin due to scar tissue, he was feeling good. He was not, as is often the case after prostate surgery, incontinent, and he was looking forward to going back to work in the coming weeks.

As Willy and I got to know each other, he began to open up. As I suspected, there was something bothering him, something he described as *very embarrassing*. The problem was that he was impotent, a common after-effect of prostate surgery. However, he felt it would seem rude or ungrateful to raise this issue with his doctor. After all, he said, he should be thankful he was alive and in remission, and not *pissing his pants*.

I asked Willy how his impotence was affecting him and the impact on his relationship with his wife. He explained that they had always had a very active sexual relationship and that they were both bitterly disappointed that they could not resume their sex life after surgery. His wife, although she knew why he was impotent, was nevertheless feeling neglected and not desired. In summary, the impotence was causing tension between them. Also, in spite of being impotent, he still had what he termed *sexual feelings*, and this resulted in a great deal of frustration on his part.

I reflected that his gratitude at being alive and well was surely a separate issue from his impotence. Also, I remarked that there were a large number of treatments available for impotence and that it might not do any harm to look into his options. As Willy had a meeting with his GP coming up, I suggested that he ask for an appropriate referral.

Willy was very happy with my suggestion and said he would ask the GP for help. He also said he would take his wife along to the consultation. As he put it, it involved her just as much as him. He thanked me for my help and we arranged to meet again in a couple of weeks. I couldn't help but notice that there was a noticeable spring in his step as he left the room.

Two weeks later Willy literally bounced into the session. He had a very funny story to tell me, he said, as a result of my suggestion and the visit to the GP. The GP was happy to refer Willy to a GU clinic and the referral came through very quickly. At the clinic, the very helpful nurse explained that for Willy's condition the best treatment was an injection into his penis, which would immediately give him an erection. There was no point taking Viagra, she explained, as it was something to do with the muscles in his groin needing stimulation, which is what the drug being injected could help with.

She showed him and his wife how to do it and they did a test run right there and then. The injection was simple and painless and it worked perfectly. She explained that the effect of the injection could last a couple of hours and gave them a large supply of ampoules and syringes to take away. When Willy and his wife got to the car, they had a great idea: why not take advantage of his aroused state, before the injection wore off?

As the clinic was a good distance from their house, they were concerned they wouldn't have enough time to get there and make love. However, they were near the airport and they knew the airport had a hotel so they drove there as quickly as they could. His wife was driving, Willy explained with a chuckle, *for obvious reasons*.

When they reached the hotel near the airport, there was a little bit of tension at check-in, as it seemed to take forever and they were very conscious of the clock ticking. At this point in the story, another big chuckle from Willy. However, they made it to the room in time, both of them laughing as they literally ran down the corridor and ripped their clothes off. Apparently the sex, although rushed, was fantastic, and they made the most of the hotel room.

I told Willy that it was a great story, and that I was delighted they had found a solution to the problem. Willy said he and his wife were very grateful for my help; it would not have occurred to them that there was help available and they would have simply been forced to accept a sex-free life.

Willy was returning to work soon and, as he felt so well, he decided to finish his sessions with me. As we said goodbye, he said, with one of his big chuckles, that he needed to go back to the nurse as they had *already nearly run out of injections* …

Emma Marx was born in 1964 and grew up in Germany, Holland, the United States and England. She attended Wadham College, Oxford, where she took a degree in Modern Languages. She lives in Scotland, where she practises psychotherapy. This is an extract from a book-in-progress.

A SUITE OF POEMS

John Glenday

AMBER

Some wounds weep precious through the generations.
They heal themselves into history by growing sticky, then hard.

What was mere sap once matures like blood in water
to dusken and burnish, and change into something useful,

almost. The Tsar had a whole room built from hurt,
but it was stolen and buried. Sometimes the grim Baltic rolls

the scars to shape those hapless jewels women like to wear;
especially treasured where they hold a thing that was living then,

something with quick, venated wings which happened
by and thought the wound looked beautiful and sweet

and that, like other wounds, it should be acknowledged
somehow, lingered over, and, if only for a moment, touched.

BRITISH PEARLS

"Gignit et Oceanus margarita, sed subfusca ac liventia ..."
                    (Tacitus Agricola 1:12)

British pearls are exceptionally poor.
They can be gathered up by the handful wherever
surf breaks, but you'll find no colour, no vitality, no lustre
to them – every last one stained the roughshod grey
of their drab, unmediterranean weather.

Imagine all the rains of this island held
in one sad, small, turbulent world.
I can hear them falling as I write. British pearls
are commonplace and waterish and dull,
but their women wear them as proudly as we wear gold.

MACAPABÁ

We rocked at anchor where the emptying river
spreads its green hand. Ochre mud thickened the sea.

On the second morning, slender boats from the forest;
they brought birds the colour of watered oil,

sallow fruit no one would taste, and a leaf folded
around a knot of gold broader than a clenching fist.

MY MOTHER'S FAVOURITE FLOWER

This world is nothing much – its mostly
threadworn, tawdry stuff, of next to little use.

If only it could bring itself to give us back
a portion of the things we would have fallen

for, but always too busy living, overlooked
and missed. So many small things missed.

So many brief, important things.
It is my intention never to write about this.

NORTHEASTERLY

Driven by sleet and hail,
snell, dour and winterly;

it fills the unwilling sail,
empties the late, green tree.

Something unreachable
lodged in the dusk of me

empties itself and fills
Like that sail. Like that tree.

STUDIE ZU DEN HÄNDEN EINES APOSTELS

after Dürer

This loophole where the light lets in; where my own breath
leaks through my hands, has damned my words to words or less.

That shim of air is God, of course, who made us all, and all
but whole, then set the wind against the world.

One of Scotland's foremost poets, John Glenday was born in 1952 in Broughty Ferry and worked for many years as psychiatric nurse and addictions counsellor. He is the author of The Apple Ghost *(Peterloo Poets, 1989),* Undark *(Peterloo Poets, 1995) and* Grain *(Picador, 2009), the latter shortlisted for both the Ted Hughes Award for New Work in Poetry and the Griffin Prize. Now retired, he lives in Drumnadrochit, Scotland, and his new collection of poems is due out in 2015.*

BYE-CHILD
(a screenplay for a short film)

Bernard MacLaverty
(after a poem by Seamus Heaney)

Vigils, solitudes, fasts.

(Editor's Note: see page 136)

> Little moon man,
> Kennelled and faithful
> At the foot of the yard ...
> (from "Bye-child", by Seamus Heaney)

1 Interior Shed Dusk

It is dusk. In the silence a dog from a distant housing estate can be faintly heard barking. Close up of a white downy feather in moonlight stuck to a beam of wood. The fluttering movement of the feather seems to be in response to breath. The camera is uncertain. The interior dark of the shed is seen but not understood. During one of its moves the camera slows down and passes on a full moon seen through a gap in the wooden wall or roof. It snags and goes back to see it properly. It remains on the circle of the moon for just slightly more than too long.

2 Exterior House Dusk

Outside a remote dilapidated two-storey farmhouse sits a grocery van. A WOMAN in her thirties has just made some purchases, which she holds in her arms. As she turns to go into the front door of the house the grocery van drives away.

3 Interior Shed Dusk

There is the sound of the van driving away. The camera tilts down from the darkening sky to a house, to an upstairs window, yellow with light from an electric light bulb. There is some angular distortion of the image (like the skull in Holbein's painting *The Ambassadors*). The landing light goes off and after a moment a light comes on in the kitchen and the camera turns quickly to investigate it. Faint sounds of dishes and cutlery rattling come from the house. The POV (Point of View) is low – again the angular distortion. It is as if it is trying to adjust the distortion – first to one side, then the other. It finally settles on normality. The WOMAN comes into view in the window, carrying her groceries. She is glimpsed as she crosses. She disappears. The camera focuses on the empty window. The woman comes into view again and this time she stops (at the sink). She sets the groceries down and stares out into the darkness.

4 *Interior Kitchen Night*

The WOMAN stands at the sink, staring out the window. She moves her head this way and that as if she sees something. But it is nothing. She wears a putty-coloured cardigan over a shower-o-hail dress. She wears an apron and flat shoes. The imagery of the room is poor and Catholic and 60s/70s.

5 *Interior Living Room Dusk*

A man in his 50s in a wheelchair sits at a drop-leaf table. He is staring across the table at a 60s television set in the corner. The programme is some review of man's journey into space. An astronaut is seen bouncing on the surface of the moon. The WOMAN comes in with a damp cloth and wipes the table. She picks up a plate with leftovers and carries it away to the kitchen.

6 *Interior Kitchen Dusk*

The WOMAN comes in and sets the plate with leftovers on the draining board. She washes and cuts up some raw carrot. The sound of the carrot chopping on a stainless steel draining board is loud.

7 *Interior Shed Night*

The sound of the distant chopping is faint but audible.

8 *Interior Kitchen Night*

The WOMAN pauses chopping.

WOMAN
(*Shouts*) Daddy, I'll make the tea in a minute.

The WOMAN fills the kettle.

9 Interior Living Room Night

The WOMAN comes in and puts the filled kettle on the range and goes out.

10 Interior Kitchen Night

The WOMAN takes the dish of food to the back door. There is a mirror hanging on the wall. She looks at herself, adjusts her hair with her free hand, putting it back behind her ear. Then with the same hand she takes a torch hanging from a nail. She opens the door quietly – as if she doesn't want her FATHER to hear her going out. But the door makes a noise. She has done all this before many, many times.

11 Interior Shed Night

The door opening is heard distantly. The POV tries to get looking through the chink in the wood.

12 Exterior Path Night

Light comes from the door but disappears when the door is closed. The WOMAN comes out and switches on the torch. The beam swings about like a sword. She walks down the path, carrying the dish.

13 Interior Shed Night

The breathing and straw noises are just about heard. The distortion of the view of the woman stooping. The flashlight waving about. It flares into the camera blindingly. Close up of the dish being pushed beneath a gap in the door into the shed on the wooden floor. The dish remains untouched but in the darkness it is a luminous circle of white. A strange high-pitched inarticulate noise of distress as the woman moves away.

14 Interior Living Room Night

The FATHER stares ahead listening to the scream of the kettle, which has grown from noise of distress in the shed. Hearing it, the WOMAN hurries in and lifts the kettle off the heat. She proceeds to make tea.

15 Interior Shed Night

The dish. A brown rat in the dish begins to feed. Something frightens it away.

16 Interior Kitchen Night

The WOMAN carries tea to the table where her FATHER sits slumped. As she sets the cup on the table his hand comes up her dress. She waits, shudders and steps back with a look almost of exasperation. She walks out of reach to pour her own tea.

17 Interior Bedroom Night

The WOMAN in her night-dress lies awake. Her bedside light is on.

18 Interior Shed Night

The lit bedroom window is seen from the shed.

19 Interior Bedroom Night

The WOMAN reaches over to switch off the light.

20 Interior Shed Night

The light disappears. Darkness. Distress noises followed by a mysterious drumming sound – like wood being pummelled.

21 Interior Bedroom Night

The WOMAN in the darkness of her bed hears the pummelling on wood from the shed outside and closes her eyes in despair. She puts her hands over her ears.

22 Interior Kitchen Day

Close up of an illustration of a ten-year-old boy. The WOMAN sits turning the pages of a well-thumbed clothes catalogue. Her FATHER sits staring at her. She stops at a page for Warm Anoraks. Then she looks up – down the overgrown garden path. In the daylight we can see the dilapidated shed in the garden.

23 Interior Shed Day

In daylight more of the interior of the shed can be seen. Light comes from an improvised horizontal window whose glass is a car side window. Outside the glass is greenery. There are roosts covered in hens' droppings with the occasional feather clinging to them. The POV moves to the back of the house. The vision is still distorted in the daylight. It adjusts. There is the sound of a carrot being slowly but noisily chewed.

24 Interior Kitchen Day

The FATHER sits slumped – "Calendar Girl" by Neil Sedaka (1961) is playing on the radio. The WOMAN comes into the room carrying a distinctive red Fair Isle man's cardigan. She holds it up to look at it with distaste. She demonstrates holes by poking her fingers through them. She sits down with a pair of scissors.

25 Exterior Road Day

Three ten-year-old BOYS, CHRIS, PADDY and FRANKIE, are clowning around. They saunter and whack the heads off nettles with sticks. They decide to play Hide and Go Seek. CHRIS turns to a wooden fence, covers his eyes and begins counting. The boys shout, "Hide your eyes." "He's not hiding his eyes." "Count to 100." "He's looking!" "You're cheating!" "Count slower." Chris counts quickly: "One two three …" "Slower!" "Five six seven eight …" "Start at the beginning again." "One two three …" When he reaches one hundred he shouts in sing-song voice, "Here I come – away or not."

26 Interior Shed Day

The sound of a carrot being chewed stops. Very faintly in the distance PADDY and his friends are heard arguing and counting.

27 Interior Kitchen Day

The WOMAN scissors off the lower half of the sleeves.

28 Exterior Field – Back of Shed – Day

FRANKIE runs across the field; PADDY runs down the field, looking back over his shoulder. He stops and wonders where he can hide so that he will not be found. He decides to hide down in leafy cover beside the shed. He hunkers down.

29 Interior Shed Day

Through the window we catch a glimpse of PADDY brushing past and hunkering down. A sound half girning, half excitement.

30 Exterior – Back of Shed – Day

When PADDY gets down and is crouched there he looks idly around him. It is a partial dump. Rusted tins of beans, magazines, a busted armchair, a naked doll with head and no arms, some nettles which he is careful to avoid. The naked doll's head has blonde nylon hair. PADDY is laughing a bit, thinking nobody'll ever find him here. He crouches beside the shed window. He looks around and a couple of inches away sees a face on the other side of the glass – very much like the doll's face, but the glass is dirty and the face unclear. It might not even be a face. PADDY looks up and sees CHRIS coming looking for him.

    CHRIS
    I can see ya. Come on out.

PADDY crouches even lower and smiles.

31 Interior Kitchen Day

The WOMAN, holding the cardigan, stands to throw the cut sleeves in the range – a circle of fire. She puts the lid back on the range, looks out the window and stiffens. She sees or hears something. It is CHRIS heading down through the field towards their back garden. She moves quickly to the door.

32 Exterior Path Day

The WOMAN, carrying the remains of the cardigan, comes hurrying out of the doorway. CHRIS is in the field, larking around, hunting the others.

WOMAN
Hey you – get away from there – yes you.

CHRIS stands defiantly.

33 Exterior – Back of Shed – Day

PADDY is aware that something is going on. He hears the woman's voice faintly.

WOMAN
This is not a public park. You're not allowed here.

He looks again at the obscured face inches away from him in the dirty window. It is staring at him from its tangle of matted hair. He looks closely at what looks like an eye. PADDY wets his finger and cleans the glass. It makes squeaking noises.

34 Interior Shed Day

Outside PADDY tries to clean the glass, his finger still squeaking against the glass.

35 Exterior – Back of Shed – Day

PADDY can't quite make out what he is seeing. Is it another doll? He stares at the eye. The eye blinks. And the mouth howls. He is startled. It's alive. PADDY is up and on his feet and half running, half clawing his way out of the garden.

36 Exterior Path Day

The WOMAN – still holding the cardigan – sees the three boys running off and shouts after them.

WOMAN
Away ye go. You've no right to be here.
I know who yis are *(to herself)* Bloody wains.

37 Exterior Fields Day

PADDY stops, panting, knowing he can't be caught, and looks back.

38 Exterior Path Day

The WOMAN stares across to the field, shading her eyes against the light. PADDY will know her again. She hears the drumming of heels on the shed floor. The WOMAN looks unsure what to do next. She realizes she has the cut-down cardigan in her hands. She moves forward.

39. Interior Shed Day

The WOMAN unfastens the door and pulls it open. She stoops and comes in. She speaks as if to calm an animal.

> WOMAN
> It's only me. It's only me. There now.

She squats in front of the HEN-HOUSE BOY, who is not seen. In the confined space the camera is behind him, facing the WOMAN. The camera stays on the WOMAN but is aware of out-of-focus hair and arms being raised from the hunched position. The WOMAN reaches out to take off the ragged thing he is wearing and replace it with the cardigan. Her murmurings are to calm the boy. He is excited by her presence and is making a sound, a strange high-pitched throat noise.

40 Flashback Interior Bedroom Day

A cardboard box for margarine sits on a dressing table. The dressing table has three mirrors facing each other so that it results in multiple images. The cardboard box contains a crying baby. A slightly younger WOMAN enters, closes the door, picks the baby up with resignation and pulls a three-legged stool towards her with her foot. This is seen in reflection in the mirrors.

> WOMAN
> Shh. You'll only annoy him. Shh.

She sits down, turns away from the door and begins to breast-feed the baby. All her movements are guilty. The door opens and the FATHER, a fit man in a vest, storms in. He is shaking with anger.

> FATHER
> If you don't get rid of it. I will.

41 Interior Shed Day

The place smells very bad and this shows on the WOMAN's face. She sniffs in and wrinkles her nose and looks critically at the HEN-HOUSE BOY.

> WOMAN
> *(To the smell)* Oh dearie me. *(Putting the cardigan on the child)* There you are. There you go. Lift. Lift up. That's you. There you are now.

Close-up of the WOMAN's face.

42 Interior Living Room Day

The WOMAN comes in with some ragged grey clothing which she throws in the range. The FATHER's eyes stare at her.

> FATHER
> Unggh?

> WOMAN
> Just a coupla boys. Messin.
> They're away now.

She stares at her father.

43 Flashback Interior Bedroom Day

The FATHER in his vest and braces is bent over the cardboard box with a pillow in his hands, trying to suffocate the baby. Again the multiple images in the dressing table mirrors. The WOMAN opens the door and enters. Immediately she realizes what he is doing and screams and tries to wrestle him to one side, screaming, "What are you doing?" But he is too strong and big and intent on what he is doing. She picks up the three-legged stool and hits him as hard as she can with it over the head. He is stunned and lurches forward over the cardboard box. She has to hit him again and again. He slides down, blood coming from his head. She picks up the baby and runs. He roars after her. He tries to rise – but goes down again like a bullock with BSE – and he roars. Not words, but a roar.

44 Flashback Interior Stairs Day

The WOMAN races down the stairs with her baby.

45 Flashback Exterior Back Door Day

The WOMAN comes running out the door. It is raining. She doesn't know where to go. Some white hens pick about the path. She hears a roar from inside the house. She dashes down the path, stoops and pushes her way into the hen house. A hen squawks and flutters out. She leaves the baby in the hen house and turns to run back to the house.

> WOMAN
> Oh Daddy? Daddy.

46 Exterior Church Day

The church sits in a rural landscape – a ragged hymn is audible. The WOMAN hurries up to the church.

47 Interior Church Day

The priest, wearing a chasuble, climbs up into the pulpit or addresses the congregation from the steps to one side of the altar. The congregation sit and look up at him. At the top left-hand side of the church sits PADDY (in different clothes – i.e. his Sunday best) with his father, HUGH. PADDY is bored. The PRIEST brings to his preaching a casual show-offery. He is the intellectual superior of anyone in his congregation.

> PRIEST
> My dear brethren, on television this week we are being treated to

Man cavorting on the moon again. There is a school of opinion which says that science and religion are opposed, are at loggerheads, if you will. I do not subscribe to that, my dear brethren. The more science finds out about the universe, the more awe inspiring it is and the MORE it makes me believe in the Almighty who made it.

Women, wearing hats, are to one side, the men, with their hats off, to the other. The WOMAN, on her own and wearing a hat, walks up the aisle. She genuflects and slides into her pew. She blesses herself and kneels.

> PRIEST
> Man is a wonderful creature – capable of greatness, capable of great evil. He has the technology to cross space, to touch down on the surface of the moon, to return to the earth. He can even shine pictures of it all back to us, sitting in our living rooms. But he cannot stop us committing sin – the million daily insults, in sins of the flesh, in sins of the mind, in sins of the heart, that are offered up to him instead of prayers.

PADDY looks idly round and sees the WOMAN. He stares across at her. The WOMAN looks at him but does not recognize him. She looks away at something else. HUGH gently but firmly turns PADDY's head and makes him face the altar.

> PRIEST
> There's a great book by an Italian poet (smiles, pronounces the name with flamboyance) Ariosto, who imagined the moon long before we could ever get to it. On his moon they treasured everything that was despised on earth – such as misspent time, squandered money, broken promises, unanswered prayers, fruitless tears. They kept wasted talent in a vase, voz, vaz labelled with the person's name ...

48 Exterior Church Day

The congregation spill out, the young ones running. The WOMAN continues to pray alone. After the release from the boredom the children are manic. Two middle-aged men in hats collect money in large St Vincent de Paul boxes. PADDY and his father come out. HUGH puts a coin in the box, then lights a cigarette. People get on bicycles and ride away. PADDY stares ahead, waiting for the WOMAN. She comes out. PADDY reaches up to tell HUGH an important secret – what he thinks he saw in the WOMAN's hen house yesterday. HUGH stares, looks at the boy, raises an eyebrow, inhales and blows out the smoke. The figure of the PRIEST in clerical black hurries past. HUGH steps forward. The WOMAN stares hard at PADDY.

> HUGH
> Excuse me, Father. Could I have a word?

They talk with bowed heads and look after the WOMAN.

49 Interior Living Room Day

A car is heard arriving. The WOMAN and her FATHER both look up. No one has called here in years. Footsteps approach. There is a loud banging from the knocker. The WOMAN and her FATHER look at each other. The FATHER rolls his eyes to the door. The WOMAN turns down the volume of the TV. The astronauts continue to move on the moon's surface.

> FATHER
> Uhhhung.

> WOMAN
> Who could it be?

She is so poorly practised at answering the door she doesn't know what to do.

> FATHER
> Uhhhung mmu.

The WOMAN looks towards the door.

50 Interior Stairway Day

The WOMAN runs up the stairs.

51 Interior Landing Window Day

The WOMAN stares down through net curtains.

52 Exterior Front of House Day

There is a car parked. HUGH moves around trying to see if anybody is at home. The PRIEST looks up at the house.

53 Interior Hallway Day

Another loud banging of the knocker. The WOMAN comes down the stairs and speaks into the kitchen.

> WOMAN *(relieved)*
> It's the priest.

She goes to the door and opens the Yale lock. She opens the door fractionally. The PRIEST stares at her.

> WOMAN
> Oh Father. It's yourself.

The WOMAN is loath to invite him in. She stalls.

> PRIEST
> Could I have a word?

The WOMAN cannot now refuse. She steps back to admit the PRIEST. As he steps inside the WOMAN looks at the car. She closes over the door but doesn't shut it.

54 Interior Car Day

HUGH sighs, looks at his watch, lights a cigarette, rolls down the window.

HUGH
You'd better be right.

PADDY stands in the back seat to see what is happening.

55 Interior Shed Day

There is a sound of movement in straw and open-mouth breathing. The HEN-HOUSE BOY's hair is seen (so it is not precisely a POV image) The HEN-HOUSE BOY stares towards the kitchen window. The WOMAN comes into sight and the HEN-HOUSE BOY becomes excited. The PRIEST comes into view. A discussion takes place. The only sounds are the ones the HEN-HOUSE BOY makes.

56 Exterior Path Night

The PRIEST, in some agitation, comes out the door.

PRIEST
It's not that I don't believe you – but if you'll excuse me, I think I'll have a look for myself. They're a very reliable family …

The PRIEST walks along the path. The WOMAN sits down on the doorstep. She puts her head in her hands. Her legs fall wide open but she is covered by her dress. The PRIEST moves towards the shed.

57 Interior Shed Day

The PRIEST approaches. The HEN-HOUSE BOY is disturbed and begins loud breathing and drumming with his heels.

58 Exterior Path Night

The PRIEST opens the shed door with some difficulty and squats and looks in. He wrinkles his nose and winces.

PRIEST
(breathed only) Jesus Mary and Joseph.

He slips off the jacket of his black suit. He reaches forward with open arms. The WOMAN sits on the back doorstep, distraught – watching as the PRIEST discovers the child in the shed. The PRIEST emerges with the HEN-HOUSE BOY in his arms. The WOMAN stands unsteadily to clear a way for the PRIEST. The PRIEST elbows past her into the kitchen. The FATHER can be seen slumped at the table. It is difficult to tell if he is sullen or stunned. The PRIEST barely stops to show him what's in the bundle.

> PRIEST
> *(shouts)* Who's responsible for this?

59 Exterior Front Door

The PRIEST backs out, carrying the HEN-HOUSE BOY. He turns slowly to reveal what he is carrying. The WOMAN follows and stands in the doorway, trying to grasp what is happening. She is stunned and bereft.

60 Interior Car Night

HUGH leaps out of the car to assist the PRIEST. PADDY stands in the back seat, unable to take his eyes off what the PRIEST is carrying. PADDY's POV to the PRIEST's bundle. The camera is unsteady and restless. The HEN-HOUSE BOY is about nine years of age but very small, utterly white, wizened and thin. There is a lot of hair and a glimpse of long nails on his bare feet. He is wearing the Fair Isle cardigan with the cut-down sleeves over some greyish, indistinguishable clothing. He is obviously terrified. The PRIEST keeps muttering.

> PRIEST
> You're okay, lad, you're okay. You're safe now. Everything's going to be all right.

Close up on the HEN-HOUSE BOY's gaping wide open mouth. He looks bizarre in the bleached-out light of day. PADDY's reaction is one of horror and guilt, which he tries not to show on his face. It's an image burnt into his mind. Freeze-frame of the HEN-HOUSE BOY's mouth. The image rotates and gradually goes to black and white. Then gradually the image turns to negative. The black orb of the mouth becomes white. Gradually becomes the full daylight moon. The voices of the astronauts are heard faintly discussing their situation.

Credits & End

EDITOR'S NOTE

The above text is the screenplay for the 17-minute short film "Bye-child", both written and directed by Bernard MacLaverty. It was conceived and produced by Andrew Bonner, and enthusiastically supported by Seamus Heaney. The original poem of the same name was written while Heaney was a teacher in Belfast in the late sixties, and prompted partly by a well-known story earlier in the poet's life about a child who had been kept by his mother in isolation at the bottom of her garden. As Heaney's epigraph to the poem has it, "He was discovered in the henhouse where she had confined him. He was incapable of saying anything." For the full poem, see Heaney's third collection of poems, *Wintering Out* (Faber, 1972).

Like the original poem – one of a number, amongst Heaney's greatest, which deal with the loss or suffering of children – MacLaverty's "Bye-child" is an act of supreme imaginative empathy. Watching the film as a CD followed by the poem recited in MacLaverty's voice, it suddenly dawns that a profound link between language and empathy is almost the *religio* (the integral bond, *geas* or obligation) of poetry itself, as an exemplar especially to the other language arts – even if the full reality must somehow always elude us.

Bernard MacLaverty was born in Belfast in 1942 and lived there until 1975, when he moved with his wife and three children to Scotland. He has been a medical laboratory technician, a mature student, a teacher of English and an occasional writer-in-residence. He has written four novels and five collections of short stories, most of which are gathered into Collected Stories *(Jonathan Cape, 2013). He has also adapted his fiction for radio plays, television plays, screenplays and libretti. As a result of an invitation, he wrote and directed the short film* Bye-child *in 2003. He lives in Glasgow and is a member of Aosdana.*

60 DEGREES NORTH: SHETLAND & GREENLAND

Malachy Tallack

I

SHETLAND
Mousa

The invisible constant.

Shetland, like other remote parts of Scotland, is scarred by the remnants of the past, by history made solid in the landscape. Rocks, reordered and rearranged, carry shadows of the people that moved them. They are the islands' memory. From the ancient field dykes and boundary lines, burnt mounds and forts, to the crumbling croft houses, abandoned by the thousands who emigrated at the end of the nineteenth century; the land is witness to every change, but it is loss that it remembers most clearly.

For some, these rocks reek of mortality. Their forms are a potentially oppressive reminder that we, too, will leave little behind us. In "The Broch of Mousa", the poet Vagaland wrote of how "in the islands darkness falls / On homes deserted, and on ruined walls; / The tide of life recedes." People have come and gone from these islands, and with them have passed "their ways, their thoughts, their songs; / To earth they have returned." We are left only with the memory of stones, which we have few skills to interpret.

The island of Mousa was once a place of people. It was once home to families, to fishermen and farmers, who lived and died there. But now the people are gone, and their homes deserted. The island has been left to the sheep, the birds and the seals. And, in the summer at least, to the tourists.

Will Self has called Mousa Broch "one of my sacred sites. For me, comparable to the pyramids." And that comparison is understandable. The broch is both beautiful and mysterious. It is imposing, and tantalisingly intact, and yet it seems that we know almost nothing of the people who built it. It is safe to assume that the architects of Scotland's brochs were a militarised people, and the towers' defensive capabilities are obvious. Indeed, in the *Orkneyinga Saga* we learn that Mousa was used by Erlend the Young and his lover Margaret in 1153, twelve centuries after it was built, to resist the assaults of Margaret's son, Earl Harald. In the saga, Mousa is described in wonderful understatement as "not an easy place to attack", and Harald is forced to give up and agree to his mother's marriage.

But there is something about this broch that suggests more than simply defence. Its massive size can't possibly have been *necessary* at the time, and the sheer excessiveness of it suggests that it was built either in a state of extreme paranoia or extreme arrogance. This latter possibility has, in recent decades, become the theory of choice for archaeologists. The brochs, very likely, were status symbols. They represent an architectural bravado like that which created skyscrapers in the twentieth century: a striking combination of functionality and showing off.

That this particular example has survived so perfectly for so long is partly a result of its remoteness, and partly, I think, because nobody has ever had the need to take it to pieces. While other ancient buildings have been plundered for useful material over the millennia, Mousa's beaches are still crowded with perfect, flat stones, providing all the material the island's inhabitants ever required. The rocks which helped to create such an incredible structure have remained plentiful enough to ensure its long life. And today, those rocks are protecting other lives too. Press your ear to the walls of the broch and you will hear the soft churring and grunting of young storm petrels, tiny seabirds that patter their way above the waves by day, returning to the safety of their nests at night. Seven thousand storm petrels – eight per cent of Britain's population – nest on this island: on the rocky beaches and in the broch itself. The building seems almost to breathe, to pulse, with the countless lives concealed within: past and present hidden, sheltered among the stones.

The people who built this broch, who lived in and around it, seem far out of reach to us today – an enigma. Archaeologists and historians examine the available clues carefully and they make assessments, suppositions. But in our desire to eradicate mystery from the past, and to understand and *know* these people, we forget, I think, one crucial point. We miss the real mystery.

Sitting on the grass beneath the broch, looking back towards the Mainland, I scratched my wrists and brushed the midges from my face. There was no wind, and the insects were taking advantage of the opportunity to feed. The clouds hung low over the sound, and draped softly onto the hills across the water. What struck me then, as I leaned back against the ancient stone wall, was not the great distance and difference that lay between now and then, nor was it the tragedy of all we do not know. What struck me was the sense of continuity, and the deep determination of people to live in this place.

Rebecca West once wrote that certain places "imprint the same stamp on whatever inhabitants history brings them, even if conquest spills out one population and pours in another wholly different in race and philosophy". This stamp is what Lawrence Durrell calls "the invisible constant". It is the thread that holds the history of a place together: the sense of *sameness* that flows through the past like a furrow through a field. In Shetland, human society has evolved in both gradual and sudden movements. For a few hundred years people built brochs, and then they stopped. In the two millenia that followed, many changes took place. New people came, bringing a new language and a new religion. Pictish culture began to take hold in the islands, and then it too disappeared when the Vikings arrived in the ninth century, overwhelming (some say exterminating) the indigenous people. Yet despite these changes, despite all that came and went in that time, always it was the land that dictated the means of survival. The Norsemen arrived as Vikings, but they became Shetlanders. They became fishermen and farmers, just as the Picts had been, just as the broch-builders had been, and all those before them. Crops were sown and harvested; sheep and cattle were reared and killed. Life moved with the seasons. The land scarred the people, just as the people, in turn, scarred the land. This is not, of course, to say that all people were the same. Clearly they were not. But, equally, we must not underestimate the significance of their ways of living. And that, always, has been determined by the one stable factor: by the place itself. A necessary relationship was formed, and that relationship, that defining *constant*, has been warped only by the intervention of economy.

The desire to pin down some kind of Shetland identity, I believe, has arisen because of an increased dis*location*: a gradual loss of that relationship with place. Fishing and crofting became industries, whose purpose was no longer sufficiency but surplus. Shetland's economy diversified, and more and more people became less and less involved with the land and the sea. Today, that division between people and place is greater than it has ever been, and it is no real surprise that Shetlanders have chosen the most vivid and colourful characters of their history – the Vikings – as symbols of who they are: the brand by which they are known. This is a shame. The question of where to locate identity is a treacherous one, but if we wish to ask it then we can do better than holding up empty caricatures of the past. We should look again, I suggest, for that "invisible constant".

II
GREENLAND
Sila

A silent inheritance.

The helicopter lifted itself calmly from the tarmac then thundered away from Qaqortoq, up and over the fjord, flying low above bare valleys and hillsides, over tundra, lakes, rocks and snow. Below, the land stretched out in a patchwork of brown and green, studded with scraps of white and grey and blue. And then, suddenly, the sea.

In the weeks I had spent travelling south along the coast I had seen a lot of ice. In the town of Narsaq, I had walked across beaches strewn with stranded bergs, slowly decomposing in the warm, spring sunshine. They were a thousand forms: some pointed, with sharp fingers and shards, others smooth, like the curves of muscle and flesh on an animal. Some were as large as cars or caravans, others I could lift and hold in the palm of my hand: tiny fragments, faded almost to nothing. I wandered among these shapes, watching their quiet disappearance, and I felt a peculiar kind of grief. Here was a difficult presence, almost alive and almost unreal, like shadows made solid, or crystalline astonishment.

Out in the water beyond, the icebergs were bigger, but still somehow precarious. They seemed out of place in the sunshine, beside the colour of the town, beneath the blackness of the mountains. Bright, blue-white against the vitreous shiver of the water, the ice took form, like clouds, in the imagination. Reclining bathers, ships, mushrooms, whales and kayakers. They seemed caught in constant imbalance, between two worlds; theirs was a transient stillness.

But now, from the window of the brash Air Greenland helicopter, I saw something else entirely. Stretched out beneath us, reaching away to the horizon and beyond, was an immense carpet of sea ice, a dense mosaic of flat white plates, like crazy-paving on the dark water. I felt immersed. As far as I could see, the fractured ice lay tightly packed. Great slabs, the size of tennis courts or football pitches, perhaps bigger, were crammed together, and between them smaller pieces in every possible shape.

This was *storis* – *big* ice: multiyear pack formed in the Arctic Ocean. Each winter, a dense band of this ice drifts southwards on the East Greenland current, rounding Cape Farewell in the first months of the year, then moving slowly up the southwest coast, where I now was, gradually disintegrating as it travelled.

The whole scene was unfathomable. There was nothing for the eye to hold on to; all sense of scale was lost. Here and there an iceberg protruded, but it was impossible to know how large they were. When we buzzed low over a solitary cargo ship, trudging a path through the solid ocean, it looked far too small, like a toy, dwarfed by the cracked expanse of white and glacial blue all around it. I took the camera from my bag and held it up to the window.

That picture hangs now above my desk as I write. A blanket of shattered ice leads out to the horizon, swollen by a blue-black bruise, reflecting the clear water beyond. I return to the image over and over, as if searching for something that I know is there but cannot seem to focus upon. Framed within that photograph is the very thing I came to Greenland to see. It is an image of the North: bright and brittle, terrifying and intensely beautiful. Looking over my shoulder now, out of the window, to the heathered hill that rises steeply behind my house, I see another North. The distance between myself and that ice-laden image stretches out and becomes an unimaginable gulf. I have tried to forge a connection, a bridge between, but the picture remains shocking, many months after I framed and hung it there.

The helicopter came to rest on the rough landing strip at Nanortalik, the southernmost of Greenland's main settlements. The village is decked out in northern Scandinavian uniform, its wooden houses coloured red, yellow, purple, green, even pink – some pastel pale, others vivid as children's paint. Nanortalik is home to around 1500 people, with a few smaller hamlets scattered through the surrounding fjords. The village itself sits on one of the many islands that pepper this southwest coast, but it is no more isolated for that. Communities here are linked by sea and by air; there are no connecting roads.

The cabin where I was to stay was located on the other side of town from the heliport. Beyond the houses and the main street, with its two supermarkets, was the tidy old harbour, complete with white wooden church and quaint timber cottages. Most of the buildings there were occupied by the town museum, but one little red bungalow served as a hostel, in which I was the only guest.

I threw my bag into the living room, where two bunk beds huddled around a furious gas fire, and went back outside to sit on the front step. The morning had cleared and warmed a little, though there was still a bitter breeze lifting off the sea. The bay in front of the hostel was loosely cluttered with ice, just clear enough for boats to make their way in and out of the harbour. There was a slow shifting of everything, almost perceptible as I sat watching, and now and then a booming crack and splash as an iceberg split and collapsed into the water.

The view from the doorway was westward, out to sea, but took in the hunched bulk of Qaqqarsuasik, Nanortalik Island's highest point. From the step I watched ravens swoop and wheel around the dark slopes, silhouetted as they rose above the peaks, then almost hidden against the blackness of the rock. Their caws, clicks and splutters echoed around the bay, puncturing the silence, as they punctured the air with their flight. A flurry of sounds – manic gulps and underwater barks – rained down on me as I sat, listening, watching, until hunger persuaded me to move.

At the other harbour, in the centre of town, old men sat outside a little shack that served as meat and fish market, smoking, laughing and talking. Some held their walking sticks in front of them, palms clasped around the handles, quietly watching the afternoon pass by. Others leaned in close towards each other, their stories told in whispers. In Qaqortoq I had seen this, too: a gathering of people near the water, as if this place, where seals and fish were brought to be cut up and sold, were the social hub of the town. I imagined the men had once been hunters themselves, and now the closest they could get was to come and watch the day's catch being brought in. But the stories they were telling would connect them to those who today were wielding knives. Those stories, and the memories they contained, would connect them, too, to their fathers, and their grandfathers, whose own knives carved into the meat, the seals, taken from the ice. These men were witnesses to a silent inheritance, a deep flash of blade and blood.

Hunting in Greenland is an issue of identity. It is an issue of culture. And it is an issue of controversy. There is an understandable belief among many Greenlanders that their traditional way of life is under constant threat from the ignorant views of people from outside. A kind of moral imperialism is suspected – the imposition of alien values onto a people for whom those values do not make sense. Individuals such as Finn Lynge, a politician who in 1985 negotiated Greenland's tactical exit from the European Community, have worked hard to convince the world that the traditional Inuit culture is entirely compatible with environmental sustainability. Others have argued that the increasing European and American focus on "animal rights", is borne not from an increased empathy and understanding for the natural world, but entirely the opposite. The Canadian activist, Alan Herscovici has written that "the animal-rights philosophy [is] widening rather than healing the rift between man and nature ... [it] may be more of a symptom of our disease than a cure". Lynge would agree. For him, the focus on *individual* animals' rights demonstrates a failure to understand nature, or to recognise our own place within it.

What the Inuit see in the European and American attitudes to Arctic hunting is the gaping distance between our people and our environment. They see a hypocritical culture that frets and recoils over the deaths of individual wild animals elsewhere, yet which engages in industrial farming, "pest-control" on an immense scale, widespread polluting and the devastating destruction of natural habitats. As individuals, we consciously distance ourselves from killing, we close our eyes to it, yet our culture is, Lynge claims, "characterized by its propensity for cruelty and death".

One evening, over dinner, a young Greenlandic couple asked me whether we ate seals at home. When I replied that there were many seals in Shetland, but that islanders had never really eaten them, the couple seemed confused. "Why wouldn't you eat them?" they enquired. I did not have a good answer. I thought, perhaps, that an abundance of fish might have made seal meat superfluous in the past. But that didn't seem plausible enough. I wondered also whether superstition might have played a part. Stories of selkie folk – seal people – were widespread in Shetland, as elsewhere in Scotland, and perhaps this notion – that seals were somehow too *human* to eat, that they might have *souls* – was the real problem. I wasn't sure, and I am still not sure. The couple seemed dissatisfied with my answer. The idea that a seal might have a soul did not seem, to them, a good reason for it not to be eaten.

A shaman once explained to the explorer and anthropologist Knud Rasmussen that "the greatest peril lies in the fact that to kill and eat, all that we strike down and destroy ... have souls as we have, souls that do not perish with the body, and therefore must be propitiated lest they revenge themselves". For the traditional Inuit, souls are not the exclusive property of human beings; they are widespread, taking many forms. Propitiation is achieved by following certain cultural traditions, and, at all times, by showing respect towards the animal that is killed. It is both atonement and thanksgiving. In our own culture, meat has been increasingly divorced, for most of its consumers, from the death that makes it possible, and from the life that it once held. Because of this, I think, there is a kind of grace that we no longer recognise, and a grace, too, that we have forgotten how to say.

In the grey light of morning, fat clouds tumbled heavily around the mountains, punctured and crushed between the peaks, rolling, blowing and inflating, from slate to black, turning over the wind. There was rain there, on the slopes. It had not reached the town yet, but it was coming.

I was stranded inside the cabin. A severe cold had struck me on my second day in Nanortalik, and had gradually worsened until I felt unable to leave the warmth of the building. I was hot and shivering; my nose blocked and sinuses throbbing; my throat was raw and my muscles ached. I felt dreadful, and sat on the sofa next to the fire, gazing out of the window. Hours passed slowly. I read, but found it hard to concentrate for long; I turned on the television, but switched it off again when I saw what was there.

Outside, the ice shifted, clearing then clotting the dark water again, as the wind dragged from east to south to south westerly. I watched its steady migration, back and forth across the bay, and something inside me moved as it moved. My thoughts drifted from the island where I sat, to my own island 1,500 miles to the east. I thought about the people in that town; I thought about the great space that lay between their lives and my own. And I thought, too, about my father, who seemed as close to me then as the ice outside, or the warmth within the room, but as distant and unreachable as the ravens across the bay – their black lives pin-pricked against the sky.

Above the water, glaucous and Iceland gulls bustled their way between the bergs, camouflaged on the ice. As they lifted up to shift themselves now and then, they shone, bright white in the air. Rain wrapped itself firmly around the town, and I opened the window a little to listen to it falling. Inland, a thick black fog was slumped heavily around the mountains, but out to sea, from where the breeze was blowing, the sky was bright. It was an illusion, of course – the reflection of the sea ice on the clouds above – but it was welcome, and added to the ever-present promise of change.

Gretel Ehrlich has written that "Arctic beauty resides in its gestures of transience. Up here, planes of light and darkness are swords that cut away illusions of permanence". In Greenland, that transience is impossible to ignore; it permeates each moment of each day. It is there in the melting icebergs on the shore, and in the meat on the market counters; it is there in the rushing clouds, and the changing climate. It is there in the air itself.

There is the sense here that, at any moment, all certainty could be undermined – that the land could reach out in an instant and wipe people away, as the Norse settlers were once wiped from this place. There is terror in that thought, but there is comfort, too.

When my father died I learned that loss is with us always. It is not a punctuating mark in our lives; it is not a momentary pause or ending. Loss is a constant force – a spirit – that moves both within and without us. It is a process – an unceasing extinguishment that we may choose, if we wish, to bear witness to. And if we do make that choice then we commit ourselves not to a lifetime of grief and melancholy. Instead, we offer ourselves the opportunity of a firmer sense of joy and of beauty. It is no surprise and certainly no coincidence that we experience our greatest appreciation of life in those things that are fragile and fleeting. We find it in the song of a bird, in the touch of a lover, or in the shimmering memory of a moment long lost. So it should be no surprise that by attuning ourselves closer to the process of loss and transience, we may in turn be brought nearer to beauty and to joy. It is in loss – in the *anticipation* of loss – that we find our most profound pleasures, and it is there also that we may find a sense of true permanence.

In traditional Inuit society, permanence was to be found in the concept of *sila*, a kind of life force or spirit, which is sometimes translated as air, wind or weather, or, more widely still, as "everything that is outside". *Sila* was the essential ingredient of life – it was breath itself – and it held the inner and outer worlds together. When a person or animal died, their life, their *breath*, returned to the world and became one with it again, or it found form in another's body. But *sila* was not a predictable permanence; it was not certainty. *Sila* encompasses both weather and climate. It is changeable, surprising, and sometimes malign. Death is part of its process and part of its force, and the Inuit understanding of the world was shaped by this belief. Or perhaps it would be more true to say that the world in which the Inuit lived shaped this understanding. For natural philosophies do not spring from empty space; they are born from the land. And this seems to me a particularly *northern* view of life and death. Here, where the seasons turn heavily, emphatically, and where impermanence cannot be disguised, *sila* makes sense.

Death is at once an ending and a continuation. A breath is given back to the wind, just as ice returns to the sea; it finds new shape. But a life, too, lives on through stories and through memories, joyful in their retelling and their fleeting recollection. Loss shapes us like a sculptor, carving out our form, and we feel each nick of its blade. But without it, we cannot *be*.

Of the many absences that I carry with me – for we all, I think, are filled with holes – the absence of my father is the one that has taught me most. It is the space through which I have come to see myself most clearly. I thought of him then, as an ice-laden wind pawed at the cabin window.

A writer, editor and singer-songwriter, Malachy Tallack was born in 1980 on Shetland and is currently working on a book about the sixtieth parallel, 60 Degrees North, *from which these chapters are taken. He was the editor of* Shetland Life *for five years, and is the editor and founder of the online magazine,* The Island Review. *He is currently based in Glasgow.*

IN HIS EIGHTY-EIGHTH YEAR

Francis Harvey

WONDERS

He'd heard of them but had never seen one
because none ever grew on the island.
Then someone gave him a picture of an oak.
He nailed it to the white-washed kitchen wall
beside pictures of Christ and the Pope.
When he was old enough he took
a currach across the gap of the sound
to Ireland. He saw wonders everywhere
but for him the greatest wonder was trees.
He moved among them like a growing child
exploring the new world of its senses,
smelling, touching, listening, running
his hands over the bark again and again
the way he'd first run them over the pelt
of a seal pup or a beached whale.
He filled his pockets with leaves and took them
back to the island like treasures from Tír na nÓg.
He kept them in a glass jar and watched them
shrivel and turn brown and rustle
like seaweed dried by the sun and the wind.
But what he was always waiting for was a storm,
the sky black as tar, the sea churning milk,
and him on the headland with his eyes closed
listening to the roar of the wind in the trees.

HOUSES OF GOD

St Peter's for the first time years ago.
The grandeur of Roman marble and gold
and me open-mouthed in front of the four
pillars of Bernini's baldachino
soaring sensuously over the altar
towards Heaven like naked human torsos
the Redemptorists might thunder about
when all that I could think of was the small
white-washed church in the sandhills that was
as cold and austere as I imagined
its Protestant counterpart down the road
must be were we allowed to enter it.

Francis Harvey, a poet and fiction-writer, was born in Enniskillen in 1925. He is the author of five collections of poetry, most recently The Boa Island Janus *(1996),* Making Space *(2000),* Collected Poems *(2006) and* Donegal Haiku *(2013), all from The Dedalus Press. He lives in Donegal Town, Co Donegal.*

THREE POEMS FROM THE IRISH
(Circa 900, Anno Domini)

Seán Hewitt

News of the world – in an age of ice.

COLD

The cold will not leave.
The weather only gets worse – glimmering
brook drowned to a river, the ford a flooded lake.

The lakes lie overweight. Each drop
of rain smacks like a stone. Each snowflake
is the sky's breaking skin.

The puddle is a well, the flatlands hills.
The moors are woods. The birds have lost
their homes, and snow saddles you to the waist.

Clenching frost has seized the roads,
crept up nightly on the standing-stone at Colt.
At every side, the weather waits,
and every word has changed to "cold".

Original:

Fuitt co bráth!
is mó in doinenn ar cách;
is ob cach etriche án,
ocus is loch lán cach áth.

Is méit muir mór cech loch lonn,
is drong cech cuire gúr gann,
méit taul scéith banna dond linn,
méit moltchrocann finn cech slamm.

Méit cuithe cach lathrach léig,
coirthe cach réid, caill cach móin,
inna helta, nís tá dín,
snechtae finn fír do-roich tóin.

Ro-íad réod rótu gribb
iar ngléo glicc im choirthi Cuilt,
con-gab doinenn dar cach leth
coná apair nech acht 'Fuitt'.

WINTER

The stag throats the cold
winter snow summer gone
the wind carves spirals of ice the sun is
low its journey short. Seas bellow
bracken rusted geese
crying on the moors
cold has seized the wings
of the birds
I wish I brought better news

Original:

Scél lemm duib:
dordaid dam,
snigid gaim,
ro-fáith sam;

gáeth ard úar,
ísel grían,
gair a rith,
ruirthech rían;

rorúad rath,
ro-cleth cruth,
ro-gab gnáth
giugrann guth;

ro-gab úacht
etti én,
aigre ré,
é mo scél.

VIKINGS

The wind is wild tonight
holding the sea by the hair and beating.
As I look out, my mind settles at ease:
trouble only crosses calmer seas.

Original:

Is acher an gáith in-nocht,
fu-fúasna fairggae findfolt:
ní ágor réimm mora minn
dond láechraid lain úa Lothlind.

TRANSLATOR'S NOTE

These secular lyrics, which reveal beautifully the ways in which nature was such a visceral presence to early Irishmen and women, were originally written down sometime around the ninth century, though the poem I have called "Winter" might be older. The poems, as with all writings from so long ago, can exert a peculiar hold on the reader's imagination; but these three in particular stand out for the vulnerability they express, both towards the power of nature and to the threat of war. In that sense, they speak more easily and directly to the modern reader than religious lyrics might at first appear to, and there is much in their openness and honesty that chimes across the centuries.

Seán Hewitt is a postgraduate student of Irish Studies at the University of Liverpool. His poetry and translations have been published in Poetry (Chicago), Poetry Review, PN Review *and* Modern Poetry in Translation, *amongst others.*

DÁN

Ailbhe Ní Ghearbhuigh

DRUMA AN CHONGÓ

San áit a labhraítear *Kele*
tá ceol tonúil na teanga
ar bhéalaibh na gCongólach
arbh íseal nó géar gach siolla.

Roimis an teileafón
bhí teanga eile acu
– teanga an druma –
a chloistí i rithimí mírialta
an bhodhráin sa dufair,
macalla á iompar
trí fhás tiubh,
buillí tolla an bhongó.
buillí géar 'gus íseal.

Bhíodh sárdhrumadóir i ngach baile
is tuiscint na ndrumaí ag cách.

Thuig na hEorpaigh go maith
nár thuigeadar puinn di.

Ach d'fhoghlaim misinéir amháin í
– an Sasanach, John Carrington –
ainneoin go raibh sí i léig,
ná raibh sí fiú á teagasc
sna scoileanna glégeala.

Is ní foláir nó gur fhoghlaim
a bhean í freisin
nuair a bhuail sí amach
an teachtaireacht seo a leanas:

Sprid an fhir ghil
sa bhforaois
Tar! Tar!
go tigh na slinne
in airde
sprid an fhir ghil
sa bhforais
bean le yams
ag fanacht
Tar ! Tar!

CONGO DRUM

There is a place where today
Kele is spoken,
a tonal language
where Congolese lips
make each phoneme a sharp or a flat.

Before telecommunication
there was another tongue here
– a language of drumming –
heard in irregular rhythms
of stretched skins in the jungle
an echo that carried through undergrowth
the hollow beats of the bongo
the sharp beats, the flat beats.

Each village chose one drum virtuoso
but all understood the percussion and code.

The Europeans who came to the jungle knew well
that tapped language for a known unknown.

But one missionary learned it
– an Englishman, John Carrington –
though by then it was weakening,
was considered hardly worth teaching
to the children in their brand-new schoolrooms.

And it was obvious
his wife had learned it as well
when she beat out to him
the following broadcast:

> *White man spirit*
> *in the forest*
> *come come*
> *to our hearth*
> *on the heath*
> *white man spirit*
> *in the forest*
> *come come*
> *a woman is waiting with yams*
> *come come*

Translated, from the Irish, by Billy Ramsell.

Rugadh Ailbhe Ní Ghearbhuigh i gCiarraí i 1984. Tá a cuid filíochta léite aici i bPáras, i Nua Eabhrac, i Montréal agus ar an mBuailtín. Tá sí ina heagarthóir Gaeilge ar an iris arlíne Southword. D'fhoilsigh Coiscéim a céad chnuasach filíochta, Péacadh, *i 2008.*

Ailbhe Ní Ghearbhuigh was born in Kerry in 1984. She has read at festivals in Paris, New York, Berlin and Montréal. She is the Irish Language Editor of the online journal, Southword. Péacadh (Germination), *her first collection, was published by Coiscéim in 2008.*

CULTÚRLANN RANT

Aodán Mac Póilin

Cad is cultúr Gaelach ann?

Tá mé an-bhuíoch as an chuireadh a bheith páirteach sa pháinéil seo. Beidh mise ag labhairt i mBéarla go príomha. Tá an méid atá le rá agam casta agus taobh istigh de chúig bhomaite déag tá sé ró-dhlúth, measaim, le go n-oibreoidh sé fríd chóras comhuaineach.

Everybody probably knows by now that Himmler *didn't* say that when he hears the word culture he reaches for his gun. When I hear the words *"cultúr Gaelach"*, I reach for my bullshit detector. Defining the word "culture" is like picking up mercury with a fork, and I don't have time to go into any of its multiple meanings, but I have a lot to say about the other word.

One of the ways I mis-spent my youth was by studying the ideology of the early Gaelic League. That experience left me with a marked, and permanent distaste for most of the baggage that goes with the word *Gaelach*. And *Gaelachas*. And sometimes I'm not too keen on the word *Gael*. I'm saying that as a *Gaeilgeoir* – I'm a *Gaeilgeoir*, I'm an Irish language fanatic (I belong to the nerdy liberal wing of the language movement, so it's not always obvious).

I'll give a couple of examples of the nonsense that made me loathe the good ship *Gaelach* and all that sail in her. This first quotation is from 1900. The writer tries to define *"an meon Gaelach"*, or *"an aigne Ghaelach"* – or in English "the Gaelic mind" or "the Irish mind".

> The Irish mind, away back in its most pagan days, was emphatically and eminently a mind inclining to religion. It was chaste, idealistic, mystical. It was spiritual beyond the ways of men; and it could not rest, or live, without contact with the other world; without the conviction of some ideal hereafter. It was clean of heart, and saw God, darkly and from afar, if you will, but with the invincible conviction of the clean heart's instinct. ... The Irish mind was loyalty itself to spiritual authority ... and this is a great part of the secret of the sound and splendid endurance of our faith to this day.

Or take Lorcán Ó Muireadhaigh speaking in 1932 in Belfast:

> The Gaelic League is fighting to keep the old civilisation of our country alive. It is a fight between the civilisation which Patrick started at Tara, Saul and Armagh, and the civilisation begun by Martin Luther ... We want to make Ireland what she was, a great Catholic and Gaelic nation that had her own pride and glory and that brought the Faith and civilisation to the rest of the world.

This bullshit, in both cases, came from priests, but laymen could also go in for weird romantic nonsense about Gaelic culture – Pearse could talk about "the patient white-souled Ireland of the Irish-speaking districts".

And then we've got *damhsaí Gaelacha* – Irish dancing. Garrison dances which had been introduced to Ireland in the 19th century were banned because they were *Gallda* and garrison dances that came in the 18th century were allowed because they were *Gaelach*. We have the world Irish dancing championships in Belfast every year in which tiny girls get more marks if they plaster themselves with make-up and wear wigs.

What worries me and what scares me about defining a culture, identifying its essence, is the way the definition becomes exclusive. The trouble with trying to define something as protean, complex, contradictory, multifaceted and many-layered as Gaelic culture is that when you say "this is *Gaelach*" everything else is not *Gaelach*.

So, by your leave, I won't talk at all about *an cultúr Gaelach*, but rather about *cultúr na Gaeilge* – the culture of the Irish language. I am going to say a couple of things that may not please everybody, but I want to begin by saying that my own personal attempts to repossess this culture have been extraordinarily rewarding. The deeper I got into the language and its culture the more I felt that in some way I was – how will I put it – I was coming home (even as I listen to myself I can hear my bullshit detector dinging like a demented doorbell). The reason I'm blethering here like some kind of new-age Celtic spirituality con-man is because I don't have any other way to account for what has sustained me through all the frustrations of being a nerdy liberal Irish language fanatic.

But what is this *cultúr na Gaeilge*? It's a culture with an extraordinary past, a fragile present and a doubtful future. The Irish language has one of the oldest and distinguished literary cultures in western Europe, and it is one of the four or five thousand languages that could be dead or moribund by the end of this century. After centuries of conquest, legal sanctions and economic and social marginalisation, the mass of the population abandoned the language and later on a minority engaged in its maintenance and revival. It's a culture in which there are forty learners of the language for every native speaker. It's a culture that is not quite broken, but it is a culture that has been severely disrupted, severely dislocated, severely attenuated. It's a culture that did not experience the organic development of most modern cultures.

Irish language culture is not an autonomous culture. By that I mean that you cannot live your entire life through Irish. If you're an English-speaker, you can lead a pretty full life speaking only English. You can't do that through Irish. If you had only Irish, you couldn't find out how to change a plug, you couldn't take a bus, you could hardly find somewhere to shop. Your communication options would be down to a very small number of people (this can be a problem – you mightn't like all of them, and if you're a nerdy liberal Irish language fanatic not all of them will like you). There's an even more important limitation. Where will you find intellectual nourishment and cultural nourishment? You would certainly find some of it through Irish, and what you find may be very significant, and it may involve things that you wouldn't get from English, but the only way you could live your entire cultural and intellectual life exclusively through Irish is to give yourself a cultural and intellectual lobotomy.

Does the fact that Irish cannot go head to head with English mean that you should abandon the language? I don't think so.

I think that it's a massive mistake to take English language culture as your template. English happens to be – at the moment anyway – the most prestigious language in the world and one of the most widely spoken, and cultural life through English is wide and varied and vibrant and has massive economic support. It's the worst possible model for a fragile minority language, but it happens to be the one we know best, and it happens to be – let us be honest – the environment in which Irish survives. But it doesn't have to be a competition. The reason you get involved in Irish is because it offers something that English doesn't. Personally, I'm not going to abandon English language culture, but I'll do my damnedest to see that Irish language culture can survive and thrive alongside it.

The arguments for maintaining languages – and their associated cultures – is one of cultural ecology. Think of *cultúr na Gaeilge* as a small to medium sized rain forest. John McWhorter speaks about a future in which most of the world's peoples will be: "subsumed into a slurry of multiethnic urban misery and exploitation voiced in just a couple of dozen big fat languages." You don't have to be a big fat language with a big fat culture to be valuable. The Irish-speaking community in Ireland today is four times larger than the population of Athens when Socrates, Aristophanes and Euripides were on the go. It's not numbers, but the intensity of the cultural life that counts.

James McCloskey has identified the cultural loss involved in the death of a language far better than I can:

> Every language that succumbs to the economic, political and cultural pressures being applied all over the globe today, takes to the grave with it an encyclopaedia of histories, mythologies, jokes, songs, philosophies, riddles, superstitions, games, sciences, hagiographies – the whole cumulative effort of a people over centuries to understand the circumstances of its own existence. It is an enormously frightening thought that nine tenths of that accumulation of wisdom, speculation and observation is to be lost within the next century or so.

Not under my watch.
And remember. When you speak Irish the landscape talks back to you.

This talk was presented at a panel discussion, Cad is cultúr Gaelach ann? *at Cultúrlann McAdam Ó Fiaich in March 2013.*

Aodán Mac Póilin was born in Belfast and now lives in the city's Irish-speaking community on Shaw's Road. He graduated from the University of Ulster with a degree and M. Phil in Irish Studies, and edited The Irish Language in Northern Ireland *(Ultach, 1997). He was the Director of an Irish-language organization, the Ultach Trust, between 1990 and 2014.*

from THE OTHER TONGUES

United by vulnerability.

EDITOR'S NOTE

Funded by generous Irish-British grants from the Arts Council of Northern Ireland, Foras na Gaeilge, the Ulster-Scots Agency and the Gaelic Books Council in Scotland, *The Other Tongues: An Introduction to Writing in Irish, Scots Gaelic and Scots in Ulster and Scotland* (ISBN 978-0-9561046-1-8) is a beautifully produced, ground-breaking and major anthology in a coffee-table-book format, aimed at the general reader in English as well as in Irish, Scots Gaelic and Scots. It was published by Irish Pages Ltd in late 2013.

With 79 texts spanning three centuries (evenly divided between each tongue: poems, prose extracts and songs), this colourful and educative anthology seeks to introduce the general reader to writing in the three minority tongues that coexist with the English language across the North Channel, in Scotland and the nine counties of Ulster.

Each text is accompanied by a striking image, a biographical note and a translation into English, making every two-page spread an elegant but succinct introduction to each author, aimed at the general public rather than a specialist or academic audience.

Drawing on the renowned production values of *Irish Pages*, the anthology is characterized by design elegance of a high order, in terms of typography, layout, paper and visual imagery. The anthology also comprises three introductions (one for each language, with translation), an index of authors, a list of illustrations, and suggestions for further reading – making this also an ideal resource for the classroom, both at secondary and university levels.

The result is a unique, beautiful and actually classic volume revealing the literary traditions of the three tongues over three centuries in Ulster and Scotland. It also represents a major and foundational entrance of Irish Pages Ltd into book publishing for Ireland and further afield.

The Foreword and three Introductions by four of the Editors of *The Other Tongues* follow below.

A TRILINGUAL *MEITHEAL*

Chris Agee

Irreplaceable facets.

According to Dinneen's famous Irish-language dictionary, a *meitheal* is "a gang or party, especially of reapers; a number of persons employed at any special work, as hay-making, or turf-cutting". That etymology of common rural endeavour, bound up with an indispensable solidarity in the task, might serve well as a metaphor for the intricate barn-raising of this unique volume. With a caveat: the assemblies involved – across one museum, two states, three tongues, five funding bodies and five universities – could hardly be described as a rapid sheaving of the literary harvest that follows.

No one editor, scholar or even literary imagination could, in fact, have assembled alone *The Other Tongues* as it now stands. There exists probably no one individual steeped sufficiently in the traditions, cultures, territories, allusions, vocabularies, orthographies and so on of *all three tongues* to venture such a quixotic and monumental solo-flight. That is why, over the course of this three-year *meitheal*, the original editorial gang of five rose to twelve. In addition to myself – part ganger, part impresario, part factotum – the initial plan foresaw four further editors, each taking on the selection of texts and the writing of authorial notes in English: Cathal Ó Searcaigh for the Irish, Peter Mackay for the Scots Gaelic, Andrew Philip for the Scots and Frank Ferguson for the Ulster Scots. It soon transpired, however, that still further scholarship was required, whether in the matter of new outstanding translations (Frank Sewell, Charles Dillon and Aonghas MacLeòid), or research, fact-checking and meticulous proofreading (Seán Mac Aindreasa and Aonghas MacLeòid). Yet, at this point, only the textual polish sat pretty.

Integral to our conception for this anthology was a wealth of visual imagery of a high and various order that would complement the texts. These images would not necessarily be directly illustrative of text and/or authorial note: they might also resonate in some atmospheric way, or collaborate visually as a whole. The research-cum-search for bespoke imagery soon revealed my own woefully limited expertise in such art-historical imagination, and it dawned that the *meitheal* would again need to be augmented. It was with good fortune that I was able to draw on the talents of three curatorial virtuosos: Murdo Macdonald and Hugh Cheape for Scotland, and Janet MacLean for all of Ireland.

As the Editor of *Irish Pages*, my role was organizational and technical, although the original editorial architecture fell to me: the number of texts, the naming of the sections, the overall design layout and the required appendixes. Another of my early choices was that the three tongues should not be grouped, but interleaved throughout, so as to reinforce the continuous simultaneity of these linguistic worlds "at the peripheries" over three centuries, both *vis-à-vis* each other and in close proximity to the daunting sway of metropolitan English. I was also responsible for the title, which immediately seemed right. *Other* catches the essential "otherness" of every language; the Scots self-description *tongue* nicely sidesteps the rather arid debate about the difference between a dialect and a language, directing our attention to the importance of self-determination in matters linguistic as well as political.

So what is the purpose of this elegant book? In my mind, its uses are threefold: educative, cultural and literary. In terms of education, the worth of such an enlightening literary distillation is self-evident. Indeed, education is simply a synonym for the transmission of inner culture, whether formally through the classroom or more informally in the invisible auditorium of solo readers. To which might be added the thought that, for virtually any writer or reader seriously interested in the literatures of these islands, *The Other Tongues* can serve as an invaluable guide to further territories of literary art not known – or, at least, not fully familiar.

The Other Tongues is also very much an Irish book, and not merely because its publisher is an all-island journal based in the northern jurisdiction. Rather, there is something both telling and refreshing about the fact that the colophon on the title page is, so to speak, a Belfast horse, derived from the Yeats-inspired 20-pence piece of the Irish Free State. This reflection is prompted by the fact that Irish and Scots in Ulster have been a matter of particular contest and some conflict in Northern Ireland before, during and after the Troubles; contrastingly, this anthology is an east–west initiative from Belfast aimed at revisioning those divisions through a Scottish–Irish cultural continuum broader than the dynamics of one island's partition.

Naturally, for the Irish nationalist or republican no less than the British-Irish unionist, such a territorial framework may involve some deep-seated discomfiture. The former pair may imagine an impugning of the integrity of the lost province of an all-Ireland state; the latter may well have to thole the thought that — despite the United Kingdom — it is not so much the planted landfall of now-vestigial Scots in Ulster as the ancient seaborne continuum of Gaelic dialects that constitutes the most substantially enduring linguistic and cultural marriage between Ireland and Scotland. But then, *Irish Pages* is nothing if not "a Yeatsian project" …

So *The Other Tongues* is a long-overdue literary *démarche* across three jurisdictions (the Republic, Northern Ireland and Scotland) aimed at bridging the Gaelic and Scots traditions on the two islands and within the two overarching states. As the following three introductions make clear, the links between the three tongues are not only persistent, but increasing in new and supple ways. Particularly noteworthy is the rich interaction between English, Scots and Scots Gaelic in contemporary Scottish writing, including a beautiful sub-vein of translation from Scots Gaelic to Scots. Alas, no similar literary cross-fertilization between Irish and Ulster Scots has hove into view across the Sea of Moyle.

During the course of this volume, I took up a post as writer-in-residence at the University of Strathclyde, Glasgow. My recurrent visits gave me the first-hand opportunity to hear the rich, colloquial and natural Scots of Scotland, especially renowned in Glasgow's tongue-meldings with English. Two observations dawned quickly.

The first thought was that, compared to its relative in Scotland, the Scots of Ulster was much weaker, both on the individual tongue and in the culture as a whole, being confined to several rural swathes in north Down and the Ards Peninsula, east Antrim, north-east Derry and the Laggan area of Donegal. Yes, it had long been recognized by scholars as one of the speech-patterns of Ireland, surrounded by Northern-Hiberno English, in which it seemed heavily embedded. Whereas in Glasgow a working-class Scots-speaker in full flow might be nearly incomprehensible, I have never once been unable to follow perfectly an Ulster-Scots-speaker, even in Donegal, where the speech seems thickest.

As I criss-crossed the skies over the Irish Sea, the second penny dropped: the literary worlds of Scotland and Ireland, including Northern Ireland, were highly sealed off, with surprisingly little mutual awareness. Antrim might be only 12 miles from the Mull of Kintyre, with a shared history of violent religious strife, but there was little general contemporary literary interchange between Ulster and Scotland, outside the auld link between Irish-speakers in Donegal and central Scotland, and with Scots-

Gaelic-speakers in the Islands. The two literary worlds now not so much face each other across the sea as stand back to back with their own vistas of historical orientation.

The thinness of contemporary Ulster Scots, allied with the separation of the two literary worlds, means that nothing remotely comparable to the creative revitalization of Scots by MacDiarmid and others has occurred in the north of Ireland. The slow honing of Scots into a literary tool of surpassing vigour has simply not migrated to Irish soil. Whilst James Fenton and Philip Robinson hold fast to the inheritance of the Rhyming Weavers, and Michael Longley aptly ransacks the Scots lexicon for loan-words, this can hardly be dubbed a renaissance. I have wondered for years as an editor why this rich Scots inheritance, still so available to the Ulster ear, has not been seized upon by some Irish writer and taken for a postmodernist gallivant.

Yet the story of literary Scots in Ireland does not quite end there. One personal pleasure attendant on this anthology was fully appreciating the strength of the tradition of Scots writing in Ulster in the wake of Robert Burns. If this literary tradition has now dwindled to a rural Ulster remnant, that is not the same as gainsaying its subterranean influence. For where did that older and intenser Scots travel in the future northern culture? A number of Ulster writers in both English and Irish, such as Seamus Heaney and Cathal Ó Searcaigh, have spoken of the influence of Burns as a potent exemplar whose language was fully cognate with the popular English spoken in the home place. Just as the Irish language has profoundly shaped the English of the island, so too has Scots clearly influenced its Northern-Hiberno branch. Is there not, for instance, something of Ulster Scots in the famed earthiness and precision, the blend of the demotic and the sophisticated, that so inflects Heaney's poetry?

All in all, *The Other Tongues* makes plain the enduring importance of bilingualism not only in these islands, but anywhere in an era of global English as the world's *lingua franca*, next to whose power over half the world's 5,000 living languages may expire this century. Against those who reckon the value of a language in terms of the number of its speakers, this book upholds the view that every language is its own world of inestimable value, a veritable inner rainforest of experience and consciousness: one irreplaceable facet of the world heritage of the human tongue. To quote Wittgenstein, "what we can say at all can be said clearly"; but, if we lose one way of saying it, we lose one part of what can be said – for good.

Chris Agee was born in 1956 in San Francisco and grew up in Massachusetts, New York and Rhode Island. He attended Harvard University and since 1979 has lived in Ireland. He is the author of three books of poems, In the New Hampshire Woods *(The Dedalus Press, 1992),* First Light *(The Dedalus Press, 2003) and* Next to Nothing *(Salt, 2009, shortlisted for the 2010 Ted Hughes Award for New Work in Poetry), as well as the editor of* Scar on the Stone: Contemporary Poetry from Bosnia *(Bloodaxe, 1998, Poetry Society Recommendation),* Unfinished Ireland: Essays on Hubert Butler *(Irish Pages, 2003) and* The New North: Contemporary Poetry from Northern Ireland *(Wake Forest University Press, 2008, and Salt, 2011). A Bosnian translation of* Next to Nothing, Gotovo ništa *(Buybook, Sarajevo), appeared in 2011. He holds dual Irish and American citizenship, and spends part of each year at his house on Korcula, near Dubrovnik, in Croatia. He is the Editor of this journal.*

STILL SINGING STRONG

Cathal Ó Searcaigh

Survivors.

For generations there have been close connections between our neighbours on the other side of the Sea of Moyle and us: bonds of race, language, music, marriage, poetry, and understanding.

There is certainly a strong link between the people of the Donegal Gaeltacht and those of the Highlands of Scotland. Both groups evolved under the same unfavourable climate and conditions. They both endured imperialist efforts to wipe out their culture and silence their tongue. But despite the hardship and hatreds directed at them, they are full of heart and song. Tribal spirit still flows in their veins. My own mother would often talk of the "Heeland" girls that she worked with, in Scotland, during the herring season. Working conditions were hard and they got little reward for their slaving. My mother was fond of those girls and often recalled this girl from Lewis or another from Uist. They were all, poor things, in the same boat.

Like my mother, they were plain-dealing girls who expected the same. So it could have been easy for some unscrupulous soul to play false with them in matters of money and, even, love or sex. Scottish readers will no doubt know the moving poems by Derick Thomson and Ian Crichton Smith in honour of these "herring girls".

My father was a seasonal worker in Scotland and was always travelling back and forth when I was young. He worked on farms around Dunbar, Haddington, and East Lothian; the Scottish Lothians, as he called it. Many Gortahork men worked in the area back then. They were well known on farms there and, with a reputation as good workers, could soon find employment. All these men, my father included, had a Scottish lilt when they spoke in English.

I should add, too, that Donegal people were deeply immersed in Robbie Burns' poetry. They heard in his work, I believe, an echo of their own struggles. He spoke to them from the depths, from something akin to their own bitter experience. "Man was made to mourn," he said. They understood that. As with our own Irish songs, his words came from the heart more than from the head. With more feeling than intellectualizing in them, his songs have (to this day) the same heartening and "hamely" quality that you find in the Irish song tradition.

Burns managed to happily marry together word and music, aptness and sweetness, sense and song-line. He understood, as our own poets did, that music transcends, takes (and brings us on) a step beyond the hurt and sorrow that can shipwreck a life or skewer a heart: "The heart's ay the part ay that makes us right or wrong". He wrote his first song, "Handsome Nell", in the year 1773, when he was just fourteen years old. That was the year in which Art Mac Cumhaigh died. Those two would have been "brother poets".

My father used to read Burns' poetry aloud to me when I was a young lad. I had no English then but the musicality of the speech went straight to my heart. I loved the musical sounds that came from my father's mouth as he recited those poems. First, he used to tell me the story (in Irish) and then he would read the poem out loud in a voice that was lithe and agile. It was easy to get carried away in the stream of music that flowed from him and to open up the sails of your imagination. That was when I realised that there was a mystical power and divine energy in words if you found the right sound-pattern, setting words and rhythm to the one pulse. Hearing my father read "The Death and Dying Words of Poor Mailie", "Tam o' Shanter", "To a Mouse", and "To a Louse" had me alternately in tears and stitches.

Notably, Nioclás Ó Cearnaigh (c. 1802–c. 1865), one of the most prolific writers among Oriel scholars in the nineteenth century, made some fine translations of Burns' poetry. Among them are songs such as "Highland

Mary" and "Sweet Afton". Burns had a sister who married and lived in the Dundalk area. That's probably why the name Sweet Afton was given to a brand of cigarettes produced by Carrolls Tobacco Company in Dundalk. The cigarette boxes bore, I recall, a picture of Burns.

———

During the troubled years that followed defeat at the Battle of the Boyne (1690), and the massacre at Aughrim (1691), the old Irish families lost power, and their lands were now in the hands of "Planter" colonists who were Protestant and English-speaking, most of them in Ulster and of Scottish extraction. In my own (Gaeltacht) area of Donegal, "Albanaigh" [the Scottish] is still a common term for Protestant people. The late seventeenth and eighteenth century was a shameful and wretched time. The Penal Laws were in operation to keep Catholics from advancement and power. They lost their rights, including the right to their own land, and suffered general degradation.

The poet Dáibhí Ó Bruadair (1625–98) defined this troubled time as the engulfment or overwhelming of the old order: "tonnbhriseadh an tseanghnáthaimh". The British authorities aimed to wipe out the ancient civilization and culture, to spread the English language, and to anglicize the entire country. The cultural heritage, language, values, and the Catholic religion had (from an imperialist perspective) to be deposed and usurped so that English rule and regulations could be established and secured in Ireland. In 1612, only eleven years after the Battle of Kinsale (1601), with most of the country falling under English rule county by county, Sir John Davies (the crown authority in Ireland) unashamedly admitted the extent and nature of England's colonial aims:

> We may conceive and hope that the next generation will in tongue, and heart, and every way else, become English; so as there will be no difference or distinction but the Irish Sea betwixt us.

Such comments indicate a policy of cultural genocide. And as the Gaelic nobility lost its land and authority, so too did it lose out in cultural terms because it was no longer in a position to provide patronage to the poet-class in society. After Kinsale, therefore, it was common for Gaelic poets to lament the decline of their leaders and of patronage itself. By the time Séamus Dall Mac Cuarta (*c.* 1647–1733) came into his own as a poet, the age of native patronage was all but over. Glassdrummond Castle, the seat of the Fews branch of the O'Neills in south Armagh, was now reduced to a battered, roofless ruin. Of all the Gaelic chiefs, the O'Neills (for their generosity and grace) had been the most celebrated by poets before the Cromwellian era when the family lost their lands and possessions. Here is how Art Mac Cumhaigh eulogised them in his poem "Úrchill a' Chreagáin" ("At Creggan Graveyard"), one of the most popular Irish-language poems in Ulster:

> Niall Frasach's fair kin who never turned music away but at Christmas gave clothes to the poets who paid them service.

The Gaelic order, which had supported the literati for hundreds of years, had been destroyed. The founts of knowledge, the ancient schools that had provided advanced training to poets in their craft and social function, were now shut down. The commanding literary form known as the Dán Díreach was on the wane, while simpler and freer forms of poetry were now coming to the fore. In matters of composition, conversational forms were now foregrounded rather than the complicated classical forms practised by the bards for thousands of years. The era of a professional poet-caste, of the Dán Díreach, was over, but the practice of learning continued. Poets from and of the people derived new possibilities from the poetic form known as the Amhrán (Gaelic song-metre).

It is thought that the Amhrán had always been used among the masses but, as a literary form, it wasn't much respected by the experts in the schools of poetry. They were more accustomed to the regular syllabic form of the Dán Díreach. However, the new poets, who were beginning to emerge, prioritized musicality over strict prosody. Despite opposition, they based their poems on the conversational rhythms and cadences in everyday speech by the people around them.

They measured the poetic line in beats (not syllables), gauged each utterance according to how it would be said in conversation, and drew music from the rhythmical flexibility of the vowels. They combined word and meaning, musicality and accuracy, momentum and emotion in a way that was new and natural; and, from that bop and beat, they jammed up a jazz from the language that had never before been heard in Irish. This was the age of the Amhrán. Despite every deprivation and distress suffered by the eighteenth-century poets, they threw their hearts into song. And their songs are still sung today. They gave and secured a hearing, you could say, for the dialect of the tribe to speak up and out in the Court of Poetry.

The question of the Stuart succession or hereditary right to the English crown was hotly contested throughout Ireland in the first half of the eighteenth century. It was difficult for any poet worthy of the name to avoid this thorny topic. Consequently, the Stuart dynasty is mentioned quite often in Ulster poetry of the period but, unlike the Munster poets who voiced loyalty and support for King James, the Ulster poets realised that the fight was lost. Apart from Art Mac Cumhaigh, who was fond of the Stuarts and sorry when James was deposed, few of the other poets felt much connection with whoever happened to wear the bloodstained crown when Gaels kept getting slaughtered during the War of the Two Kings. In fact, the poet Peadar Ó Doirnín was so fed up with the Stuarts *et al.* that he made a mockery of the crown itself in his poem "Tá Bearád i Londain" ("There is a Hat in London").

The kingdom of Oriel, in north-east Ulster, is where the first texts in my section of this anthology were written. It was in Oriel in 1707 that the poem "Fáilte don Éan" ("A Welcome for the Bird") was composed. From 1700 to the end of the nineteenth century, this region was synonymous with learning and had a corresponding reputation for literary creativity. It was there, in the eighteenth century, that the highly accomplished work of Mac Cuarta, Ó Doirnín, and Mac Cumhaigh marked a new flowering in poetry. And it was there that a new impetus was given to prose writing in the same period. For example, a text such as *Eachtra Aodha Mhic Oireachtaigh* is worthy of interest not least because it is one of the earliest texts containing features that we associate with the novel as a genre. It is, in fact, a comic novella, a scathing satire in powerful and well-wrought prose. Another text that displays exceptional skill in its use of prose is *Fealsúnacht Aodha Mhic Dhomhnaill* (*The Philosophy of Hugh McDonnell*). With its precise account of plants and herbs, fish and birds, it is more of a nature almanac than a treatise of heavy ruminations. The text reveals a breadth of knowledge that the author clearly gathered from the ancient Greeks, the Bible, folklore and, of course, his own observations. He deftly manages to capture elements of nature and the living world in accurate and concise language.

It's worth mentioning that Mac Domhnaill was one of the collectors sent out by Robert Shipboy MacAdam (1808–95) to gather manuscripts from all over Ulster and to note down the songs and poems that were still being sung or recited before all such Gaelic learning and craft would be lost to the world forever. MacAdam was a Protestant from Belfast, a talented entrepreneur who made his money from iron manufacture. In his time, industry and commerce were spreading all over the city, mills and factories were in production, and shipbuilding was at its height. It was not uncommon then for members of the wealthy middle class to form societies and take an interest in cultural pursuits. Soon every aspect of intellectual life was coming to light in Belfast, evidence of which is found in the number and names of the various societies formed: The Belfast Literary Society, The Harmonic Society, The Historic Society, The Natural History and Philosophical Society, The Rhetorical Society, The Irish Harp Society, and The Ulster Gaelic Society or Cuideachta Gaedhilge Uladh. It has to be said that not all Protestants turned a deaf ear to Irish. After 1798, there were a small dedicated few who wholeheartedly cared about the language and who devoted themselves to preserving and promoting the language. Among them were Unionists such as the Rev William Nelson, a Presbyterian minister and Head of the Classical School and Professor of the Classical, Hebrew and Irish Languages at the Belfast Academical Institution, who wrote *An Introduction to the Irish Language*, and others such as MacAdam. It was clear to the latter from his field research that Irish was in decline throughout the whole of Ulster. The ongoing loss of the language hurt him deeply as he regretted that a young generation was growing up and turning its back on the language, lore, and stories of the older generation: "I am sorry," he said, "that the young are not learning it [Irish] directly from the old tradition-bearers who are dying out one by one."

    He himself learnt the language and he determined to save as much Gaelic lore as he could. He used the wealth at his disposal to buy manuscripts, to send out collectors, and to set scribes to writing. He employed not only Aodh Mac Domhnaill but other Gaelic poets and scribes including Art Mac Bionaid and Peadar Ó Gealacáin, who are among the most renowned authors of their time.

    These poor scholars, who were barely subsisting, welcomed any pay at all that helped them to survive. No wonder then that Mac Domhnaill, Mac Bionaid, and Ó Gealacáin spent a period of their lives teaching in Church of Ireland Bible schools. One of the Protestant organizations most to the fore in such missionary work was The Irish Society for Promoting the Education of the Native Irish through the Medium of Their Own Language, whose aim was to equip its students with enough Irish to read the Bible. Of course, they were hoping for conversions as a result.

Although there were various small groups working here and there for the good of the language during the nineteenth century, there wasn't any large-scale nationwide movement until the Gaelic League was formed on 31 July 1893. By that time, the English language was in command and ascendancy in every aspect of national life. Irish was in decline and had *no* official status from the government down. It was viewed as a backwoods language, a badge of poverty ... You need English, it was said, to get anywhere in this life. Even the "Liberator" Daniel O'Connell shared that opinion and had no shame in openly expressing it:

> Although the Irish language is connected with many recollections that twine around the hearts of Irishmen, yet the superior utility of the English tongue as a medium of all modern communication is so great that I can witness without a sigh the gradual disuse of the Irish.

It's worth remembering that O'Connell himself could speak Irish and that it was his own aunt, Eibhlín Dhubh Ní Chonaill, who composed "Caoineadh Airt Uí Laoghaire" ("The Lament for Art O'Leary"), a major poem in the Irish canon.

The view of Irish as worthless was common to the "gombeen" men, the new middle-class Catholics who were beginning to advance slightly but who were still disrespected on the grounds of their Gaelic heritage. To the gombeen or provincial mind, anything foreign was necessarily superior to the local or native. In order to "progress" in the world, gombeen men (and women) preferred to ape foreign culture, the modes and mores of the dominant class which they thought were superior, more fashionable and, above all else, more suitable for material advancement. From their point of view, Irish was a rural and restricted/restrictive language.

The Gaelic League aimed to transform that negative attitude and to promote across the nation a much more favourable opinion of the language. The League did not revive the language completely but they did succeed, during the early years at least, in explaining to the Irish people the importance of the language, and in raising the profile of a unique world heritage. From those beginnings came the "autumn flowering" that we refer to as twentieth-century literature in Irish.

While most eighteenth- and nineteenth-century writing and preservation of literature and learning in Irish occurred in Oriel, it was in Ranafast (Donegal) that Ulster writers first adopted that role again in the twentieth century. The Mac Grianna family, brothers Séamus and Seosamh, paid a great service to literature in Irish. Séamus (Máire as he was better known) was the more prolific of the two but Seosamh is rated as the best prose writer of his generation. He had many talents: intelligence, imagination, and linguistic ability. But, for all that, he was laid low by depression. Sadly, it silenced him for half his life, his mind locked away in an asylum in Letterkenny.

In his major prose work *Mo Bhealach Féin* (*My Own Way*), he acknowledges at the start of the novel that he has inside him the odd strain that marks out the loner or poet whose views fall foul of society's narrow norms. He wishes to avoid the barren paths of the middle class and to turn instead towards his own visions: "What I would like to do is to turn the world upside down so that everything would be magical as long as you perceived it in your own way." This is the poet's *reveille*, the odd-man-out resisting the manacles of the mundane world. No wonder that *Mo Bhealach Féin* left a very deep impression on all of us who came to be influenced by this extraordinary work. And that goes for most of the Ulster writers who emerged in the second half of the twentieth century and whose work is gathered in this anthology.

Didn't Mac Grianna beg us "in the name of God, go where others don't, even if all you see are hen houses"? That is inspirational advice for any would-be author. And Mac Grianna's influence is evident in the daring new work that has been wrought from Ulster Irish in the past sixty years. The most impressive and heartening writers in the language are those imbued with such a spirit of deep curiosity and adventure. Such are Mac Grianna's natural heirs – in keeping with their culture and open to change.

Breandán Ó Doibhlin paid close attention to Mac Grianna. This is clear from his 1964 novel *Néal Maidine agus Tine Oíche* (*Morning Cloud and Night Fire*), a perceptive book written in masterful style. More like a work of philosophy than anything else, it is a poetic fable in which the author has weighed every word. You could imagine the narrator as an Old Testament prophet, his mission to lead his people back to their culture. This is a text that deserves more attention than it has hitherto received; an exceptional book. Ambitious, it contains profundity of thought and some of the most intelligent discussion in contemporary literature of our country's cultural quagmire.

Séamus Mac Annaidh's revolutionary 1983 novel *Cuaifeach Mo Lon Dubh Buí* (*The Squalls of My Yellow Blackbird*) challenged and changed our expectations of storytelling. In one go, he deconstructed the narrative form to make us fundamentally question the nature of the novel. He turned upside down the basic rules of storytelling that we (as readers) were long used to. Then, having removed the usual signposts that we had come to expect, Mac Annaidh deliberately placed us in uncertainty, making us seek out strands in the narrative that could lead us towards firmer ground and out of the depths that he had constructed for us. This is a prized cult novel which more than deserves its status.

As we see from the selection included in this anthology, Ulster poetry is in fine voice and busy practising its scales throughout the whole province. Gréagóir Ó Dúill (an anthologist, perceptive critic, and established poet who guides and encourages the new generation of writers) has been publishing regularly for over forty years. Belfast poet Gearóid Mac Lochlainn is in full voice. Mature, learned, a master of his craft, he takes on the linguistic schizophrenia which we (minority-language speakers) live and endure, and he turns it to creative use and to revelation. Each of the poets included here has found her or his own way to make the language supple and malleable. Colette Ní Ghallchóir, Pól Ó Muirí, Máire Wren, Diarmaid Ó Doibhlin, Proinsias Mac a' Bhaird, Réamonn Ó Muirí, and Philip Cummings are refashioning the ancestral craft to the needs of today. They are re-engaging the language and revivifying the tradition. There are even more new and daring voices that cannot be included here due only to lack of space, important poets such as Celia de Fréine and Pádraig Mac Suibhne, Tom Mac Intyre and Pádraig Ó Croiligh, Antaine Ó Donnaile and Cathal Póirtéir, Caitríona Ní Chléirichín and Seán Ó Dúrois. These contemporary Ulster authors are extending the scope of poetry, their work demonstrating how the genre is currently flourishing and adapting.

Tight editorial restrictions also dictate that I cannot (here, at least) give due space and attention to the new generation of Ulster prose writers: Peigí Rose, Pádraig Ó Siadhail, Fiontán de Brún, Deirdre Nic Grianna, Eoghan Mac Giolla Bhríde, Pádraig Ó Baoill, Antain Mac Lochlainn, Eoghan Ó Néill, and Lillis Ó Laoire. These are all writers of talent who have produced accomplished works in prose.

Clearly, that little blackbird who "whistled from the end of its bright yellow bill" centuries ago near the River Lagan is still singing strong.

Translated, from the Irish, by Frank Sewell.

Cathal Ó Searcaigh was born in 1956 and raised in Meenala, near Gortahork, an Irish-speaking district in Co Donegal. He was writer-in-residence in the Irish language at the University of Ulster and Queen's University Belfast for three years in the early nineties. His poetry collections are Súile Shuibhne *(Coiscéim, 1983),* Suibhne *(Coiscéim, 1987), the bilingual* An Bealach 'na Bhaile/Homecoming *(Cló Iar-Chonnacht, 1993),* Na Buachaillí Bána *(Cló Iar-Chonnacht, 1996), the selected* Out in the Open *(Cló Iar-Chonnacht, 1998),* Ag Tnúth Leis an tSolas *(Cló Iar-Chonnacht, 2000),* Gúrú i gCluídíní *(2006),* An tAm Marfach ina Mairimid *(2011), and* Aimsir Ársa *(2013). His prose works include* Seal i Neipeal *(2004),* Light on Distant Hills: A Memoir *(2009), and* Pianó Mhín na bPreachán *(2011). He is also the author of several plays in Irish, and a selection of English translations of his poetry,* By the Hearth in Mín a' Leá *(Arc), appeared in 2005. He is the Irish Language Editor of this journal, and continues to live in Meenala.*

LASTING LINKS

Peter Mackay

A long conversation.

For millennia the Sea of Moyle has been a sea-road, carrying people and goods, songs and stories across the waves, connecting Scotland and Ireland; it was the crossing point for a continuous cultural community stretching – at its height – from Mizen Head to Dunnet Head. But, since the eighteenth century, the ties across the straits have weakened. According to tradition, Niall Mac Mhuirich, who died in 1726, was the last Scottish poet to write in the classical language shared by Gaelic poets in Scotland and Ireland. Scottish Gaelic vernacular literature – if traced back to the publication of Alexander MacDonald's *Ais-eiridh na sean Chánoin Albannaich* in 1751 – has risen from the ashes of this lost shared classical culture; and for much of the near-three hundred years that have passed since, the Gaelic literatures have gone their separate ways, divided by differences in language, historical context and political status. But as Gaelic literature has developed, there have always been glances back or across, starting with MacDonald's own "Galley of Clanranald", which uses the metaphor of a journey from South Uist to Carrickfergus to create a political parable and virtuosic soundscape.

Since this breach with the shared classical tradition, Scottish Gaelic literature has tended to be diverse and (often) international in scope. Although MacDonald was the first to publish secular Gaelic poetry, there was also a wealth of songs and stories retained in the oral tradition, and a large number of published religious texts – both original sermons and translations – from the 1567 translation of "Knox's Liturgy" (the *Book of Common Order*) onwards; a great deal of Gaelic literature from the eighteenth century to the present day draws on this store of religious writing and folk and vernacular songs, as well as the classics of Greek and Roman literature. Although verse has tended to dominate discussions of Gaelic literature, in the nineteenth century a sizeable body of prose (and a much smaller dramatic corpus) was also developed. The plays of Archibald MacLaren – mixing Gaelic and English – gained some popularity at the beginning of the century, and factual prose was brought to a wide readership in Scotland (and Canada) in journals and newspapers such as *An Teachdaire Gaelach* or *Cuairtear nan Gleann*, edited by Norman MacLeod,

"Caraid nan Gàidheal"; it was not until the twentieth century, however, that short stories and novels came to be published with any frequency.

As a result of the work of James MacPherson in gathering and publishing Ossianic material, and the scandal surrounding the authenticity of these songs, there was great interest in the late eighteenth and nineteenth century in the folk myths, stories and traditions of Scotland and Ireland. However, although the work of collectors such as John Frances Campbell and Alexander Carmichael became hugely popular, the Ossianic scandal served to set the scholarly communities in Scotland and Ireland against each other, with rights to these ancient songs at stake. This was symptomatic of a deeper rift in how aware the two communities were of each other: in the nineteenth century, it was only rarely that Ireland featured as a subject in contemporary Scottish Gaelic literature. When it did, it was most commonly to explore the shared problems of emigration, clearance and famine – as in the songs of William Livingston and Lady Jane D' Oyly – or as an ally in the Land League agitations.

It was not only the relationship with Ireland that was changing, but also the manner in which place and landscape were portrayed in Gaelic literature. To some extent this reflected the growing influence of European Romanticism, with place being used to explore and display the emotions of the individual. But place has always also been used as a metaphor for political systems and in nineteenth-century Gaelic songs these two ways of describing place coincided: the frequent descriptions of cleared landscapes spoke both of the individual loss and misery felt by thousands in the Highlands, and also of a way of life (and the political system that supported it) that no longer existed. These poems of dislocation, lament and longing therefore always had a political element, even if they rarely encouraged a political response.

Where much of the nineteenth-century experience was common to Scotland and Ireland, one effect of the political upheavals of the early twentieth century – the First World War and the Easter Rising, the War of Independence and the Civil War in Ireland, Irish independence, Irish neutrality during the Second World War, sectarianism in Northern Ireland and the west of Scotland – was that Ireland and Scotland felt very far from each other. Some looked enviously over at the new country that took Dublin as its capital, but Irish political independence also highlighted cultural differences. It was not until the 1930s, and the emergence of Sorley MacLean that lasting links between the literatures of Gaelic Scotland and

Ireland started to be forged again. MacLean was a hugely important figure in bringing the literatures together. This was, on the one hand, because he still envisaged Gaelic Scotland and Ireland as part of the same cultural continuity – for him, "the old wound of Ulster is a disease / suppurating in the heart of Europe / and in the heart of every Gael / who knows he is a Gael". On the other – and perhaps most pertinently – he had strong personal attachments to Ireland, through his love and friendship for Nessa O'Shea, his brother Calum's work for the Irish Folklore Commission, and through his admiration for W.B. Yeats and James Connolly.

In Scotland, MacLean was the foremost of a generation of poets that encouraged a renaissance in Gaelic literature to rival the era of Alexander MacDonald and Duncan Bàn MacIntyre. George Campbell Hay, Iain Crichton Smith, Derick Thomson and Donald MacAulay – along with MacLean – raised the profile of Gaelic poetry dramatically both in Scotland and abroad. At home, this was largely through engagement with the different waves of the Scottish Renaissance, in part through translations between Gaelic and Scots, and personal relationships with the likes of MacDiarmid, Douglas Young and Robert Garioch; in Ireland, the Bardic Circuit trips greatly aided the creation of new links and understanding between the sea-bound Gaels. Overall, there was an extremely lively (and occasionally contentious) literary scene, centred around the quarterly magazine *Gairm*, which had been founded by Thomson and Finlay MacDonald in 1952 and which for 50 years provided a road to publication for generations of aspiring and established writers, offering translations, critical work and non-fiction alongside short stories by the likes of Alasdair Campbell, Norman Campbell and John Murray.

Since the 70s there has been a resurgence of Gaelic poetry matched by an outpouring of all types of writing, with Gaelic literature in ruder health than it had been for centuries. New poets such as Meg Bateman, Anna Frater, Rody Gorman, Iain S. MacPherson, Fearghas MacFhionnlaigh, Christopher Whyte, Aonghas MacNeacail, Catriona Montgomery and Morag Montgomery have emerged from a diverse range of backgrounds – natives and learners of Gaelic, from Scotland and abroad. The opportunity has arisen to write for the stage, radio, TV and film. Music groups like Runrig and Capercaillie have had international success with a mix of traditional and new Gaelic songs. And since 2002 there has been a huge increase in the number and range of novels in Gaelic, with the Ùr-Sgeul series establishing new (for Gaelic) genres of fiction, and in the process encouraging new writers such as Alison Lang and Caitriona Lexy Campbell and more established writers, including Norman MacLean and Angus Peter Campbell.

Part of the buoyancy of Gaelic literature has come through a strengthening of links with Scots and Irish writing. It is now much more common than at any point since the 40s to find translations between Gaelic and Scots; the historical links between Scottish and Irish Gaelic, meanwhile, have been marked by projects such as *An Leabhar Mòr*, links continued through Rody Gorman's annual anthology *An Guth*. These connections are part of a conversation (sometimes a debate, sometimes an argument, sometimes a trysting) that has been taking place across the Sea of Moyle for centuries; we hope that this selection will give you a sense of the manifold ways in which that conversation has risen, ebbed and flowed.

Translated, from the Scots Gaelic, by the author.

Peter Mackay is a poet, writer, academic and broadcaster. He has a PhD from Trinity College Dublin, and has worked as a researcher at the Seamus Heaney Centre for Poetry, Queen's University Belfast, an associate lecturer at Trinity College Dublin, a broadcast journalist for the BBC in Scotland, and as the Sgrìobhadair or writer-in-residence at Sabhal Mòr Ostaig. He is the author of Sorley MacLean *(RIISS, 2010) and* From Another Island *(Clutag, 2010) and the co-editor of* Modern Irish and Scottish Poetry *(Cambridge University Press, 2011). He has also written widely on contemporary Scottish and Irish literature, and Scottish Gaelic literature in general. Originally from the Isle of Lewis, he is now a Lecturer in the School of English, University of St Andrews, Fife.*

THE MITHER TONGUE

Andrew Philip

Muckle life.

Writing in the Scots language is the bearer and the *bairn* of a rich tradition born in disputed space, a mix of persistence and discontinuity. It shares these features with writing in Irish and Scottish Gaelic, so it is entirely appropriate that the three tongues provide each other with context in this book for more than geographical reasons. When we speak of Scots, we are referring not to a Celtic language as in the case of Irish or Scottish Gaelic but a Germanic language, a close relative of English. It should also go without saying that we are speaking not of a dialect but a language. Like any language, Scots has a number of dialects with distinct accents, vocabulary and even grammatical features. Ulster Scots, which is descended from the speech of the Scottish settlers in the seventeenth-century Plantation, is one of these. However, its literature forms a stream of its own.

The Scots language developed largely from the Scandinavian-influenced Northern Old English spoken by the servants and retainers of the twelfth-century Anglo-Norman and Flemish landowners. By the fourteenth century, it had become the dominant spoken language of all ranks in Lowland Scotland, supplanting Gaelic, and began to be used in poetry, prose and record. This included, from 1424 onwards, the statutes of the nation's parliament.

Literature in Scots began in earnest in the fourteenth century. Its first major work was John Barbour's poem *The Brus* (1376), which recounts the exploits of Robert the Bruce in the War of Independence. Roughly a century later, Blind Harry followed Barbour's lead for an earlier hero with *The Wallace*. Harry's poem is perhaps Scottish literature's first genuinely popular major work. It has been said that, at one point, the two books found in every Scottish household were the Bible and *The Wallace*. As source material for Mel Gibson's *Braveheart*, Harry's poem has continued to make its presence felt.

Poetry in Scots reached a golden age in the fifteenth century with Robert Henryson, William Dunbar, Gavin Douglas and Sir David Lyndsay – collectively known as the Makars. These are justly celebrated writers of subtlety, range and quality, in touch with European literary trends and creating masterworks of late medieval vernacular literature. Douglas's *Eneados* is the first complete translation of the *Aeneid* into a language descended from Old English. It is also provides one of the early instances of the name *Scottis* being applied to the language.

In the ensuing three centuries, three events played significant parts in eroding Scots as a language of status: the Reformation (1560), the Union of the Crowns (1603) and the Union of the Parliaments (1707).

The Reformation, which gave Scotland a religious flavour quite distinct from England or Ireland, might seem a strange culprit. Although some portions of the Bible were translated into Scots at the time, the shepherds of Scotland's reformed church adopted an English Bible and Psalter. Henceforth, God spoke English, although for some time it was English pronounced as Scots.

The prestige of the Scots *leid* was dealt a further blow when the royal court moved to London after James VI acceded to the throne of England. Until this point, Scots had been the language of court. Although *Jamie Saxt* continued to speak Scots, the concentration of royal power in the south meant that ambitious Scotsmen began to look in that direction for advancement and consequently began to modify their writing and their speech.

If this was the case while Scotland retained its identity as a separate state, the tendency became even more acute after the Union of the Parliaments. This was the era in which some began to compile lists of Scotticisms for polite folk to avoid, yet it was also the era in which others began to lament the passing of the Scots language – a dolorous duet that has continued with variations down the years.

Perhaps paradoxically, poetry in Scots experienced something of a renaissance in this difficult context. The most renowned figures of this vernacular revival, as it is frequently termed, are Robert Fergusson and Robert Burns. They demonstrated that Scots was still capable of range and depth of expression. In particular, they explored and exploited the Standard Habbie stanza to its fullest scope. So close is the association that this verse form, although found in eleventh-century Provençal poems and medieval English romances, is now often simply known as "the Burns stanza". Regardless of whether Burns and Fergusson were aware of this wider connection, its existence demonstrates that Scots writing has never been a mere linguistic backwater.

Burns, of course, is also one of Scotland's great folksong collectors, editors and writers. This work, and that of Sir Walter Scott on the border ballads in his *Mistrelsy of the Scottish Borders*, helped to ensure that the vital (in both senses) oral tradition, and the Scots language of the common folk in which it was formed, remained in the eyes and ears of literate Scots. We should not underestimate the importance of this, as that tradition continues directly and indirectly to feed the imaginations of Scottish writers to this day, regardless of whether or not they employ Scots.

Scott, although a major Scottish and world literary figure, was not a Scots writer as such. Nonetheless, his command of the language is shown in dialogue, such as the morsel from *Heart of Midlothian* now included among quotations that adorn the Scottish Parliament's exterior wall. Therefore, despite the demise of any serious prose tradition in Scots, the language still found a foothold in fiction. James Hogg amply demonstrated how powerful this could be in his *Private Memoirs and Confessions of a Justified Sinner*. This approach to Scots in fiction lasted through the nineteenth century. Even William Alexander's *Johnny Gibb of Gushetneuk*, for all the density and frequency of its Scots, maintains the same division between the language of authorial voice and that of dialogue. Although a vein of popular writing in Scots continued, it was not until the twentieth century that any substantial attempt was made to create serious prose in continuous Scots.

In the twentieth century, literature in Scots was dominated by the figure of Hugh MacDiarmid – the pen name of Christopher Murray Grieve – whose poetry, criticism and polemical writing revitalised Scots as a literary language in the 1920s. MacDiarmid reached back to the oral tradition and the medieval Makars, fusing these influences with contemporary European poetics to produce powerful, innovative work. "Dunbar not Burns" was one of his rallying cries and he showed himself a worthy successor to the earlier poet in the range and vitality of his poetry. MacDiarmid's Scots was consciously literary or, as he termed it, "synthetic" – a base of Borders dialect bolstered with vocabulary from previous eras and other regions. Controversial as this was, it was not a new approach. Robert Fergusson, for instance, had done much the same; MacDiarmid was merely more systematic and forthright. In any event, his method continues to provide the model that Scots writers either follow or kick against.

MacDiarmid was at the heart of a group of writers dedicated to revitalizing Scottish literature. They included the great modernist Gaelic poet Sorley MacLean, translated into Scots by Douglas Young. That interchange with Gaelic has blossomed into, for example, *Sangs tae Eimhir*, Derrick McClure's 2011 Scots version of MacLean's *Dàin do Eimhir* and Angus Peter Campbell's 2007 collection *Meas air Chrannaibh*, published in Gaelic with Scots and English translations. Aonghas MacNeacail has also recently begun writing in Scots. Such a level of engagement between these neighbour tongues is long overdue.

Translation has played an important role in the modern revival of Scots. William Laughton Lorimer's New Testament was not the first attempt to put scripture into *the mither tongue*, but is by far the best known and most substantial of such modern versions. In striving to replicate the stylistic diversity of the Greek, Lorimer affirmed the plasticity of Scots and nurtured a serious Scots prose that has still to take a wider hold.

Subsequent generations have continued to engage with other tongues. The ever-inventive Edwin Morgan frequently turned to Scots for translation, not least in his marvellous Glaswegian rendering of *Cyrano de Bergerac*. Liz Lochhead has used it powerfully in her translations and versions of Greek and French drama as well as her own poetry and stage plays.

The success of James Robertson and Matthew Fitt's Itchy Coo children's books may indicate that there is still hope for Scots prose to take proper root. There are isolated examples, such as James Kelman's novels in urban Scots and Fitt's cyberpunk novel written entirely in a denser Scots. This is still a rare approach; it is more common to find passages – even extensive passages – in the language, as in Robertson's fine literary fiction.

However, Scots remains strongest in poetry. Generation X produced a fine and diverse crop of poets working in the *leid*. Among the best known are Kathleen Jamie, Robert Crawford, W.N. Herbert, Jackie Kay and David Kinloch, but Rab Wilson is also a voice of note. Tom Leonard's approach to urban Scots has proved influential on, for instance, Alison Flett, while the use of Shetlandic Scots by Christine De Luca and Robert Alan Jamieson continues with younger poets such as Christie Williamson.

Reports of the death of Scots have long been exaggerated – a situation doubtless familiar to speakers of Irish and Scottish Gaelic. Scots is at last beginning to find a space in the education system, and the Scottish government now has a minister whose portfolio explicitly includes both the Scots and Gaelic languages. There is still a long way to go before the future is secure and there is no room for complacency, but there is *muckle* life in the *auld tongue* yet.

Andrew Philip was born in Aberdeen in 1975 and grew up in a former mining village near Falkirk. He lived in Berlin for a short spell in the 1990s, an experience which, in part, led him to study linguistics at Edinburgh University. He has been interested in Scots from a young age, having grown up in a Scots-speaking community. His first full collection of poetry, The Ambulance Box *(Salt, 2009), was shortlisted for the Aldeburgh First Collection Prize, the Seamus Heaney Centre Prize for Poetry and in the Scottish Book Awards.* The North End of the Possible *(Salt, 2013) is his second collection. He is the Poetry Editor at Freight Books in Glasgow, and the Scots Language Editor of* Irish Pages. *He lives in Linlithgow, between Glasgow and Edinburgh.*

SLEEKIT LOANENS

Stephen Dornan

The iconic and the couthy.

The census is designed to provide a snapshot of the easily quantifiable. It deals in statistical certainties; it is a tool for the collection of immutable data. In Northern Ireland this means that it is primarily treated as a sectarian head-count and an opportunity to resuscitate millennial hopes and doleful fears of demographic tilting points. However, in the midst of the 2011 census in Northern Ireland, there was a moment of refreshing dissonance, of joyous unclarity, of egregious ambiguity. In 2011 the populace were invited to ponder the following: "Can you understand, speak, read or write ... Ulster-Scots?" The disarming simplicity of the question conceals a labyrinthine wheen of sleekit loanens. In a sense Ulster-Scots was the skelf under the skin of statistical functionality, the gellick in its lug; a skifter skiting over its drouthy prose.

The question is not simple. Scots is a slippery, nebulous enough entity: it danders in a hinterland between familiarity and incomprehensibility and maggs in that ambiguous, slabbery sheuch which imperfectly separates language and dialect. Ulster-Scots introduces a further layer of complexity. Not only is its relationship to English ambiguous, but its relationship to Scots is problematised by the hyphen, which seems to imply linguistic distinctiveness. The question of what constitutes linguistic ability in Scots is tricky enough, but ability specifically in Ulster-Scots is even more difficult to ascertain.

But there are tangibles: Scots and English are both cognate dialects of Old English. But by the seventeenth-century Scots, was already declining from its position as the fully functioning language of an independent state. The Union of the Crowns (1603) and the Union of the Parliaments (1707) meant that English became the language of the court and the parliament and official discourse in general. This process was arguably started by the Scottish Reformation which favoured English translations of the Bible. By the beginning of the eighteenth century, therefore, Scots had become a predominantly spoken language used in everyday life, but largely excluded from official, public discourse and consequently often expunged by the socially and educationally aspirant. The eighteenth and early nineteenth century Scots literary revival, in which numerous Ulster writers participated, bolstered Scots' profile to an extent and culminated with Robert Burns, its sensational poster boy.

Traditionally Ulster-Scots has been something of a blind spot for enthusiasts and commentators on Scots in Scotland. Scots in Scotland is usually divided into four main dialect areas: insular (Orkney and Shetland), northern (Aberdeenshire and and Angus), central (a large swathe of central, eastern and south west Scotland) and southern (Borders). Ulster-Scots occupies a nebulous, indefinite space. In recent years, due to its increased visibility, it has emerged as a debatable fifth dialect area, with close connections to the sub-section of the central dialect spoken in the south west of Scotland.

The problematic relationship between Ulster-Scots and Scots in Scotland has more to do with the different political contexts on either side of the North Channel than linguistic difference. Whilst Scots is not central to the political project of Scottish Nationalism, enthusiasm for the tongue tends to correlate fairly strongly with separatist sentiment. Scots has tended to be used as a cultural resource that denotes difference from standard English and the cultural and political hegemony that it represents. There are echoes of this in the sense of dissenting, crabbed, independent-mindedness, and thrawn, plain-speaking truculence that vaguely coheres around Ulster-Scots stereotypes. But there is a crucial difference: Scots in Ulster has often been emblematic of cultural distance from Irish nationalist identity. This is not a new phenomenon. The first distinctively "Ulster" regional novels, written in the 1820s by James McHenry and John Gamble, use Ulster-Scots dialogue to signify the cultural difference and diversity of Ulster, and establish the cultural complexity of Ireland, in an age where other novelists were depicting Irish identity politics in terms of a negotiation between an Anglo-Irish ascendancy and a pre-existing indigenous Gaelic culture. It is a feature of Ulster-Scots, and arguably one of its key virtues, that it has the potential to problematise limiting binaries.

Certainly Ulster-Scots seems to cultivate paradox. It is the tongue of a fragile, marginal and fragmented speech community which has been startlingly elevated into public discourse in Northern Ireland. There are clearly pockets of enthusiasm for Ulster-Scots – in the aforementioned census, 8.08% or 140,204 people in Northern Ireland – claimed to have some knowledge of Ulster-Scots. On the other hand, the idea of an Ulster-

Scots language continues to provoke a variety of hostile responses: it has been dismissed as a DIY language for Orangemen, and condescendingly denigrated as bumpkinish County Antrim farmer-talk.

A crucial aspect of Scots, whether from Ulster or Scotland, is that it exists in intimate relation to English. Scots and English have a large shared vocabulary and shared grammatical structures. They are simultaneously forenent and throuither. Linguists working on Scots speak of a Scots continuum along which speakers move depending on the context and content of an utterance. At one end of this continuum is dense Scots with standard Scottish English at the other. Such swithering fluidity defies the feckless simplicity of a census. Writers also use this fluidity and the best make it a central virtue. Burns, for example, demonstrates a facility for moving along the Scots continuum depending on his topic or the fluctuations of his speaker's mind. Scots blossoms and dissipates.

It is in such paradoxical fluidity that the creative and aesthetic possibilities of Ulster-Scots exist. In Scotland, Scots has a distinguished literary pedigree and remains an important and versatile resource for a wide variety of contemporary writers. For some writers it provides a sense of realism in dialogue, whilst for others it provides the basis for bold aesthetic experimentation. Traditional forms co-exist with representations of urban demotic, regional varieties and synthetic, overtly literary forms. Overall, Scots is an important and colourful strand in the rich linguistic tapestry that makes up Scottish literature. In Ulster too, a literary tradition in Scots exists, although this has been largely neglected, partially forgotten, or even occluded until fairly recently.

There has been a fairly modest revival in Scots writing in Ulster over the last few decades, but it has hardly established Scots as functioning literary medium in the way it is in Scotland. Certainly Scots provides interesting possibilities for writers. On one hand, the distinctive lexicon of Scots enriches English, and provides colourful, evocative lexical items – guldering hallions of words, alive with viscera and energy. Inscribing even a sprinkling of words with familiar standard English cognates, on the other hand, micht tak a reader oot o their comfort zone an mak them engage wi the text in a different way. It tends to have a disorientating and alienating effect on readers used to encountering only the standard English cognates in print. This simultaneous familiarity and strangeness can be effective in evoking challenging, marginal voices. Traditionally the disruption of linguistic orthodoxy could generate a sort of edgy political subversion, or denote a wholesome distance from cosmopolitan norms and mores. Scots can be a versatile medium that oscillates between the ironic and the couthy.

In Ulster, perhaps some realignment between identity and aesthetics is required. This might encourage increased awareness of, and engagement and interaction with, contemporary Scottish writing. It is perhaps doubtful if there is an audience comfortable with and literate in Scots in Ulster given its twentieth century decline. The existence of a corpus of work from Ulster that uses Scots suggests that historically audiences were comfortable with it. The more thorough retrieval of this tradition might be a first step. Despite the onset of the digital age, and although some progress has been made, it requires a degree of determination to access even some of the most significant Scots texts from Ulster. The gates to these loanens have been long cleeked and the entrances culfed. If they can be redd up and hoked out, their sleekit jooks might be re-discovered.

Glossary

sleekit – twisting; *loanen* – lane; *wheen* – several; *skelf* – a small splint of wood under the skin; *gellick* – earwig; *lug* – ear; *skifter* – light rain shower; *skiting* – moving quickly/skimming; *drouthy* – thirsty; *danders* – walks lazily; *maggs* – rampages; *slabbery* – thick and wet; *sheuch* – wet ditch; *crabbed* – ill-tempered; *thrawn* – stubborn; *forenent* – opposite; *throuither* – mixed together; *swithering* – changeable; *guldering* – shouting; *hallions* – rough fellows; *micht* – might; *tak* – take; *oot* – out; *mak* – make; *wi* – with; *cleeked* – locked; *culfed* – blocked up; *redd up* – tidied up; *hoked out* – dug out/cleared away

Stephen Dornan was born in 1978 in Newtownards and grew up in Comber, Co Down. He was educated at the Royal Belfast Academical Institution and the University of Aberdeen. His essays on Irish, Scottish and Ulster Scots literature have appeared in a number of academic journals and books, including Scottish Studies Review, Journal of Irish and Scottish Studies *and* Romanticism and Ireland, *edited by Jim Kelly (Palgrave, 2010). He currently teaches English at Cults Academy in Aberdeen. He is the Scots Language Editor (Ulster) of this journal.*

SEVEN POEMS

Iain Galbraith

AUSPICES

First, raise your eyes. Look up into the sky.
                            Euripides

In the window square I watch
a buzzard chased from the branch by jays.
I have come to join my mother
who does not know where she lives, her name,
but wake to find my own son's head
wrapped in a sheet in my arms. Surely
there has been some error? Cries
the raptor, fainter, *gone for ever*
is the house you founded once in brick
and not even you, so many lifetimes
later, know who you are or why, when
autumn slips and the light grows silver
and thin, the gossamer chorus flies.

COLUMBA

What does the morning bring?
This wood pigeon's call
in a late summer's garden
so long ago?
              What
quartering memory finds
is not the dove but an oak
at the edge of a lawn, and goalposts
long out of use.

          Beyond
are rows that stretch
to stunted elms, the yew, desire paths
through a gap in the wall
to links and the open sea.

But soon our calling pigeon too
is flown to a different land,
the view of it splintered, the voice
unbodied and sheer.
                  And something
is reaching down
through the skylight, leaving us
used for a moment longer
in this endlessly turning cell.

QUAIL SONG

after Horace

The outlook for the winter months reversed:
the herded waves reared up and left
the race of fishes lodged in tops of elms,
the storms drove wolves from the heights.

Do you think we trembled with fright?
Not once did we yearn for city lights —
instead in the hardy woods we thanked
each dawning day, the blaze we plied

with logs, and wrapped in blankets drank
from the Sabine jar. When springtime
came the pylons floated high above
the haze, and but for a white-cap far

to north the snow soon burned away.
Carefree one evening down by the stream
she grasped my wrist — a voice sang out
in the corn: *wet-my-feet* they'd called

the quail in the place where she was born.
Deep in the sedges reeled the wren
and marking the lull between incoming planes
ice-melt sighed on a stone.

THE LITTLE EGRET

Come along the river and we'll finish
the job. A shelf of crime thrillers
and a wooden cross: into the skip.
Lop the magnolia's branches off,
later sell the trunk. Doubtless
we shall dream of things that wear
this cruelly with our early years. You saw
the little egret settle in the stubble
by the lake? Then let us redeem some
right away. The surface we cannot inhabit,
watery, grey — sublimities here and there ...
all of this can be scrubbed. The voices
in the furrow are no longer ours —
a slow wing beat as we go.

HOOPOE

Paladin caller of the early hours
he bustles among the pine-nuts,
bathing in dust, probing the dead,
an augur in the pathways of ants.

Gentleman of these parts he left
us his name, but when you threw
back the shutters he took his hat,
hiding in the cloak of the sea.

We watched out for him daily.
The islands sparkled in showers
of spring light – his morning, ours.

Why did we doubt his return?
Come with him to my table, love –
cover my hand with your own.

RAGS!

Standing beside ourselves in the glass
we thought at first a raucous
crow had passed. We glanced to follow
its path, then heard the heavy hooves.
Outside, a strip of shadow lay
across the house and barred the yews,
and faster whirled the dead vine
leaves. The day was bright, a cold
wind tore at the trees. I'd seen
the flash of brass, but when it tossed
its head and cartwheels scraped the kerb,
you'd gone: the years had slipped between.

SNIPE
(Gallinago gallinago)
   for Christiane

Back we'll go, in we'll go,
tumbling through the years
into a forest of eyes:

here the balm and bleeding meet,
as if through all of life
we'd stepped

into this field of buttercups.
And down they glide again,
swooping over our heads –

the male's whummering
courting song
that cups the heart –

while windows flame
at the edge of the land,
our sky grows small

and the cows' tongues
tear at the pasture
in the failing northern light.

Born in Glasgow in 1956, Iain Galbraith grew up in the west of Scotland and studied at the universities of Cambridge, Freiburg and Mainz. His poems have appeared in many anthologies and journals, including the TLS, Poetry Review, PN Review, The Edinburgh Review *and* New Writing. *He is also the editor of five poetry anthologies including* Beredter Norden *(2011), a substantial selection of Scottish poetry from 1900 to the present in German translation. His other recent translations include a selection of W.G. Sebald's poetry,* Across the Land and the Water *(2011), a "Selected John Burnside" in German,* Versuch über das Licht *(2011), and* Self-portrait with a Swarm of Bees, *a selection of the German poet Jan Wagner, due out in 2015. Besides translating poetry and fiction, he is a widely performed translator of British and Irish drama into German. He lives in Wiesbaden, Germany.*

BENDS IN THE ROAD

Tom Mac Intyre

One of Ireland's best.

THAT DOG AGAIN

There's a dog at the window,
sturdy Alsatian, involved, you
can tell that, not concerned,
divil the bit, but yes, involved.

A travelling company, one of
the "fit-ups", arrives – God be
with you, Louis D'Alton, by
your show we shall know all
that we are like to know!

Somebody's wake, is it? Gottit
in one. Herself is lowering (by
winch) the coffin onto a bed,
I'm in that coffin, alert
cadaver. E'er a worry, Mate?
Zilch. Heart compliant. All set.

The Alsatian's now in the room.
Approaches me. I place my hand
in the dog's mouth. (Head in
the lion's, 'prentice hand in
dog's, early lesson.) And the dog,
ould butty, licks that hand.
There goes needful anointing.

I sing it again:
first time we met,
flick of his paw
left me on
the hasp of my arse,
cobbles beneath me,
the lisp of water,
no hurry on it
caressing the stone.

NEWS FROM THE FRONT

Exists, after all, a cure
for hernia, inoperable
due to weight of the calendar.

I have it straight from lips
of The Goddess, whose face, need
I say, one is not permitted
to view. That's fine, her words
are what matter. "Be careful,
Pilgrim, you find the comedy,"
she counsels, "the tears of the music."
And gone. They don't hang around.

I lie there, happiest man
this side of Cahersiveen.
The bit out of puff, sure.
Find the comedy, the tears,
of the music. How simple, how
complete. The comedy. Tears.

Sure isn't that it?
Of the music.

from MEMOIRS

Lavin

"I owe you an apology," she said, "One shouldn't take sides. I did. I'm sorry."

That was in respect of marriage turmoil and separation.

"Thank you, Mary."

I'd gone to visit her – first time in years – bringing a copy of *The Harper's Turn* (1972) which Gallery Press had just published.

"*The New Yorker* don't publish my kind of story anymore," she said, "they publish your kind of story." I nodded muted assent. The sixties – when we first met, when I was – with Kilroy and McGahern, for example – a member of the circle of young writers about her, regular visitors to The Mews, there off Merrion Square.

She was looking well, very much in charge of herself, no sign of the dementia which would blight her final years. When she was made a *Saoi* of *Aosdána* she was there but not there really, had no idea of what was going on.

My first meeting with her? I was somewhere in my late twenties, a raw aspirant writer. Was there – a basic question – an established writer in the vicinity who, in some sense of the word, would mentor me? There was Lavin – twenty miles or so to where she lived in Bective, out the road from Navan. A visit was arranged. One Sunday evening, summer, I arrived. Lavin *en famille*, her daughters around her, success around her, some melody of happiness adjacent. I distinguished myself that evening by asking how much *The New Yorker* paid her for a short-story. She – effortlessly – pretended not to have heard my gauche enquiry. It was an exciting evening, just being in her company. Rambling chat, now and then about writing, and now I'm on my way home. We'd meet again. That was agreed.

Didn't know it but I was on the verge of an event – ordinary and not – which spoke eloquently of the charge Lavin carried, the impact of her energy on the hungry aspirant. Thumbing home, I get to Virginia. Short walk now and I have the shelter of a relative's farmhouse a couple of miles out the road to Bailieborough, my home town. To my left as I walked, a bog. My roving eye arrested. A bog-hole in view. And I see reflected in bog-water the starry sky. I meet the bog of stars. That's my Lavin story *non pareil*. Coming away from our first meeting, I meet the fabled Bog of Stars. Don't know that I ever told her that – but I certainly told it to the assembled mourners at her graveside.

Lavin, Lavin, Lavin – what was it about Lavin? A born story-teller, and an impressive body of work. Innumerable lessons for your aspirant story-teller – but there's something, it seems to me all these years later – something missing. Was she, I ask myself, was she a prude? And it seems to me – she was Irish-American, remember – seems to me that your Irish-American carries a puritan reserve that makes the Wasp congregation seem positively libertine. You wait a long day for mention of the cock or the cunt in Lavin. A missing dimension? Yes. A notable absence.

On a lighter note she did have a delicious sense of fun. I recall a journey to Galway, Lavin driving, Tom Kilroy and myself aboard. Kilroy, if I recall correctly, will be delivering a paper on Faulkner in UCG. Somewhere west of Loughrea the singing starts – Kilroy and I the performers of *The Galway Shawl*, Lavin the enchanted listener … "Near Aramore in the county Galway/On a summer's evening in the month of May …" – Kilroy and I pulling out all the stops of a classic comeallye, Lavin – hadn't she heard it before – in stitches at the gusto of the singing, the unabashed heart-throbbery of the lingo – "She sighed and kissed me/And then she left me/But she took my heart in her Galway Shawl … " Call the above vignette "Lavin in ecstasy …"

Lavin. In summary? A born storyteller. The work marred, in my reckoning, by a notable absence. A censorship. An Irish-American prudery, I think that there was a great writer lost in her. And I tend to make – validly or no – a connection between the dementia of her closing years and the censorship by which she lived – the censorship which kept watch over every line she wrote. Lavin in dementia, receiving the highest award *Aosdána* (the writer's association) can bestow, that's an image that – cruelly or not – refuses to go away. Reflect on it. I do, frequently. As I do on our first meeting, her vivid presence, and, later that evening, the clarion signal of the bog of stars.

Brodsky

It was Coleman Barks (the acclaimed translator of Rumi) who told me that Brodsky habitually referred to me as "that rogue Mac Intyre". I was shocked, even affronted, but, on reflection, had to concede the throwaway accuracy of the description. It gave me something to chew on, I'll warrant you. Anxiety an ingredient? Not really. On reflection, I was flattered. *Rogue*

– such a resonating word, isn't it, explore it, I counselled myself. Have the rogue talk back to you. Surely there is a rowdy play in it for the staid Abbey Theatre? I was full of virtuous intent concerning my forehead's badge of roguery but, being a rogue, I promptly forgot all about it. So. There y'are now, as we say in East Cavan. An' not in Shercock.

But Brodsky: I think firstly of his vehemence – unadulterated where The Muses were concerned. He was a pupil, remember, of Akhmatova's – "we called her The Hobo Queen" – and that decreed acceptance of – dedicated pursuit of – the highest standards. Pasternak – hint of forgiveness – was given the nod, Yevtushenko consigned to the flames. On the matter of Desmond O'Grady – "He hits it now and again", Paddy Kavanagh – "Never washed they say, but the lines wash." "Heaney" long pause. "Yes, Josef?" A sigh. Then an explosion – "*He doesn't hate himself enough.*" In Brodsky's company – if you want my reading – you either rejoiced in your pupil status or got out of there at a fair lick.

"He doesn't hate himself enough!" Plumb the implications of that, Sir! The lesson? You have to loathe yourself – healthily. They didn't have that in the Catechism where I was reared. The pair of us now loitering outside The Lion's Head, in Sheridan Square, NYC. Noise and crackle of noontime traffic. "Marina Tsvetayeva?" Her, I was aware, he revered. "A few stanzas, Josef, please." He begins to recite. The traffic dims. Brodsky reciting Tsvetayeva? You don't need fluency in Russian to hear the music. And it will stay with you – I believe I may confidently vouch for this – stay with you while you live. God's truth, it would give hearing to the deaf.

Russia behind him, Brodsky was free to roam. He landed on Inishboffin – this was the 70s, everyone made time for The Island of The White Cow, poets in the van. The islanders loved him. "Josef – a comical class of a man" – loosing the phrase reserved for poets, audible in it a salute, regard, respect not lightly vouchsafed. Josef was (wherever he landed) impossible, did his own thing, went his own way, and they understood, approved, and, likely, to some degree envied his low-slung swagger. I can see him in a hayfield on 'Bofin, pitch-fork in his hands, working easily among the men, the boys, of a limitless summer day. A rest period decreed – by Josef, likely. I continue working. "Tom, *sit down!*" He's right. Spare us your automaton spasms.

"He doesn't *hate* himself enough." Loosed with apostolic vehemence. Unforgettable, such a sermon.

And what else? He had a Puritan fear of the body, and, accordingly, took palliative steps. For example, loosing Beethoven on the hi-fi (volume up, please) as he went to have a shit. I was once an intrigued witness to that trope. Nobel Prize winner invokes final movement of Beethoven's Ninth to quench brass and wind rumpus of uppity bowel movement. Makes wonderful sense, if you pause to consider, in its meticulously balanced way. Only Brodsky would come up with such an answer to the latrine that follows us around. And I'm thinking – as, job done, he quenches the music – the child in him was such an essential part of his numen.

"That rogue Mac Intyre …" He got that right, you have to admit it.

"*You want to kill me,*" he shouted – this was in Paris, within days of our first meeting. He wasn't far off. Everyone wanted to kill him. Envy, clearly. He had it – the *bejasus* factor, had it to fumes of incense. He was one of the identifiable Apostles, a Jesus freak, and he spoke in tongues, multitudinous and oracular. A halo? You couldn't be in his company and not remark it. Naturally, this created problems, one in particular: everyone, just about, had an urge to do away with him. How could you breathe easy in the proximity of that earned – and have no doubt that it was earned – and sumptuously flickering halo? And, by the way, his hidalgo lack of awareness touching the halo inevitably enhanced its effulgence. How did the Apostles *stand* the Saviour? There's a question.

But. Over a period – three or four years – or five or six – you'd come to savour Joseph's virtues, his foibles, his faiblesse … They have, don't they, a phrase in the limping English language – "the one undoubted genius I ever met." In this instance, it pertains. His generosity – did I mention? "I have no money, Josef." Fifty dollars into your pocket – a hundred – no demur. He didn't give tuppence for money. But if *you* were in need, he was there.

I believe – coming now to his early death – I think he wanted to die. And quietly went about the arrangements, non-stop smoking being germane. He'd sung his song, rabbinical, plangent, unrelenting. Time to be moving on. Leaving wife and child. So be it.

My luminous abiding memory of this genius? His rant on the subject of his companion laureate Heaney. "He doesn't hate himself enough, he doesn't hate himself enough …" Brodsky stating the conditions of engagement. An articulate and dedicated Rabbi. A friend in need. Gifted to look and to know. "Rogue, rogue, where hast thou been aroguing?" Helping you – helping the other – in so many ways, most of all in finding deference to the axiom of which the hermits chant and the poets sing – "Know thyself, hate yourself enough, and the traffic-lights will clear the road, clear the road, and wave you on your way."

A Lad From The Erne

NYC, sometime in the early 70s. I'm forty plus, and shapeless. People are beginning to talk. Tom Kinsella stopped me one day on Grafton Street. "You realise you're no longer young and promising." "Correct," I responded, "And there's only one thing to be done about that!" "Which is?" "Deal with it." And so we parted. But I hadn't dealt with it. Cowardice is a fearful word. Who are you? I'm one of Ireland's standing army of ten thousand poets. The droop in my eye would fool only the indolent. Or the innocent. I was in po-faced, well-shaven despair.

Sheridan Square, lower Manhattan. I wander into The Lion's Head, a roomy tavern with a certain Bohemian cachet. It's deserted, bar a man I recognised as Liam Clancy, youngest of the fabled Clancy Brothers. He's sitting at the counter, head bowed, fingering his guitar. I recognised the tune he was caressing – *I'm a Lad from The Erne*. Without hesitation, I approached quietly, positioned myself directly behind him, and – he hadn't noticed my arrival – began to sing – "Buachaill ón Eirne mé 's bhréagfainn féin cailín deas óg. / Ní iarrfainn bó spré léithe tá mé fén saibhir go leor ..."

Simply as that, we were into our adventure. Strangers, we met in the song, in the *mise en scene*; intimately as we were positioned, I wouldn't – I couldn't – wouldn't see his face, nor could he see mine – but the music of the love song bound us. The tension was tender, a tender tight-rope. We could have been rehearsing song, music, choreography, for years. Who had choreographed this duet? We neither knew nor cared ... "A chuisle 's a stór ná pós an seanduine liath / Ach pós a' fear óg, mo lao, mur' maire sé ach / bliain ..." We loosed the last stanza, saw the song to its close – "Nó beidh tú go foil gan ó nó mac os do chionn / A shilfeadh a'n deor tráthnóna nó'r maidin go trom ..."

There was a rattle of applause from the far deeps of the bar. Now we faced each other. "Who are you?" Clancy enquired. I hesitated. "Don't you know?" He pursued, a merry glint in his eye. "I half know," he said, "on the head of meeting you – and the container we found for a meeting." Pause. He studied me affectionately. "Show me your hands, like a dacent man," he requested. I showed him my hands, what the mother always referred to as my "artist's hands." He examined the hands carefully. "Tailors among your ancestors?" "Correct." "But you – you're a poet – in the making." "Am I?" "Go for it," he said. We spent a hell of an evening together. Late in the evening, he said – "The stage comes into your future. Plays, that kinda thing. You know what they say about hurling, the key thing – it's a *touch*. So with the writing. The father said to me – "The problem's twofold, firstly to *hear* what you're meant for, then to *be* that – get it?" "Got it," I said, lick of a tremble in my voice, "Got it." He smiled, a ripe Munster smile.

One of those evenings that shape a bend of the road.

THE WRITIN'

Afternoon quiet of the street, her
howl from the other footpath, I
have to say, caught me unaware –
"Y'ould reprobate!" I looked. There
she was, nondescript middle-aged
shopper, firm of step, jut of chin,
striding on about other business.
God's truth, my heart lifted for her,
every last sinew taut in the rant …
I took it, yes, for a kind of applause.

Another peach while I'm in
the vein. Your local landlady
greets an American couple, dis-
covers they have come to visit me.
She steadied, took aim, fired.
"That fella, is it? With the long
red hair and the tramp beard!
You know his trouble? Too many
brains! What's he supposed to
do with them? Wrap them around
his head?" The tickle of pardon –
I love it. And the livid phrasing.
I welcome them all. Long on
the road, dear heart, long on
the bockety road … Quill in hand …

Have I your ear? Prize cameo?
I go, decades since, to pay fair
respects to my sometime nanny,
now an aging postmistress in
a windy corner of the eggs-in-a-
basket hills. The tiny post-office,
stillness pendant. I knock. Again.
An old woman appears from
behind the curtains of muted green
studies me through her bifocals.
"You're one of the Mac Intyres,"
she states confidently. I nod
confirmation. She coughs gently
to herself, examines me again.
"Are you the one" – she's alert,
on her toes, "are you the one
who does be at" – now lends her
right hand to the mime of writing.
Breath giddy, I nod agreement,
could have, yes, embraced her.
In my heart I did. *Surement.*

And for why? She'd lent her hand
to the motion of writing, wouldn't
utter the word itself – the confined
space now resonating to her
impeccable sense of the taboo,
mesh of the arcane and sacral,
that pertains to the art, craft,
of writing, exaltation of The Muse.
The air around us was now
stirring with the word made song.
I'd come to meet my nanny,
salute again her caring breasts,
and oh how intimately the pair
of us had renewed our vows.
"Mna," I said – thus the version
of "Mary Anne" our youngling lips
had fashioned for her, "Mna, how

are you?" She smiles. Views me.
I could feel myself tumbling
in her arms. Did I lisp in
numbers? To be sure I did.
And the numbers came? Pent-
ameter on pentameter. Mna's
head stirs a lovely silence.
We could be there yet. We are.

MULDOON

Late night Belfast bar,
last orders a while ago,
the quiet, quiet's a spur …
"What are ye on about anyway?"
Of a sudden, I'm in his sights,
shivered, I did, and visibly.
"Carrying on a conversation
with myself, times fair wind,
times – often – the stray sod, will-
o'- the-wisp, the bog, bog-hole,
sour of their spit from Dradram
Ó Dré, Glé, and Gliogram Ó Gleo."
"Best conversation you'll ever have."
Then he went off to Amerikay.
I stayed put, carried on
the conversation, distracted by
beauties lost, flesh and phantom,
savouring, every now and then,
his question, my litanied reply,
the pair of us going to it,
so contentedly at one,
stravaygin' the sacred slopes,
hooked, hooked on The Nine,
The Nine, The Nine, The Nine, The Nine,
Nine Lanterns in Their Hands.

Editor's Note: "The Nine" alludes to the nine muses.

THE ELEPHANT

is alpha and omega and
I'm the one that knows it.
We shared a merry intro
years back, the elephant as
youngling, gambolled we did,
I knew myself thrice blessed,
knew myself to be, to grow,
in the urgent company
of The Self. What's The Self, pray?
Who or what? Where it's at.
Just that. Things rested so.

Met again of late, kingly
the elephant, sovereign the rage,
he went through me for
a short-cut, never have I
known a fear to compare with
the fright that reamed me,

and knew, on the second knew,
a fly-blown stain for mine,
rogue gene loose I'd drifted,
I'd strayed from deference,
I'd blasphemed. A deal to rue.

King Elephant hammered
the holy ground – water streamed,
hammered again – sheets, sheets
of flame. My pulse was flight
but the legs gave. There I stood,
shitless. Withered, did you? Yes.
Tusked Majesty knows to an ounce
when the mercy plea no longer
adheres. Mercy was back there. Years.

Is laziness, laziness the greatest
sin? Let us be precise where
truth's at last on the table.
Laziness, and I'm the one that
knows it, beds it, laziness
is letting go. Of? Deference.
No less. Defer. Defer. Defer.
Know thyself in the high Marvel
Precincts of The Self. Listen, nothing
else pertains. "Nothing," intones
my Lord Elephant, voyager eyes
on the intimately far horizon,
"nothing matters but the longest journey."

Editor's Note: the elephant is a traditional Indian symbol for the self.

THE WOMAN IN THE WHEEL-CHAIR

Brings a lot together, doesn't she?
She was plain as she was
beautiful, and she posed the one
question, question that was
a request, request being, in turn,
a question: are, Sir, you willing,
you that has all your limbs
about you, to take me, lift
and transport me, John Galahad,
Prince Royal, Ian Fleming, Don
Flamingo, you have been chosen,
act now, land me where all

ache to be, brown eyes, alert
brown eyes unrelenting, this,
this is a first, I'm thinking,
the question unuttered, the more
audible for that, soft-loud, clear,
never been, have you, before
or since, sought for by such,

The Woman In The Wheel-Chair,
waiting for you, wasn't she, Mister?
I got outa there, it was an
interview situation, in-depth
interview you might fairly say,
week later she's on my door-
step, up-country, middle of no-
where, take and place me, it
isn't too much to ask, take
and land me where I burn
to be, come in, I said, gave
her tea and scones, I did, yes,
(I have no shame left, none),
wondered what it would be
like – and, surely, she heard me
so ponder – be like to take
her in my arms, solace, have
her fondle me in turn, there
was little spoken, our entire
conversation, loud, clear, was
unspoken, that second aborted
meeting was our last, if you
omit the eternally recurring
meetings of agility and passion
stemmed, where are you now,
my beauty, my last chance to –
to? – to learn, to gather, to

study mutual consent, assent,
on twenty-seven levels of eur-
eka, she was soft-spoken, she
was, no need to stress, she was
no daw, I suppose – I know – I
confess – some terror once again
took hold of you, great chance
gone, easy to purr it now, to
taste the world, the other, your
wispy self. Next time, you'll

learn better – except there won't
be a next, that's a once only,
such a simple, direct, humble,
prideful question, are you willing,
you that has your entire be-
longings, open, to take me,
land us where four roads meet,
the cross-roads of event, divan,
feather-bed, seraglio, sunset and
streaky dawnlight where we
all dance unimpaired, crutches
no more, no more, no more ...

Long short of it? She belongs,
belongs, belongs to your doorstep,
she's there now. Stride to the door,
open it. Say! – "Come in!" See
to her. (She's yours, isn't she?)
See to her while you've breath.
Learn. Learn her Swahili, love,
love, love her, aye, unto death.

A poet, dramatist and fiction-writer in both English and Irish, Tom Mac Intyre was born in Cavan in 1931. He is the author of eight collections of poetry, most recently ABC *(New Island Books, 2006),* Encountering Zoe: New and Selected Poetry *(New Island Books, 2010) and* Poppy's Leavetaking *(2012), all from New Island. His plays for The Abbey Theatre include* The Great Hunger *(1983),* Good Evening, Mr Collins *(1997) and his version of Brian Merriman's* Cúirt An Mhean Oiche/The Midnight Court *(1999). A collection of short fiction,* The Word for Yes: New and Selected Stories, *was published by the Gallery Press in 1991. He is a member of Aosdána, and lives in Lurganboy, Co Cavan.*

SUPPORT US NOW
Friends of Irish Pages

NAME

ADDRESS

COUNTRY   POSTCODE/ZIP

EMAIL

☐ I would like to become a *Friend of Irish Pages* with a contribution of £250/€300/$400 or more.

☐ I would like to become a *Supporter of Irish Pages* with the following contribution: _____ .

Enclosed is my cheque/money order to IRISH PAGES for the amount of _____ .

Please charge my ☐ Visa ☐ Mastercard

Card Number ☐☐☐☐ ☐☐☐☐ ☐☐☐☐ ☐☐☐☐

Expiry Date ☐☐/☐☐   Signature _____

Please post a copy of this form to:
IRISH PAGES
129 Ormeau Road, Belfast, BT7 1SH
Email: editor@irishpages.org
Tel: +44 (0) 2890 434800
or visit our website at www.irishpages.org

FRIENDS OF IRISH PAGES

Supporting the culture of classic print.

The *Friends of Irish Pages* is a new and generous group of readers, writers and business organizations whose financial contributions help advance the work of IRISH PAGES: A JOURNAL OF CONTEMPORARY WRITING. The journal gratefully now acknowledges this financial assistance on one dedicated page of every issue.

Manus Charleton	John McGinley
Joe and Geraldine Duffy	McKibbin Commercial
Joseph Hassett	Modern Office Supplies
Philip Haughey	Nicholson & Bass
Enda McDonagh	Tony Skelton (bookseller)
Robert McDowell	Timothy Vignoles

In this difficult economic climate, not only the book trade, but the culture of classic print itself, is under pressure as never before. The new support of the *Friends of Irish Pages* is essential to the vitality and independence of Ireland's premier literary journal.

With the largest print-run of any Irish literary periodical, IRISH PAGES represents – uniquely for the island – the intersection of a large general readership with outstanding writing from Ireland and overseas. Each issue assembles a carefully-edited mix of English and Irish, prose and poetry, fiction and non-fiction, style and subject matter, in an overall fit aimed at a wide range of reading tastes. For the Irish resident, no less than the Irish expatriate or the overseas reader, IRISH PAGES offers an unrivalled biannual window on the literary and cultural life of these islands – and further afield.

Please send your contribution, photocopying the form overleaf, to IRISH PAGES at the address given; or ring our office directly at + 44 (0) 28 90434800, where your contribution can be taken by credit card. Alternatively, you can pay directly via PayPal at http://tinyurl.com/friends-of-irish-pages, making sure to notify us at sales@irishpages.org of your name and address.